Christian Education Curriculum for the Digital Generation

Christian Education Curriculum for the Digital Generation

A Case Study of Second-Generation Korean Australian Youth

Jong Soo Park

Foreword by
Michael A. Kelly

WIPF & STOCK · Eugene, Oregon

CHRISTIAN EDUCATION CURRICULUM
FOR THE DIGITAL GENERATION
A Case Study of Second-Generation Korean Australian Youth

Copyright © 2015 Jong Soo Park. All rights reserved. Except for brief quotations in critical publications or reviews, no part of this book may be reproduced in any manner without prior written permission from the publisher. Write: Permissions. Wipf and Stock Publishers, 199 W. 8th Ave., Suite 3, Eugene, OR 97401.

Wipf and Stock
An Imprint of Wipf and Stock Publishers
199 W. 8th Ave., Suite 3
Eugene, OR 97401

www.wipfandstock.com

ISBN 13: 978-1-4982-0736-2

Manufactured in the U.S.A.   02/16/2015

Dedicated to my wife
Yoo Mi Park

And my beautiful princesses
Celine and Haerin

Contents

Tables | viii

Foreword by Michael A. Kelly | ix

I Theoretical Review

1 Introduction: Toward a Paradigm Shift | 1

2 Religious Education Curriculum | 15

3 Understanding of Faith | 55

II Case Study: Qualitative Analysis

4 Socio-Historical Background of the Korean Australian Church | 89

5 The Lives of Second-Generation Korean Australian Adolescents | 114

6 The Religious Educational Performance in the Korean Australian Church | 150

7 An Analysis of the Current Religious Education Curriculum of the Korean Australian Church | 176

III Toward a New Horizon

8 A Model of Religious Education Curriculum for the Digital Generation | 201

Epilogue | 235

Bibliography | 237

Tables

Table 1 Negative Effects of the Paradigm of Transmitting Knowledge-Out-of-Context on Religious Education in the KAR Church | 14

Table 2 Information of SGKA Teenage Informants | 115

Table 3 Information of Youth Group Teacher Informants | 115

Table 4 Information of Youth Group Pastors Informants | 116

Table 5 Three Filters for Designing a 4R Movement Embedded Unit | 221

Foreword

THE RELIGIOUS EDUCATION OF the next generation is an important concern in every culture as parents, teachers and pastors seek to pass on their faith and values to their children. This challenge is even more complex when the parents and faith communities of the young people come from another culture. The older generation understandably wishes to preserve the language and culture of their country of origin while ensuring that their young people are formed in the faith which they profess. However, while these concerns are legitimate, this generation is not as challenged as their children's children, who seek to find an appropriate personal and religious identity in a new world.

Dr. Jong Soo Park addresses a number of key questions which are pertinent for all migrant church groups. How are culture and language preserved? What is the language in which religious education is being conducted? What is the source of the texts that are being used in the learning-teaching project? How is religious observance maintained and enhanced as their children, members of the digital generation, make their way in a new cultural context? How does their religious formation and education induct them into a new context and help them to form a faith commitment? These questions reflect the challenges of every migrant group as they try to sort matters of identity, formation, and education in their religious tradition.

The focus of this research is refreshingly specific in addressing these questions as it engages with four Korean Australian communities and the participants in their religious education programs. Pastors, religious educators and students are interviewed, and their programs are assessed against the background of a serious reading of their different approaches and a delineation of their concerns, strengths and limitations.

Together with the examination of the educational programs there is an assessment of the limitations of the current curriculum model which focuses on the formation of ethnic identity in a monocultural way. These programs take place in churches that are dominated by first-generation members among whom there is a shortage of trained and prepared teachers. Jong Soo's critique calls for a paradigm shift from "the model of transmitting knowledge-out-of-context" to a new curriculum model, so that students can move from programs based on an outmoded objectivist epistemology to ones that enable them to engage their religious tradition in the context of contemporary society which is increasingly multicultural and digital.

The outcome is a proposal for a new approach to the religious education curriculum that is grounded in the reality of the students and a curriculum design based on the model of software programming which offers a four stage approach to contemporary religious education. This approach is grounded in a spiral movement from analysis to design, simulation and service. The learning-teaching process is then proposed as the 4R movement of reflection, reinterpretation, re-formation and re-creation.

This book is an important contribution to new curricular approaches to religious education for second-generation migrant youth living in today's multicultural and digital world. Considering that there is little published research on religious education curriculums suitable for second-generation migrant young people of the digital generation, I am sure that this work will be a meaningful resource for many ethnic teachers, parents, and pastors. I also believe that his groundbreaking insights into digital-based religious education curriculum will be helpful for a diverse range of Christian educators who are struggling with the challenges of designing learning and teaching that is appropriate for today's digital-generation students.

Associate Professor Michael A. Kelly, YTU

Chair, Academic Board of University of Divinity

September 16, 2014

1
Introduction
Toward a Paradigm Shift

For a long time I taught second-generation Korean Australian (SGKA) children and teenagers, prepared learning materials for them, and trained teachers in a Korean Australian (KA) church. In the course of the Sunday School ministry, I, like many other pastors and teachers in the KA churches, struggled to educate SGKA young people to be Christians, with few textbooks or methods suitable for the life context of immigrant teachers and students.[1] Some educators of the KA churches imported Korean-produced materials, especially graded lessons developed by Korean denominations, and utilized them in teaching their students, while others have sought English materials produced in Australia or America. However, both groups have often found that these resources are not suitable for their educational environments.

In the case of Korean textbooks or teaching-learning materials, most of the SGKA adolescents cannot read or fully understand them because of language barriers or cultural gaps. In addition, almost every Korean textbook seems to be unconcerned with Australian culture or issues, or with Korean immigrant contexts in Australia. This means that these materials are likely to be used out of context, which seems to cause a significant educational problem because true knowledge is context based.[2] By contrast, in the case of English texts, most first-generation teachers tend to feel uncomfortable using English materials mainly because of the language barriers. Also, English resources do not refer to the Korean migrant's culture, issues, or life contexts.

Thus, I began to use Korean and English resources eclectically, in a self-developed one-year curriculum. In general, English learning

---

1. Sunday School is a program of religious education for children and teenagers held on Sundays. It is the primary context of religious education for most Korean Australian churches.

2. Niebuhr, *Faith on Earth*, 34.

materials were provided for students, and teachers were trained in Korean a week before the lesson. When a Korean text was used, it was translated into English. However, in the course of designing a one-year curriculum and organizing lessons according to the curriculum every year for five years, I became aware that there were a number of hidden key issues other than language barriers or culture gaps which should be addressed to enable appropriate education of SGKA young people.

First of all, Christian religious education in the KA church is ethnic identity–promoting education. The ethnicity issue is directly related to the first-generation churchgoers' concept of the ethnic church as a Korean culture–keeping institution as well as a religious organization.[3]

From the early days the Korean ethnic churches in Australia have been a meeting place not only for Christians, but also for non-Christians, because the Korean migrants could meet other Koreans and form warm friendships.[4] In the interests of meeting other Koreans and educating their children to preserve Korean traditions, many non-Christians could come to the church with little hesitation. As a result, the KA churches have become centers for preserving Korean cultural traditions, values, and language. Not only the Christian gospel, but also Korean language, ethnic values, culture, and ethnic identity have been actively taught and transplanted to future generations under the church education system. In *A History of the Korean Church of Melbourne*, Gi Young Nahm, one of the founders of the church, recollects that in 1974 its Sunday School was organized for the first time into two classes: a lower-grade class and a higher-grade class.[5] The curriculum for the lower-grade class was dance and fairy tales and that for the higher-grade was Korean language and Korean history.[6] This shows clearly that one of the primary purposes of religious education of the KA church has been to pass on Korean culture and values.

This ethnic identity–focused religious education has consequently led to a monocultural education which is not particularly relevant to the

---

3. The concept of ethnic church is very important in relation to the religious education of the Korean ethnic churches because the contents and direction of religious education are based on ecclesiology. See Oh et al., *Gidokgyo gyoyukron*, 149.

4. Yang, "Hanindeului jonggyo hwaldong," 142.

5. Including the Catholic Church and the Protestant Church, the first Korean Australian church is the Korean Church of Melbourne, which is a Uniting Church, established in Melbourne on July 8, 1973.

6. Nahm, *Melbon-haningyohoeui yeoksa*, 29.

multicultural context of the KA church. Above all, the KA church is a multicultural institution because it is inevitably a contact zone between Korean and Australian cultures, values, issues, and Christian characteristics which are naturally expressed through the ideas and behaviors of first and second-generation church members. In addition, in the KA church there are varieties of people with diverse backgrounds such as first-generation, second-generation, 1.5-generation,[7] multicultural families, long-term international students and their guardians, short-term language students and various sojourners. These facts mean that religious education in the KA church should be a multicultural education which meets the diverse demands of various members of the congregation. However, many first-generation church leaders who have grown up in an intense monocultural society in Korea seem not to fully recognize the necessity of multicultural religious education within the ethnic church.

The current ethnicity-stressing and monocultural religious education is likely to narrow the perspectives and attitudes of SGKA young people to different cultures and to the values of the wider society by educating them with only a Korean world view.[8] James Banks argues that teachers should educate students living in a multicultural society to be able to understand and analyze concepts, issues, events, and subjects with various racial and cultural perspectives by interpreting their educational content from various cultural viewpoints. He believes these students would then grow up as healthy and balanced citizens.[9] Furthermore, *religious education with multicultural perspectives* seems more persuasive to SGKA adolescents who are accustomed to a multicultural orientation in Australian society.

In this respect, some English-speaking ministry designed for SGKA young people in some Korean Australian churches which emphasize English proficiency, Australian culture and values seems also not to be appropriate for educating SGKA young people for faith. This tendency is a reaction to the ethnicity focused religious education, but it is also another type of monocultural education. The appropriateness of the ethnic identity–promoting and monocultural religious education for SGKA young people should be researched and analyzed so as to set the best direction for adequately educating SGKA children and adolescents.

---

7. In this work, 1.5 generation means those who were born in Korea and migrated to Australia after the age of five with no Australian-born parents.

8. Lee, "Damunhwa gyoyukgwa goyyukgwajeong," 53–54.

9. Banks, *Introduction to Multiculutral Education*, 47–49.

The second hidden issue is the first-generation-dominated climate of the KA church. This first-generation-centered church structure has caused SGKA adolescents to feel underestimated, uncomfortable, and even hostile toward church structures including the Confucian way of thinking, authoritarian and hierarchical leadership and decision-making systems, and the unilateral pressure to learn Korean language and values without enough comprehension of their life contexts. In many cases, the young generation's egalitarian preference, multicultural orientation, postmodern relativism, and digital ways of communication tend not to be considered seriously and addressed appropriately in the process of religious education.

Consequently, the church tends to become a place of conflict among church members, especially between first and second generations, which mitigates against effective religious education for future generations. This conflict seems to close SGKA young people's minds rather than opening them. This first-generation-dominated structure of the KA church has been a major stumbling-block to satisfactory religious education for SGKA young people. There are negative effects of the unbalanced church administration as follows:

> [The KA church] is a contact zone between two cultures, two values, and two types of Christianity of the first-generation and the second-generation Koreans....
>
> However, most of [the KA churches] are very much dominated by the first-generation's style and perspective because of the lack of comprehension of the immigrant church as a contact zone....
>
> The first-generation's perspectives and ministry methods have dominance, while the second-generation's perspectives and needs are underestimated relatively; parents have been inclined to force their children to accept totally their ways of thinking, dressing, living, and even their way of believing in God....
>
> Consequently, the church has been likely to fall in a context of conflict between two generations.[10]

As a result, many SGKAs tend to leave the mother church after they graduate from secondary school or become independent of their parents.[11] In order to nurture SGKA young people toward becoming a people of God, educators and leaders of the KA church should transform the

---

10. Park, "Study of Religious Education Pedagogy," 34.
11. Ibid., 40–42.

church from a context of conflict to a context of reconciliation between two generations. As John Westerhoff argues, "When the faith community's story becomes our story, God's presence among us as historic actor becomes a part of our experience,"[12] so it is essential for appropriate religious education that the ethnic church becomes a context of reconciliation among church members. This change to a context of harmony seems to start from considering the ethnic church as a contact zone rather than a first-generation-dominated organization.

The third hidden issue is about untrained teachers in the KA churches. I have worked with more than sixty teachers in a KA church in Melbourne. Among them, some were well-trained and faithful teachers, while others were untrained and uninterested in their students. Through educational ministry experience, I became aware that there is nothing more important than a faithful teacher in religious education, as there can be amazing transformations within students' lives just because of a teacher's commitment. From the same perspective, Sang-Jin Park emphasizes the role of the religious education teacher as follows:

> The teacher's personal image is very influential, having a lifelong influence on learners. Even though the learners cannot remember the teacher's words, the image of the teacher remains and grasps the learners' imagination. The teacher's image, which consists of beings and doings of the teacher such as a smile, silence, eye contact, tears, attitude, loving relationship with students, and faithfulness, has a life-long influence on the life of a student.[13]

For me, however, it was not easy to meet a teacher who fully committed him/herself to educational ministry in the KA church. This phenomenon might be related to a misconception about the role of Christian religious education. Many Korean migrant teachers are inclined to consider religious education as transmitting Christian dogmas and Bible stories to students effectively at an appointed time in the Sunday School of the church. This tendency is closely related to the fact that most Korean immigrant educators are thirsty for practical teaching-learning methods and effective textbooks or materials suitable for their contexts. An example is the 2011 teacher survey conducted by the Melbourne Korean Minister's Association in which fifty-three teachers in ten Korean ethnic

---

12. Westerhoff, *Will Our Children Have Faith?*, 35.
13. Park, "Curriculum Model," 278.

churches participated. The survey results show that the most popular topics identified by survey participants were *small group management* and *teaching skills* (both 22.6 percent).[14]

Because most teachers of the KA church commit themselves to the Sunday School teaching ministry, they tend not to have contact with their students outside the Sunday School sessions, and consequently, there is a weak relationship between the teacher and students. Considering S. Park's argument that "the personal loving relationship of the teacher with learners is crucial in Christian education for faith,"[15] this shallow relationship between the teacher and students developed only on Sundays at a given time might deal a significant blow to every effort to nurture learners as a people of God. The assumption that religious education is about knowledge transmission at the Sunday School should be overcome in order to correctly educate SGKA young people.

To resolve the issue of untrained teachers, especially their misunderstanding of religious education as teaching in the Sunday School, there should be a well-organized process of teacher recruitment and regular training sessions for teachers to be equipped appropriately. However, when pastors and church leaders of the KA churches recruit teachers for their church education, they tend to accept most volunteers to be teachers in their groups without a certain period of discernment and completion of a preparation program as there is always a lack of teachers. Although most pastors know the importance of a committed teacher and want to develop an appropriate process of teacher recruitment, in reality they have little room to fully consider the process with limited human resources in their context. In addition, in many cases there are limited opportunities for teacher training in a local church and such education tends to focus mainly on distributing teaching resources and/or techniques.

As such, beyond language barriers and cultural gaps, there are three significant hidden issues related to the current Sunday School–centered religious education of the KA church: the ethnic identity promoting and monocultural education, the first-generation-dominated church structure, and the shortage of trained and prepared teachers. These three hidden issues are interconnected and seem to be critical parts of the hidden

---

14. Korean Ministers Association in Melbourne, "2011 Teacher Survey."
15. Park, "Curriculum Model," 277.

and null curriculum of religious education of the KA church and thus have a huge impact on the process of nurturing students multidimensionally.

A remarkable thing is that these three matters of religious education of the KA church seem grounded in a curriculum model: *the model of transmitting knowledge-out-of-context*.[16] The term *knowledge-out-of-context* comes from Arthur Applebee's theory. He argues that true knowledge can be obtained not from the cramming of knowledge-out-of-context, but from actively participating in the conversation with the tradition. This is called *knowledge-in-action*.[17] From the epistemological perspective, knowledge-out-of-context seems similar to what Parker Palmer says about knowledge under the modern objectivist epistemology:

> The mode of knowing that dominates education creates disconnection between teachers, their subjects, and their students because it is rooted in fear. This mode, called *objectivism*, portrays truth as something we can achieve only by disconnecting ourselves, physically and emotionally, from the thing we want to know.[18]

From the curricular view, the model of transmitting knowledge-out-of-context is closely related to the Tylerian curriculum model.[19] The Tylerian curriculum model relates to those theories which have something in common with Ralph Tyler's schooling-instructional paradigm.[20] Tyler's rationale is based on the modern objectivist epistemology which assumes that only objective and measurable knowledge can be obtained. Thus, Tyler believed that objective and quantifiable knowledge could be transmitted to students effectively through scientific and rational curricular procedures.[21]

---

16. This paradigm is not only about general approach for planning curriculum of educators of the KA churches, but also about their general concept of religious education.

17. Applebee, *Curriculum as Conversation*, 11–12.

18. Palmer, *Courage to Teach*, 52.

19. Since his book *Basic Principles of Curriculum and Instruction* came out in 1949, Tyler's model has had a marked impact on the theories and practices of religious education curriculum as well as those in the field of general education. Elliot Eisner argues that Tyler's rationale for the creating of curriculum has been the most influential theory in the field of curriculum. Tyler's curriculum theory will be covered in detail in chapter 2. See Eisner, *Educational Imagination*, 16.

20. Park, "Curriculum Model," 106.

21. See ibid., 146–56.

The paradigm of transmitting knowledge-out-of-context seems to have strong roots within most KA churches and has had considerable influence on the religious education of their members. This model is intertwined with the three hidden educational issues of the KA church discussed earlier. Above all, this model is closely related to the poor quality of volunteer teachers in the KA church because it tends to assume that religious education is a teaching ministry in the Sunday School alone. Under this paradigm, many educators of the KA churches seem to consider Christian faith as knowledge-out-of-context and believe that they could make learners understand Christian truth and accept it by imparting Christian dogmas and Bible stories in the Sunday School class. This is a major reason why Korean ethnic church educators are mainly interested in teaching-learning methods or techniques and effective resources rather than improving other important characteristics for pastoral care, loving relationships, and spiritual guidance, although religious education for faith is more than teaching practice.

Under this paradigm, many Korean migrant educators have also been caught with a language problem because language is critical to teaching. Those who speak Korean at the Bible study session so as to help their SGKA learners maintain a Korean identity tend to be sceptical about good communication with students who have poor Korean proficiency and about building a close relationship with them, while others who speak English for their learners tend to have a complex about *perfect English* and thus feel uncomfortable in reaching out to SGKA students in a personal way.

In the case of my former ministry, in order to develop warm relationships between the teacher and learners for satisfactory pastoral care, Korean-speaking students and English-speaking students were divided into two groups. Korean-speaking teachers were in charge of the Korean-speaking classes, while native speakers of English took charge of SGKA students. I found that this change made little difference with respect to creating a warm environment for pastoral care and loving relationships. That is, religious education is more than language-proficiency. Nevertheless, a considerable number of Korean educators of the KA church tend to be overwhelmed by language proficiency and refuse to employ many creative possibilities to connect with their students, because they assume that religious education is about teaching. Under this model, many teachers, except for some bilingual ones, may not feel free from the shackles of limited language proficiency.

In addition, the paradigm of transmitting knowledge-out-of-context has strengthened the ethnic identity promoting religious education and has generated conflict in the KA church. With the modern objectivistic perspective, many first-generation church leaders regard identity as knowledge given like an inheritance, so identity is believed to be established by unquestionable truths or authorities.[22] This assumption is also connected to a primordial understanding of ethnicity which regards ethnic identity as fixed and unchangeable according to lineage and regardless of contexts.[23] This background explains why first-generation Koreans have made efforts to transmit Korean traditions and values to SGKA young people in order to help them develop a Korean identity, going as far as to adhere to the ethnicity-centered and monocultural religious education in spite of the many problems this creates such as conflicts within the church.

However, as Miri Song argues, many recent analysts of ethnicity do not consider ethnicity from a primordial perspective any longer. They view ethnic identity as socially constructed rather than as given by birth and consider ethnic identity as one's sense of belonging to an ethnic group in which shared values and behaviors associated with the group are prevalent.[24] Bernardo Ferdman and Gabriel Horenczyk argue that these shared elements are not static or fixed, but are transformed or modified in the process of transmission from generation to generation. Components of ethnic culture such as signs and symbols may be in a continuous state of transformation, being filled with new meaning and equipped with new functions and expressions during communication with fellow group members and others outside the group.[25]

Joane Nagel describes these processes of reconstruction, creation, and recreation of ethnic culture as follows: "Culture is not a shopping cart that comes to us already loaded with a set of historical, cultural goods. Rather we construct culture by picking and choosing items from the shelves of the past and the present. In other words, cultures change: They are borrowed, blended, rediscovered, and reinterpreted."[26] Cheryl Holcomb-McCoy similarly insists that people are able to choose the degree

---

22. Gergen, "Psychological Science in a Postmodern Context," 804.
23. Song, *Choosing Ethnic Identity*, 7.
24. Phinney and Ong, "Conceptualization and Measurement," 274.
25. Ferdman and Horenczyk, "Cultural Identity and Immigration," 84.
26. Nagel, "Constructing Ethnicity," 162, quoted in Ferdman and Horenczyk, "Cultural Identity and Immigration," 84.

of their group membership by dealing with their assigned ethnic categories individually and interpreting ethnic values and symbols according to each experience and situation.[27] These emphases on the individuals' subjective construction of ethnicity in the process of ethnic identity development are totally different from the supposition of first-generation Korean Australians who believe they can pass on a Korean identity to their children under the model of transmitting knowledge-out-of-context.

Likewise, all three significant issues discussed above are directly associated with a curriculum model focusing on transmitting knowledge-out-of-context. In addition, in the course of investigating the paradigm of passing on knowledge-out-of-context in relation to the three educational issues, I found that the model causes two more fundamental problems in educating SGKA young people for faith: (1) the paradigm based on the modern objectivist epistemology is not adequate for nurturing faith because its concept of knowledge is totally different from the Christian perspective of faith as knowledge of God, and (2) the model is not appropriate for educating SGKA young people as a digital generation because transmitting knowledge-out-of-context is distant from digital ways of learning.

First, the model of transmitting knowledge-out-of-context has an epistemological problem in developing faith. Since it is grounded on modern epistemology, it considers knowledge as objective, positivistic, and individualistic, which is distant from the Christian understanding of knowledge of God. In *Institutes of the Christian Religion*, for example, John Calvin argues that faith is the knowledge of God which has different characteristics from objective knowledge.[28] John McNeill insightfully exposes a core meaning of Calvin's knowing of God in his editorial footnote as follows: "Knowledge, whatever the word employed, is for Calvin never 'mere' or 'simple' or purely objective knowledge. . . . Probably 'existential apprehension' is the nearest equivalent in contemporary parlance."[29] For Calvin, knowledge of God is personal and existential rather than objective knowledge-out-of-context. Further, he thinks that personal and existential knowing of God is grounded in personal assurance resulting from obedience to God's commandments.[30] For him, obedience to God means

27. Phinney and Ong, "Conceptualization and Measurement," 275.
28. Calvin, *Institutes*, trans. Battles, 1.1.1.
29. Ibid., 35–36.
30. Ibid., 1.2.1.

Introduction

to participate in the mutual process of developing a sincere relationship with God.[31] Thus, knowing God is inevitably participatory knowing rather than spectator-like knowledge.

Calvin also emphasizes the importance of the Bible in terms of knowing God. For him, human beings might be able to recognize the presence of God through nature and reason, but knowledge of God through general revelation is not perfect because of the ontological and existential gulf between God and human beings.[32] He argues that people can know God clearly only through the Scripture as God's special revelation. For this, however, the role of the Spirit is indispensable because without the inner illumination of the Spirit people cannot understand the Bible.[33] In this regard, faith is spiritual knowledge of God.[34] To improve spiritual knowledge, Calvin draws attention to contemplating God rather than speculating about Him.[35] Maria Harris argues that contemplation enables "attending, listening, being-with, and existing fully in the presence of Being."[36] Finally, Calvin stresses the role of the community of faith in developing knowledge of God. He argues that God gives us the visible church as our Mother who educates and nurtures us to be the people of God.[37] In this respect, for Calvin, knowledge of God is communal knowing rather than individualistic.[38]

For Calvin, knowledge of God is personal, spiritual, participatory, and communal knowing, which is totally different from the notion of knowledge in modern objectivist epistemology which argues that knowing is objective, positivistic, and individualistic.[39] Therefore, knowledge of God cannot be proposed and improved within the paradigm of transmitting knowledge-out-of-context. Calvin's idea of knowing God will

---

31. Ibid., 1.6.2.

32. Ibid., 1.4.1.

33. Ibid., 1.9.2.

34. Today there are many definitions and many meanings to spirituality. A key feature of contemporary spirituality is to separate the meaning of spirituality from religion. However, the meaning of the term *spiritual* in this book does not accord with contemporary spirituality. It is *religious* spirituality focusing on living in the divine mystery following Calvin and Barth.

35. Calvin, *Institutes*, trans. Battles, 1.5.9.

36. Harris, *Teaching and Religious Imagination*, 21.

37. Calvin, *Institutes*, trans. Battles, 4.1.1.

38. Ibid., 4.1.2–28.

39. Palmer, *Courage to Teach*, 51–61.

be further elaborated along with Karl Barth's understanding of faith in chapter 3.[40]

Second, the paradigm of transmitting knowledge-out-of-context is not in accord with the learning style of a digital generation such as SGKA teenagers. Marc Prensky argues that today's students have changed radically and they are totally different from the older generation because they are the digital generation who grew up with new technology.[41] He calls these students of today *Digital Natives* in that they are "native speakers of the digital language of computers, video games and the Internet."[42] He describes Digital Natives in more detail as follows:

> Digital Natives are used to receiving information really fast. They like to parallel process and multi-task. They prefer their graphics *before* their text rather than the opposite. They prefer random access (like hypertext). They function best when networked. They thrive on instant gratification and frequent rewards. They prefer games to "serious" work.[43]

Diana Oblinger and James Oblinger also agree that those born in the digital generation generally have the high-level digital literacy skills because they tend to be exposed to technology from a very young age. They argue that today's digital-generation young people are highly mobile, always connected, good at multitasking, social, comfortable in multimedia environments and very fast in receiving information.[44] Based on these characteristics of the digital generation, Ian Jukes, Ted McCain, and Lee Crockett describe digital learning styles, comparing with traditional ways of teaching as follows: (1) digital learners prefer obtaining information quickly using multiple resources while many educators prefer controlling release of information in sequence and logic; (2) digital learners prefer

40. Sang-Jin Park also argued that faith as knowledge of God cannot be nurtured under the modern objectivist epistemology. After analyzing the faith understanding of the four Reformed theologians, John Calvin, Karl Barth, Emil Brunner, and Richard Niebuhr, he proposed that the Reformed faith is personal, imaginative, participatory, and communal knowledge of God. I agree with his ideas of the Reformed understanding of knowledge of God, but in the course of appraising the faith understanding of John Calvin and Karl Barth in detail I needed to more focus on spiritual dimension than on imaginative dimension. I will deal with this topic in chapter 3. See Park, "Curriculum Model," 27–54.

41. Prensky, "Digital Natives, Digital Immigrants Part 1," 1.

42. Ibid.

43. Ibid., 2.

44. Oblinger and Oblinger, "Is It Age or IT," 2.2–2.7.

multitasking while many educators prefer processing one thing at a time; (3) today's students are primarily visual learners while many educators still focus on text based teaching; (4) today's students prefer team-project learning while many teachers prefer teacher-centered instruction; and (5) digital-generation students are accustomed to instant feedback and rewards in a digital culture while many teachers underline delayed rewards such as a good grade or a good school, which might be distant from what students need now. They argue that the huge gap between the digital learning styles of students and the analog ways of teaching should be overcome so as to educate today's students appropriately.[45]

The model of transmitting knowledge-out-of-context is based primarily on the analog ways of teaching described above, so it is not an appropriate approach for educating SGKA teenagers growing up in a digital culture. It is grounded on traditional non-digital perspectives about teaching and learning.[46]

As such, the model of passing on knowledge-out-of-context has been a major foundation of religious education in most of the KA churches, resulting in negative effects on educating SGKA young people for faith as shown in table 1.

---

45. Jukes et al., *Understanding the Digital Generation*, 35–45.

46. This does not mean that analog ways of learning and communicating are useless in educating the digital generation and should, thus, be renounced in a new curriculum for them. On the contrary, the teacher should be able to utilize both ways in a balanced mode depending on topics, students, and situations because analog ways still have strong points in terms of education. In addition, many digital gen students prefer a balanced approach between analog and digital ways. See interview findings of digital culture in chapter 5.

Table 1. Negative Effects of the Paradigm of Transmitting Knowledge-Out-of-Context

Effects of the Paradigm on Religious Education

1. Considering Knowledge of God as Purely Objective Knowledge
2. Inappropriate for Educating the Digital Generation
3. Three Hidden Educational Issues: (1) Ethnic Identity Promoting and Monocultural Religious Education, (2) First-Generation-Dominated Church Atmosphere, and (3) Teacher's Misunderstanding of Religious Education for Faith

Through field experience, I became aware that unless the paradigm of transmitting knowledge-out-of-context can be shifted to a new curriculum model of religious education for faith which is adequate for the lives of SGKA young people and the unique context of the KA church, the problems discussed above are not likely to be fully resolved. Thus, an alternative model for planning a proper religious education curriculum is needed and this will require a paradigm shift.

The purpose of this book is to propose a new religious education curriculum model for SGKA teenagers growing up in the context of the KA church. To achieve this purpose, three research methods were used: a critical review of the current religious education curriculum of four KA church youth groups, semi-structured interviews with SGKA teenagers, teachers, and pastors affiliated with the selected youth groups, and an analysis of written documents related to the religious education of the groups.

There are a number of basic criteria required in order to construct a new curriculum paradigm for religious education for SGKA adolescents in the KA church as follows: (1) a new curriculum model should be suitable for key features of faith; (2) a new curriculum model should address and engage the sociocultural life contexts of SGKA adolescents who are living in a multicultural and digital society; and (3) a new curriculum model should resolve the specific educational issues of the KA churches.

2
Religious Education Curriculum

SINCE FRANKLIN BOBBITT PUBLISHED a book titled *The Curriculum* in 1918, the first full-length book on the subject, many curriculum theories have been presented.[1] Among them, Elliot Eisner argues that Ralph Tyler's rationale for curriculum planning has been the most influential theory in the field of curriculum.[2] For Tyler, curriculum is a means of achieving the concrete objectives of educational programs in schools.[3] Influenced by Tyler, his followers have considered curriculum to be a plan or a strategy for a teaching-learning class and the means of achieving educational purposes. Tyler's curricular rationale has long influenced many religious education curriculum-makers as well. A considerable number of significant religious education curricula have been developed following Tyler's procedure including the Cooperative Curriculum Project and Christian Education: Shared Approaches.[4]

From the late 1960s, however, the concept of curriculum as schooling began to be criticized by some curricularists called reconceptualists in religious education as well as in general education. They believed that curriculum is more than what is called schooling and chose, instead, to explore the wider curriculum of "education" in general. Since then, various new definitions and approaches to curriculum have attempted to overcome the Tylerian curriculum model. However, Tyler's curricular rationale is still referred to and used critically in the field of religious

---

1. Kliebard, "Curricular Objectives and Evaluation," 241.

2. Eisner, *Educational Imagination*, 16.

3. Thus, Tyler thought that proposing concrete educational purposes is the most important step in creating a curriculum. See Tyler, *Basic Principles of Curriculum and Instruction*, 3–5.

4. These curricula were strongly influenced by the curriculum theory of Campbell Wyckoff who followed Tyler's scientific curriculum approach. For more accounts of Cooperative Curriculum Project and Christian Education: Shared Approaches, see n76 and n81 in this chapter, respectively.

education curriculum, although there are changes in the definition and use of Tyler's original concepts.

This chapter consists of three parts. First, basic concepts of religious education curriculum will be discussed referring to those of the general education curriculum. Second, the history of religious education curriculum theory will be examined in detail according to William Pinar's classification: *traditionalists, conceptual-empiricists, and reconceptualists*. Finally, I will investigate limitations of the analog curriculum approach on which many current curriculum models seem to be based including the reconceptualized ones, and then propose the necessity of a digital curriculum paradigm for those born in the digital era.

Understanding of Curriculum

The term *curriculum* originated from the Latin word *currere* which implies a running course around which runners would run and finish.[5] Thus, traditionally, curriculum has been understood as the learning track in which there is a starting and finishing line. In this understanding, curriculum is a course, plan, or means for obtaining particular educational objectives. Tyler's approach was traditional. He believed that "education is a process of changing the behavior patterns of people"[6] and viewed curriculum as "a functioning instrument of education."[7] William Pinar, however, tried to reconceptualize the concept of *currere*, emphasizing more the runners than the track.[8] Through Pinar's reinterpretation of *currere*, the learners' experience or context gained more attention in the educational process.[9]

In Eisner's approach, the balance between the runner and the course is emphasized more. He argues that *"the curriculum of a school, or a course, or a classroom can be conceived of as a series of planned events that are intended to have educational consequences for one or more students."*[10] With this definition, Eisner states that curriculum is a series of activities and a planned process of education to achieve some educational objectives. For

---

5. Smith and Lovat, *Curriculum*, 7.
6. Tyler, *Basic Principles of Curriculum and Instruction*, 5–6.
7. Ibid., 1.
8. See Pinar, "Currere: Toward Reconceptualization," 396–414.
9. Pinar, "Method of 'Currere.'"
10. Eisner, *Educational Imagination*, 31, italics in original.

Eisner, to accomplish the purpose of curriculum, it is essential for curricularists to consider differences in cognitive forms among learners. He believes that students possess different kinds of intelligences, so curriculum designers should lead "to programs that intentionally provide for the development of multiple forms of literacy" so as to expand "educational equity in the classroom."[11]

Understandings of religious education curriculum have changed along with these major paradigm shifts in the general theory of curriculum. However, since the main purpose of religious education—nurturing faith—is different from that of general education, religious educators have critically accepted theories from the general education curriculum and modified them for their own purposes. For Christian educators, a capacity for theological reflection on the meaning of faith and the realities of students' lives and experiences is absolutely essential.[12] In this regard, a religious education curriculum can be considered as both a theological and educational enterprise.[13]

For example, Campbell Wyckoff, being influenced by Tyler's rationale, argued that "a curriculum is a plan by which the teaching-learning process may be systematically undertaken."[14] However, Wyckoff was especially interested in systematically providing students with opportunities for Christian experience. So, he argued that "the curriculum of Christian education seeks to reorder experience so that it may become Christian in quality."[15]

In the late 1960s and 1970s when a number of curricularists began to reconceptualize curriculum, Dwayne Huebner criticized the Tylerian scientific and technocratic curriculum approach to schooling because textbook-centered schooling was not appropriate for developing faith in the church context. He argued that schooling did not provide students with enough opportunities to converse with the text itself. For him, the confrontation between the student and the text is the essence of

---

11. Ibid., 82.

12. Seymour, "Clue to Christian Religious Education," 275–78.

13. Sara Little also understands religious education as a theological and educational discipline. "Truth is the experienced reality of the relationship: theology, the interpretation of that reality, informed by the biblical witness; education, the nurture of the experience and the activity of interpreting the meaning to be found there." See Little, "Expressions of Gratitude," 294.

14. Wyckoff, *Theory and Design*, 17.

15. Wyckoff, *Task of Christian Education*, 127.

education. Thus, religious education curriculum should be a dialectic and hermeneutic process in which students are able to participate in cultural traditions and liturgies and interpret them themselves so that they can construct and reconstruct meaning. Only then, he thought, can they be transformed into Christians.[16] Huebner's ideas of curriculum influenced many religious education curricularists. Since then, various approaches to the religious education curriculum have been proposed to overcome the limitations of the Tylerian curriculum models and formulate curriculum suitable for faith development.

Eisner argues that there are three forms of curriculum in educational institutions, namely the explicit, the hidden, and the null curriculum. First, he talks about what the teacher intends to teach. This is the explicit curriculum. Eisner thinks, however, that educators unintentionally teach far more than they expect or prepare. Students learn to decode what values educational institutions like schools pursue through various channels.[17] This is the hidden or implicit curriculum. John Westerhoff III underlines the significance of hidden curriculum in educating for faith.[18] He argues that the informal hidden curriculum is more influential than the explicit intended curriculum.[19] Finally, Eisner refers to the null curriculum, which is a kind of paradox as it exists because it does not exist. The null curriculum is about what students learn that schools do not teach. He claims that the null curriculum is as important as the explicit and intended one.[20] As such, "schools have consequences not only by virtue of what they do teach, but also by virtue of what they neglect to teach."[21] Maria Harris argues that church curricularists should consider these three forms in creating curriculum.[22]

Dimensions of Curriculum Planning

Understanding the dimensions of curriculum planning is crucial in apprehending what curriculum is. In the process of curriculum planning,

16. See Huebner et al., "From Theory to Practice," 363–74.
17. Eisner, *Educational Imagination*, 92.
18. Westerhoff, *Will Our Children Have Faith?*, 17.
19. Ibid., 18.
20. Eisner, *Educational Imagination*, 97.
21. Ibid., 103.
22. Harris, *Fashion Me a People*, 68–69.

there are a number of dimensions to be appraised. Tyler suggests four factors as basic dimensions of curriculum planning such as objectives, learning experiences, organization of learning experiences and evaluation. He argues that these four aspects should be identified concretely and coherently step by step in order to develop an appropriate learning program. Among them, he particularly emphasizes the importance of concretely identifying educational objectives because educational purposes are "the most critical criteria for guiding all the other activities of the curriculum-maker."[23]

Since Huebner criticized the Tylerian curriculum of schooling in the late 1960s, many religious education curricularists have raised significant questions about the appropriateness of using Tyler's rationale for their own enterprise.[24] Among the theories that try to overcome the limitations of Tyler's model, I will select Eisner's approach and compare Tyler's rationale with it, because his theory, based on the aesthetic approach to curriculum and cognitive pluralism, has considerably influenced many religious education curriculum models. In the course of comparison of the two paradigms, a number of controversial curricular issues will be raised: standardized/hierarchical vs. personalized/contextualized process, intelligence-centered vs. holistic/cognitive plural approach, linear vs. nonlinear organization, and quantitative vs. qualitative evaluation. These issues are critical factors which determine the character of a specific curriculum.

1. Educational Objectives

Tyler argues that all dimensions of curriculum are primarily for achieving the selected educational purposes of an educational institution. Thus, educational objectives are considered the criteria by which learning experiences are selected and organized, and methods of evaluation are formulated.[25] For him, educational objectives mean "the kinds of changes in behavior that an educational institution seeks to bring about in its students"[26] because he views education as "a process of changing the

---

23. Tyler, *Basic Principles of Curriculum and Instruction*, 62.
24. See Harris, *Fashion Me a People*, 168–70.
25. Tyler, *Basic Principles of Curriculum and Instruction*, 3.
26. Ibid., 6.

behavior patterns of people."[27] It is notable that he emphasizes the importance of a scientific approach in the process of making decisions about educational objectives, allegedly to increase the validity and reliability of the selected objectives.[28] He argues, therefore, that curriculum-makers should investigate various factors in order to collect adequate data, such as the needs of the learners, the opinions of subject specialists, educational philosophy and psychology of learning.[29]

After analyzing these factors and selecting a number of educational objectives, it is significant, for Tyler, to state concretely the selected objectives so that learning experiences and teaching methods may be decided appropriately. To do this, he argues that educational objectives should be stated in a two-dimensional chart indicating the behavioral aspect and the content aspect of the objectives: "The most useful form for stating objectives is to express them in terms which identify both the kind of behavior to be developed in the student and the content or area of life in which this behavior is to operate."[30] He believes that the two-dimensional chart can provide solid guidance on the subsequent process of curriculum planning.[31]

Eisner also agrees with the importance of objectives in curriculum planning. He even argues that no concept is more essential.[32] However, he criticizes Tyler's emphasis on behavioral objectives. Especially, he disparages the tendency to make them standards and apply them generally, to all students, in order to judge their development.

> Standards are crisp, unambiguous, and precise. A person can swim five lengths of the pool or cannot. Someone can spell *aardvark* or cannot. Someone knows who the 27th president of the United States was or does not. Someone can multiply two sets of three-digit figures correctly or cannot. For such performances, standards are specifiable and applicable by anyone or by any machine that "knows" the rules through which the standards are to be applied. But what about the rhetorical force of a student's essay? What about the aesthetic quality of her painting? What about the cogency of his verbal argumentation? What about

---

27. Ibid., 5–6.
28. Ibid., 4.
29. See ibid., 5–43.
30. Ibid., 46–47.
31. Tyler explains the two-dimensional chart in detail. See ibid., 51–62.
32. Eisner, *Educational Imagination*, 108.

her intellectual style, the ways she interprets the evidence in a science experiment, the way in which historical material is analyzed? Are these subject to standards? I think not.[33]

Thus, he proposes the term *expressive outcomes* as an alternative to behavioral objectives.[34] In the concept of expressive outcomes, curriculum activities precede the formation of educational objectives. That is, educational objectives are not provided one-sidedly by curriculum-makers, but created through the dialogue between teacher and student on the expressive outcomes generated as a result of curriculum activities. In this model, the different abilities and interests of each student in the class would be taken into account in the process of curriculum planning.[35]

2. Learning Experiences

Tyler views learning experiences as the essential channels through which the selected educational objectives can be achieved. He argues that learning takes place variously depending on experiences in the class. For example, even if two students are in the same class, they may learn differently according to the extent of their interests and participation in the course. Thus, he emphasizes that curriculum-makers should choose learning experiences which are suitable for the selected objectives and provide appropriate opportunities for their students to have the desired learning experiences so as to attain the objectives.[36] For Tyler, learning experiences mean "the interaction between the learner and the external conditions in the environment to which he can react," which is not the same as the content nor the activities that the teacher provides in the course.[37] That is, learning experiences are about what a student does, learns, and feels during the course, not about what the teacher teaches and provides.

To appropriately select learning experiences, Tyler suggests five principles. First, learning experiences should be opportunities for students themselves to practice the desired behavior to attain the selected

33. Ibid., 114.

34. Eisner says that he chose the term *expressive outcomes* rather than *expressive objectives* as "the term *objective* implies a preformulated goal." See ibid., 118.

35. See ibid., 118–23.

36. Tyler, *Basic Principles of Curriculum and Instruction*, 63–65.

37. Ibid., 63.

learning objectives. For example, if one of the learning objectives is to develop skill in numeracy, students should have opportunities to solve various mathematical questions. Second, the selected learning experiences should be satisfactory for students. To achieve this, curriculum-makers should understand their students' interests and background. Third, the expectation of the selected learning experiences should be suitable for the students' current levels and environments. Otherwise, the learning experiences might be out of context. Fourth, curriculum-makers should be creative in providing various learning experiences to achieve the same objectives. A wide range of learning experiences prepared for the same educational purpose increases the possibilities that more students can actively participate in the learning process. Last, curricularists should understand that the same learning experience may result in several outcomes. That is, they should prepare for unexpected as well as desired outcomes.[38]

Eisner names learning experiences as learning opportunities, but his concept of learning opportunities is almost the same as Tyler's. Eisner argues that once educational goals are decided after discussing expressed outcomes, such goals and aims should be transformed into appropriate learning opportunities that satisfy students' interests so that students may gain educational benefits. To do this, teachers should develop an educational imagination in order to provide students with various opportunities that are suitable for their environments.[39] Arthur Applebee also argues that such learning opportunities should be in forms suitable to encourage students' participation in conversation with subjects. Applebee believes that true knowledge can be obtained only through actual participation in significant domains for conversation rather than studying about, and terms it *knowledge-in-action*. He argues that only knowledge-in-action can transform student behavior and life, not knowledge-out-of-context that comes from studying or memorization. Thus, for Applebee it is essential to provide students with a wide range of opportunities for entering into subject matters.[40]

---

38. Ibid., 65–68.
39. Eisner, *Educational Imagination*, 138–41.
40. See Applebee, *Curriculum as Conversation*, 1–50.

3. Organization of Learning Experiences

Tyler argues that the selected learning experiences should be formed into units, courses, and programs. The main purpose of organizing learning experiences is to accumulate enough educational experiences to make important changes in human behavior, and the process of changing behavior patterns might not be successfully achieved with only a single learning experience.[41] In the process of organizing learning experiences, Tyler underscores three major criteria: continuity, sequence, and integration. Continuity means "the vertical reiteration" of significant curriculum elements such as concepts, values, and skills.[42] Sequence is also related to the vertical reiteration, but it more particularly refers to the progressive development of crucial curriculum elements in terms of level and depth. Integration is "the horizontal relationship of curriculum experiences" which focuses on raising the integrating ability of students to connect all single elements to other subject fields and to their life contexts.[43]

Tyler then suggests four steps for organizing learning experiences, considering the three criteria mentioned above. First, major curriculum elements should be selected to organize the selected learning experiences. Tyler argues that major elements can "serve as the threads running from the nursery-primary through the middle school and the high school to provide the basis for continuity, for sequence, and for integration in the curriculum."[44] Second, curriculum-makers should decide on organizing principles on which the curricular threads can be interwoven. Third, organizing structures, namely units, courses, and programs are needed to systematically form the major curriculum elements by using the selected organizing principle in order to amplify the effectiveness of the selected learning experiences. Last, there should be an agreed process for deciding curriculum details so teachers can use the curriculum effectively.[45]

According to Eisner, Tyler's model for organizing learning experiences is a kind of staircase model. The staircase model assumes that there are a series of steps which students should master in order to progress to a different level. Thus, the movement is upward like climbing a staircase and the process is linear. In this model, it is believed that students can

---

41. Tyler, *Basic Principles of Curriculum and Instruction*, 83.
42. Ibid., 84.
43. Ibid., 85–86.
44. Ibid., 87.
45. See ibid., 86–103.

progress step by step from one stage to another.[46] Eisner introduces another model for organizing learning experiences: the spiderweb model. This model is not linear and standardized. Instead, it focuses on individual variation. In this model, teachers are encouraged to use learning events as a set of heuristic materials or activities according to the students' situation.[47] The spiderweb model is appropriate for Eisner's concept of learning opportunities that focus on the differences of individuals. However, he argues that since there are strengths and weaknesses in both models, it is not possible to conclude that one model is better than the other. Rather, curriculum-makers should develop the ability to judge which model is most adequate for their educational programs.[48]

4. Evaluation

Tyler thinks that evaluation is a scientific and positivistic process to assess the effectiveness of the curriculum by comparing evidence about behavior changes in students with the original educational objectives. The following statement shows the meaning of evaluation in his theory:

> It should be clear that evaluation then becomes a process for finding out how far the learning experiences as developed and organized are actually producing the desired results and the process of evaluation will involve identifying the strengths and weaknesses of the plans. This helps to check the validity of the basic hypotheses upon which the instructional program has been organized and developed, and it also checks the effectiveness of the particular instruments, that is, the teachers and other conditions that are being used to carry forward the instructional program. As a result of evaluation it is possible to note in what respects the curriculum is effective and in what respects it needs improvement.[49]

For Tyler, who considers curriculum planning a production process for efficiency improvement, evaluation is a significant stage for collecting data in order to produce a better education program next time. Thus, he underlines the importance of getting objective, valid, and reliable data,

---

46. Eisner, *Educational Imagination*, 141.
47. Ibid., 142.
48. Ibid.
49. Tyler, *Basic Principles of Curriculum and Instruction*, 105.

and explains in detail the procedures and methods for analytically judging the results of implementing the curriculum.[50]

Eisner criticizes Tyler's scientific and quantitative approach to evaluation. He argues that such evaluation focuses primarily on the measurement of student achievement based on preselected educational objectives and concludes the extent of the effectiveness of curriculum with the results. Consequently, the scientific model tends to neglect lots of curricular aspects such as quality of teaching and quality of multiple student outcomes.[51] Eisner argues that the main problem with the scientific and quantitative paradigm is the conclusive nature of curriculum assessment:

> The problem with such [scientific] procedures is that they provide conclusions rather than disclosures about the character of the work done and the sorts of progress and problems children encounter. To do the latter would require, first, close attention to what a given child or class has created. If the work is an essay, one might describe how a child has organized his or her essay, the quality of the arguments or evidence he or she employs, the extent to which his or her imagination has been used to create the work.[52]

To overcome the limitations of quantitative evaluation, Eisner prefers using the term *assessment* rather than the term *evaluation*. For him, assessment provides more appropriate concepts for decoding the subtle qualities of a program, taking the educational temperature within a class, and offering feedback to teachers.[53] In addition, he introduces the term *educational criticism*. The main purpose of educational criticism is to illuminate "something's qualities so that an appraisal of its value can be made" rather than a negative judgement.[54] For appropriate educational criticism, it is essential for educators to have *educational connoisseurship*, the art of appreciation, because well-founded criticism depends largely on adequate appreciation.[55] He explains educational connoisseurship as follows: "It is an appreciative art, similar in some respects to learning how to see a football game, a polo match, a play, or how to really hear music.

---

50. See ibid., 105–25.
51. See Eisner, *Educational Imagination*, 195–210.
52. Ibid., 191.
53. See. Eisner, "Reshaping Assessment in Education," 224–32.
54. Eisner, *Educational Imagination*, 214. He considers educational criticism as *the art of disclosure*. For more information about educational criticism, see.ibid., 212–48.
55. See ibid., 215–19.

Connoisseurship is a learnable skill having to do with the appreciation of subtle and complex forms of performance."[56]

In summary, Tyler's rationale is standardized/hierarchical, intelligence centered, linear, and a quantitative curriculum, while Eisner's is a personalized/contextualized, holistic, nonlinear, and qualitative curriculum. In addition, unlike Tyler, Eisner argues that these dimensions are not sequential: "*The sequence of these dimensions is, to a large degree, arbitrary. One need not begin or end with the factors or aspects as they appear here.*"[57] These two different approaches also indicate significant paradigm shifts within the religious education curriculum.

History of Religious Education Curriculum Theory

Since Wyckoff introduced Tyler's curriculum ideas into the field of religious education curriculum, concepts and models of general education curriculum have led the way in religious education curriculum.[58] However, this does not mean that religious education curricularists lost their identities as educators for faith. Although influenced by theories of general educational curriculum, curriculum planners in religious education have tried to hold on to the uniqueness of religious education to help people realize God's grace in their lives, interpret God's revelation from their experience, and thus have faith in God.[59] Here I will review the development of religious education curriculum theory by using Pinar's historical classification of curriculum paradigms.

In an article titled "The Reconceptualization of Curriculum Studies," Pinar categorizes curriculum into three types: *traditionalists*, *conceptual-empiricists*, and *reconceptualists*. According to his perspective, traditionalists based on Tyler's rationale have a lively interest in the actual construction of curriculum, focusing the teaching-learning process in the school setting, whereas conceptual-empiricists draw attention to the verification of developed curriculum in terms of practical efficiency by using typical social scientific methodologies, such as proposing hypotheses, testing them, and analyzing the test results.[60] Although

56. Eisner, "Preparing Teachers," 105.
57. Eisner, *Educational Imagination*, 134, italics in original.
58. See Mitchell, "What Is 'Curriculum'?," 362–66.
59. Seymour, "Clue to Christian Religious Education," 278.
60. See Pinar, "Reconceptualization of Curriculum Studies," 205–9.

conceptual-empiricists are different from traditionalists in that they are concerned with how a curriculum works in the actual teaching-learning field, their ideas are still connected to Tyler's model in that they tend to view curriculum as a plan and their curriculum theories are both scientific and technocratic. The concept of curriculum as systematization and efficiency based on Tyler's scientific model began to be criticized by emerging scholars called reconceptualists in the late 1960s and 1970s.[61] Pinar argues that the reconceptualists' concern was to understand or study curriculum itself, with the aid of various intellectual disciplines, rather than to develop or implement curriculum.[62]

As Pinar argues, these three types of curriculum are not separate, but are interrelated; they have strengths and weaknesses respectively. Thus, he claims that one should be open to other stances for creating a more satisfactory curriculum:

> I am convinced that this intolerance among curricularists for work differing from one's own must be suspended to some extent if significant intellectual movement in the field is to occur. Becoming open to another genre of work does not mean loss of one's capacity for critical reflection. Nor does it mean, necessarily, loss of intellectual identity. One may remain a traditionalist while sympathetically studying the work of a reconceptualist. One's own point of view may well be enriched.[63]

Traditionalists

Since his book *Basic Principles of Curriculum and Instruction* came out in 1949, Tyler's model has had a marked impact on the theories and practices of religious education curriculum as well as those in the field of general education. Alison Kreider claims that Tyler's model has made "an indelible mark on the field of curriculum theorizing, as well as on teaching practices in the American public schools."[64]

Tyler's rationale consists of four simple steps as discussed earlier: (1) proposing concrete learning objectives; (2) selecting useful learning experiences for achieving the proposed objectives; (3) organizing learning

---

61. See ibid., 209–11.
62. Pinar, "Crisis, Reconceptualization, Internationalization."
63. Pinar, "Reconceptualization of Curriculum Studies," 212.
64. Kreider, "1949."

experiences so as to maximize their effect; and (4) evaluating the process and revising weak points.[65] For these four steps, Tyler argues that the first step, proposing concrete learning objectives, is the most important stage. He insists that educational purpose decides the rest of the steps of his rationale as it serves as the most essential criterion for the process of curriculum planning. That is, depending on learning objectives, necessary learning experiences will be selected, the methods to organize the selected learning experiences will be developed, and an evaluation process will be proposed.[66]

Mary Boys claims that Tyler's model takes root in the scientific management theory of Frederick Taylor.[67] Taylor emphasized technocratic rationality which operated on three assumptions: (1) truth is something objective and independent from the knower; (2) reality can be divided into parts, and the sum of these parts is equal to the whole of reality; and (3) concrete objectives may guarantee certain results.[68] These assumptions are largely grounded in modern objectivistic epistemology. Parker Palmer argues that modern epistemology considers truth as objectivistic, individualistic, and positivistic rather than personal, communal, and participatory.[69] For Palmer, in the modern understanding of knowledge truth is "an object to be manipulated and owned."[70]

Consequently, Tyler's approach causes a dichotomy between objectives and means in the course of effectively achieving educational purpose and tries to control the process of education with extrinsic goals proposed by teachers.[71] In this setting, students' participation and concern tend to be underestimated. From the same perspective, Kreider criticizes Tyler's rationale based on the four basic principles:

> As a result of the basic principles, the role of the curricularist and teacher shifted to that of scientist. In the development of any curriculum using the Tyler method, hypotheses are to be established in direct relation to the expected learning outcomes for students. As the curriculum is enacted, teachers and curricularists become scientific observers, determining whether or not

---

65. Tyler, *Basic Principles of Curriculum and Instruction*, 1.
66. Ibid., 3.
67. Boys, *Biblical Interpretation*, 206–7.
68. Lee, *Haeseokhakjeok sangsangryeokgwa gidokgyo gyoyukgwajeong*, 70.
69. See. Palmer, *To Know as We Are Known*, 48–68.
70. Ibid., 65.
71. Lee, *Haeseokhakjeok sangsangryeokgwa gidokgyo gyoyukgwajeong*, 73.

their curricular hypotheses are in fact demonstrated by student behavior. Following the application of the curriculum, educators return to the curricular plans to make any adjustments so as to ensure the proper outcomes in the classroom. In this case, students do not participate on any level in the planning or implementation of their education; rather, they solely assume the role of object of study.[72]

Tyler's model started to influence religious education curriculum studies when Wyckoff incorporated Tyler's rationale into his religious education curriculum theory. As Wyckoff's model based on Tyler's scientific and technocratic curriculum has been one of the most influential theories in the field of religious education curriculum, it is reasonable to argue that Tyler's rationale has strongly influenced the theories and practices of the Christian religious education curriculum.[73]

For Wyckoff, religious education curriculum is an important tool for achieving the purposes of Christian education. He argued that curriculum must be intentionally organized and planned in accord with the goals of religious education.[74] From his viewpoint, Tyler's scientific and systematic approach was a satisfactory framework for designing religious education curriculum. Thus, Wyckoff introduced Tyler's basic principles into the process of religious education curriculum planning.[75] For example, the five components of the Cooperative Curriculum Project (CCP) based on Wyckoff's theory were Objective, Scope, Context, Learning Tasks, and Organizing Principle, which seem to be in accord with Tyler's basic principles.[76] Like Tyler, he emphasized the concreteness of educational purpose for the effective designing of curriculum.[77]

Although many of his ideas are based on Tyler's rationale, his concept of the *organizing principle of curriculum construction* seems different from Tyler's concept of *organizing learning experiences*. While Tyler tends

72. Kreider, "1949."
73. Park, "Curriculum Model," 125.
74. Wyckoff, *Theory and Design*, 29–31.
75. See Park, *Gidokgyo gyoyukgwajeong Tamgu*, 185–90.
76. Cooperative Curriculum Project is a representative ecumenical curriculum developed in 1965 with the cooperation of sixteen Protestant denominations in United States and Canada. From the curricular view it is based on Wyckoff's ideas of curriculum, while its theological approach is influenced by Neo-orthodoxy. C. Ellis Nelson argued that CCP is one of great achievements in religious education curriculum. Lee, *Haeseokhakjeok sangsangryeokgwa gidokgyo gyoyukgwajeong*, 80–87.
77. Ibid., 82–84.

to draw attention to the role of the teacher in effectively controlling and organizing necessary learning experiences even though such learning experiences are basically for students, Wyckoff seems to stress very strongly the experiences of students[78] and thus, viewed curriculum as all of the planned experiences of learners.[79] He emphasizes student responses to God's calling and student participation in a faith community in his curriculum design.[80]

Conceptual-Empiricists

Wyckoff's thinking on curriculum influenced many religious education curricularists, including Iris Cully. Cully joined in the Joint Educational Development committee and had a leading role in developing Christian Education: Shared Approaches (CE: SA).[81] In the course of designing this ecumenical curriculum, she was affected considerably by Wyckoff's Cooperative Curriculum Project, especially its philosophical concepts and educational strategies.[82] However, in this project, Cully concentrated on the efficiency of curriculum rather than on its systematization.[83]

The change from Wyckoff's systematization to Cully's efficiency in the field of religious education curriculum resulted from the emergence of new curricularists around that time who are called the conceptual-empiricists. The efficiency of curriculum on which Cully had focused is one of the essential characteristics of the conceptual-empiricist approach which relies on research methodologies and social-scientific research in its study of curriculum.

Influenced by the research trends of conceptual-empiricists, Cully concentrates on the effectiveness of the organization of religious education curriculum in the actual teaching-learning contexts, which is different from Wyckoff who was concerned with developing church curricula

---

78. Wyckoff, *Task of Christian Education*, 127–29.

79. Wyckoff, *Theory and Design*, 29.

80. See Lee, *Haeseokhakjeok sangsangryeokgwa gidokgyo gyoyukgwajeong*, 80–87.

81. Christian Education: Shared Approaches is an ecumenical curriculum developed by Joint Educational Development in 1967. Twelve Protestant denominations in the United States and Canada participated in the Joint Educational Development. This curriculum is based on the curriculum theory of Iris Cully focusing the efficiency of curriculum. For analysis of this curriculum, see Oh et al., *Gidokgyo gyoyukron*, 356–72.

82. See. Lee, *Haeseokhakjeok sangsangryeokgwa gidokgyo gyoyukgwajeong*, 87–92.

83. Ibid., 28.

systematically as a traditionalist. To increase curriculum efficiency, Cully expands her research interests beyond curriculum itself to educational environments, the teacher's ability, and the learner's age. She draws attention to developmental psychological theories in order to understand how the child develops because she believes that such knowledge provides an important basis for selecting learning experiences.[84] Furthermore, she claims that such theories would be particularly helpful for voluntary, untrained church teachers in deciding which subjects or materials would be useful for their young students.[85] She also favors setting measurable and objective behavior goals as criteria for checking the efficiency of the teaching-learning process.[86] Cully believes that such behaviors achieved in the classroom can result in action for Christian living. In her mind, learning in religious education should be connected to living as a Christian.[87]

Reconceptualists

The movement of reconceptualization began in 1969 when Joseph Schwab published an article, "The Practical: A Language for Curriculum."[88] In this essay, he argued that "the field of curriculum is moribund, unable by its present methods and principles to continue its work and desperately in search of new and more effective principles and methods."[89] Schwab presents the following six signs as evidence of his claim: first, that the role of problem-solving in the field of curriculum is often done by scholars in other areas like psychology; second, there is a tendency to move from concrete discourse or theory about the subject of curriculum to abstract discourse or meta-theory; third, there are fewer principles relevant to curricularists in the field; fourth, curriculum scholars have become sidelined; fifth, there has been nothing but a repetition of old knowledge or principles of curriculum for a long time; and finally, there is an increase in disagreements or arguments within the field of curriculum studies.[90]

---

84. Huebner et al., "From Theory to Practice," 412.
85. Ibid., 413.
86. Cully, "New Approaches to Teaching," 379.
87. Cully, "Christian Education," 257.
88. Schwab, "Practical," 103–17.
89. Ibid., 103.
90. Ibid., 104–5.

His sense of the curriculum crisis at that time spurred a movement to reconceptualize curriculum anew, questioning the traditional scientific and technocratic approach.[91] As Pinar maintains, "Bureaucratized curriculum development—associated with the Tyler protocol—was replaced by a multi-discursive academic effort to understand curriculum."[92]

These reconceptualizing efforts have been closely related to a movement seeking an alternative epistemology to the modern scientific and positivistic one on which Tyler's rationale is embedded. Patrick Slattery argues that new curriculum based on postmodern epistemology should encourage *multiple forms of representation* as follows:

> In modern curriculum research we emphasize—often exclusively—linear logic, propositional language, universal truth, and fixed meaning. . . .
>
> Postmodern curriculum . . . wages war on totality of representation that reduces learning to information transmission, disciplinary structures, grand narratives, and concepts of "reason" that continue to foster the bifurcations that ignite racism, patriarchy, homophobia, colonialism, and classism. Postmodern curriculum research refuses to be bound by rigid modern bifurcations and the divisive linear logic that follows.[93]

To overcome the express limitations of Tylerian scientific and technocratic curriculum, lots of reconceptualized curriculum theories have been formulated. Among them, three representative approaches will be dealt with in some detail: critical theory, hermeneutical approach, and aesthetic approach.

1. Critical Theory

In order to reconceptualize the curriculum, critical theorists review the justification for curriculum in public schools. They focus especially on social ideologies and concerns of the ruling class hidden behind the official curriculum of public schools and believe that the hidden curriculum in schools reveals the ideologies and interests of the minority rulers.[94] Eisner explains the hidden curriculum as follows:

---

91. Lee, *Haeseokhakjeok sangsangryeokgwa gidokgyo gyoyukgwajeong*, 331–32.
92. Pinar, "Crisis, Reconceptualization, Internationalization," 5.
93. Slattery, "Postmodern Curriculum Research."
94. Eisner, *Educational Imagination*, 73. Patrick Slattery and Dana Rapp argue that

The hidden curriculum consists of the message given to children by teachers, school structures, textbooks, and other school resources. These messages are often conveyed by teachers who themselves are unaware of their presence. "Hidden" implies a hider—someone or some group that intentionally conceals. Concealment, in turn, suggests a form of subterfuge in order to achieve some gain. Hence, the hidden curriculum is often believed to serve the interests of the power elite that the school, often unwittingly, is thought to serve.[95]

Critical reflection on the hidden curriculum in schools tends to promote the idea of education as humanization, education seeking an all-round development of human potential beyond schooling. Paulo Freire is one of the leading scholars who advocate education for freedom and humanization. He criticizes schooling as banking education, and reveals ten incorrect assumptions about schooling as follows:

(a) The teacher teaches and the students are taught. (b) The teacher knows everything and the students know nothing. (c) The teacher thinks and the students are thought about. (d) The teacher talks and the students listen-meekly. (e) The teacher disciplines and the students are disciplined. (f) The teacher chooses and enforces his choice, and the students comply. (g) The teacher acts and the students have the illusion of acting through the action of the teacher. (h) The teacher chooses the program content and the students (who were not consulted) adapt to it. (i) The teacher confuses the authority of knowledge with his own professional authority, which he sets in opposition to the freedom of the students. (j) The Teacher is the Subject of the learning process, while the pupils are mere objects.[96]

As an alternative to banking education, Freire proposes *problem-posing education* through which the teacher could pose, reflect, resolve students' real problems, and build true communication with them.[97] His

---

such understanding "sets free what is hidden from view by layers of tradition, prejudice, and even conscious evasion." Slattery and Rapp, *Ethics and the Foundations of Education*, 96, quoted in Pinar, "Crisis, Reconceptualization, Internalization," 5.

95. Eisner, *Educational Imagination*, 73.
96. Freire, *Pedagogy of the Oppressed*, 46–47.
97. The practice of problem-posing education demands a resolution of the teacher-student contradiction, by presenting dialogical relationship between them. "Through dialogue, the teacher-of-students and the students-of-teacher cease to exist and a new term emerges: teacher-student with students-teachers. The teacher is no longer merely

concepts of *dialogical theory of action* and *cultural synthesis* seem insightful and helpful for teachers seeking to understand students.[98]

Many religious educators have criticized the schooling model of religious education. John Westerhoff III is a representative religious educator who criticizes the schooling curriculum of religious education. He argues that "Christian educators and local churches have functioned according to a *schooling-instructional paradigm*. That is, our image of education has been founded upon some sort of a 'school' as the context *and* some form of instruction as the means."[99] As a result, he claims that many church educators have adhered to teaching-related aspects such as teaching skill and resources, and confined religious education to the Sunday School, which resulted in a broken ecology of religious education.[100]

According to Westerhoff, there have been six institutions working together in religious education: community, the family, public schools, church life, religious literature, and Sunday School. Among the six organizations, he argues that the Sunday School has played an important role organizing other institutions to work together in order to produce an ecology relevant to religious education.[101] Since the curriculum of schooling began to dominate in religious education, the church school has been isolated from other institutions and has wrestled alone with nurturing people for faith.[102]

Westerhoff maintains that church educators cannot nurture faith under the schooling-instructional paradigm because faith cannot be taught by teachers. "Faith cannot be taught by any method of instruction; we can only teach religion. . . . Faith is expressed, transformed, and made meaningful by persons sharing their faith in an historical, tradition-bearing community of faith."[103] For him, all aspects of church life are crucial

---

the-one-who-teaches, but one who is himself taught in dialogue with the students, who in their turn while being taught also teach. They become jointly responsible for a process in which all grow." Ibid., 53.

98. See ibid., 96–150. Freire argued that the dialogical theory of cultural action has a feature of cultural synthesis. In cultural synthesis, teachers "do not come to *teach* or to *transmit* or to *give* anything, but rather to learn" with the students, about their world. They "become integrated with [the students], who are co-authors of the action that both perform upon the world." Ibid., 147.

99. Westerhoff, *Will Our Children Have Faith?*, 6.

100. Ibid., 13.

101. See ibid., 13–16.

102. Ibid., 16.

103. Ibid., 23.

experiences that directly influence one's faith formation. He underlines the importance of the informal hidden curriculum of socialization in the church for faith more than the formal curriculum of schooling. Formal curriculum based on the schooling-instructional paradigm is a small part of religious education, not the whole.[104] However, he agrees that the term *socialization* might give the impression that "someone does something to someone else."[105] So, he chooses the term *enculturation* instead of socialization to emphasize the mutuality of socialization in the process of faith development in a faith community.

> Christian faith implies the need to focus on the mutuality of our engagements with each other, thereby eliminating all categories such as teacher and student, adult (the one who knows) and child (the one who needs to know), socializer and socializee. For these reasons, I have chosen the word "enculturation" to characterize educational method in a faith community.
>
> While much socialization literature has a tendency to emphasize how the environment, experiences, and actions of others influence us, enculturation emphasizes the process of interaction between and among persons of all ages.[106]

Westerhoff argues that the religious education curriculum should be designed to promote the process of enculturation in faith education and focus on every aspect of life in the church. To do this, the church should be a faith community suitable for the faith-enculturation paradigm.[107] It is remarkable that critical theory criticizes intentional socialization in education by the minority rulers, but Westerhoff found some implications for religious education in the concept and broadened the context of religious education to underscore the hidden curriculum of enculturation in the church.

2. Hermeneutical Approach

Huebner is another leading religious educator who criticized the use of the curriculum of schooling in religious education. Although agreeing

---

104. Ibid., 17–23.
105. Ibid., 79.
106. Ibid., 80.
107. Ibid., 50–54. For a practical example of the faith-enculturation paradigm, see Westerhoff, *Tomorrow's Church*, 105–27.

in many respects with Westerhoff's perceived problems in the schooling paradigm, Huebner's approach is quite different from that of Westerhoff in that he disapproves of Westerhoff's emphasis on the role of socialization in faith education. Huebner thinks the term *socialization* is not educational. For Huebner, socialization just means *hidden forms of control*: "Socialization points to the way the adult tries to shape the child to fit into adult perceptions of what the world should be and what the child should be.... Behind it lie questions concerning power and control."[108] Huebner claims that education is, by its very nature, political and related to power and control. Thus, it is very important for educational authorities to use power appropriately in their efforts to educate rather than control, but he thinks that socialization seems to be a misuse of such power.[109]

For the same reason, as mentioned above, Westerhoff introduced the term *enculturation* in order to avoid the image of intentional control. However, Huebner criticized the new term—enculturation—because he thinks the term does not focus on *the interaction of persons and culture* which seems essential in using educational power creatively. While Westerhoff draws attention to the interaction between and among persons in a faith community in the process of religious education, Huebner concentrates on the interplay between persons and culture because he believes that *the impact of cultural wealth* could lead to *the transformation of persons*.[110]

Westerhoff criticizes the schooling curriculum of religious education because he thinks it tends to prevent students from being mutually socialized (enculturated) with the teacher in a faith community, while Huebner disparages church education in a school setting as it is likely to hinder students from being confronted with the truth itself by controlling them through intentional socialization.[111] For Huebner, the confrontation between students and their faith tradition is essential in

---

108. Huebner et al., "From Theory to Practice," 364.

109. Ibid. Craig Dykstra totally agrees with Huebner's opinion on the political character of education: "Curriculum issues always of control, of power. There is no doubt that educators have power and seek to use power. But the question is, given our power, how will we use it?" Ibid., 407.

110. Ibid., 364–65.

111. Ibid., 370. For example, he argues that, in the case of the catechism, if only already fixed answers or directions are provided to learners, it would be socialization for control rather than education for transformation. See ibid., 366.

Religious Education Curriculum

religious education for faith, and it is the difference between socialization and education:

> Especially, I am concerned about the way we use textbooks in schools. The textbook itself is a destruction of the texts, because it removes the confrontation between the person and the text itself. When the religious educator went to the secular traditions of building religious textual materials it was text*book* material. Rather than dealing with the texts and the confrontation of the community with the texts, and the way meaning is established out of that confrontation, the church school moved towards textbooks. Textbooks do not honor the texts.[112]

In this respect, Huebner defines curriculum as *the content* which means knowledge, heritage, or cultural wealth. His definition was contrary to the then dominant concept of curriculum as all the experiences of students in school.[113] He thinks that there are two curricular problems in the Tylerian scientific curriculum for schooling.

First, Huebner argues that Tyler's emphasis on learners' needs or experiences as a crucial starting point for designing curriculum has caused curriculum-makers to rely too much on social science and psychology to understand students.[114] Consequently, "the curriculum field lost its sense of identity."[115] Huebner claims that "one of the major stumbling blocks to the redevelopment of education and to the redevelopment of curriculum is the domination by psychological language today.... We need to break the tremendous control of our technological, scientific orientation."[116] Especially, he strongly criticizes the thoughtless application of insights of developmental psychology theorists like Piaget, Kohlberg, Erikson, and Fowler into the field of education because such theories tend to prevent the teacher from considering children's individual differences by making them stick to the prescribed developmental path, which could lead to "a faithless response to the individual."[117]

Second, Huebner indicates that the understanding of curriculum as all of the experiences of the person in school seems to provide teachers

---

112. Ibid., 370.

113. Ibid., 363.

114. Huebner criticized both traditionalists and conceptual-empiricists that depend on Tyler's scientific and technocratic approach.

115. Huebner et al., "From Theory to Practice," 363.

116. Ibid., 372.

117. Ibid., 374.

with plenty of room to control the experience of the student. As discussed above, many curriculum theorists stressing students' needs or experiences like Tyler, Wyckoff, and Cully underline setting concrete behavioral goals in their curricula and controlling learning experiences to achieve the selected goals. Huebner criticizes goal-driven education because it is likely to degenerate into control. Furthermore, this production-oriented curriculum tends to weaken religious educators' historicity which is very important in dealing with Christian heritage in the present and past.[118]

To overcome these two problems related to the long-standing appreciation of curriculum as experience, Huebner reconceptualizes curriculum as content and is concerned about the way in which it would become available to people. For example, he argues that liturgy is curriculum as content because it contains lots of meaning. In addition, for Huebner, the way that liturgy is made available to students is critical.[119] Clarisse Croteau-Chonka accurately describes what Huebner thought about liturgy as curriculum as follows:

> The point is made that when the student searches for meaning in the liturgy, the teacher must also try to re-understand the ritual. In that way the community as a whole can be encouraged to understand its liturgical activity anew. This example further clarifies Huebner's intentions with respect to curriculum. The word is used to refer both to content of education and the meaning which comes from that content. In this usage, curriculum is not a passive educational form imposed on the student, but rather an educational activity into which the student enters, with which the student has dialog.[120]

As such, Huebner considers curriculum to be a diverse form of cultural wealth and draws attention to the dialectic and hermeneutic communication between the text and students. He believes that this is the way in which "this cultural wealth can transform the child and be transformed by the child."[121] By narrowing the concerns of the curriculum field into

---

118. See Huebner, "Curriculum as Concern," 325. Sara Little describes his curriculum as goal-free curriculum which values process rather than production. Huebner et al., "From Theory to Practice," 377.

119. Huebner et al., "From Theory to Practice," 367.

120. Ibid., 422.

121. Ibid., 413. As Robert Browning indicates, this is the goal of his curriculum theory although he rejected to use the term "goal" or "purpose" of curriculum. Ibid., 416.

content, Huebner shows that the most significant role of religious educators is to help students confront the truth by encouraging a hermeneutic dialogue with what they learn. By proposing the dialectic-hermeneutical approach for religious education, he attempts to help religious educators escape not only from the long-standing schooling paradigm, but also from dependence on social science and psychology.

To facilitate this process, the teacher should try to constantly reinterpret what they have taken for granted and be open to new understandings of Christian traditions through active communication with learners. Then, there might be a mutual transformation between the teacher and students and even the whole community could be renewed.[122] Likewise, for Huebner, students are "co-creators of meaning in a setting of mutuality."[123] This is Huebner's proposal for using power rightly. James Michael Lee describes Huebner's dialectic and hermeneutic curriculum of religious education as "his vision of shared curricular power."[124] Huebner's reconceptualized thinking on curriculum has had a huge impact on the field of religious education curriculum.[125]

However, there have also been various critics of Huebner's curriculum theory. For example, conceptual-empiricists like Cully, Lee, and Browning questioned Huebner's criticism of the reckless application of developmental theories in the context of religious education. They also criticized his goal-free curriculum because they thought that every curriculum has, by its nature, some direction for curriculum planning and its implementation.[126] In addition, James Michael Lee criticized Huebner's cognition-centered approach, arguing that "the exclusive or even primary identification of religion with the cognitive domain blinds a person to the deeper, more pervasive, and more potent lifestyle dimensions of religion."[127] He also argued that Huebner's exclusivistic cognitivism is based on rationalism[128] which seems a primary reason for the decline in

---

122. See ibid., 367–71.

123. Ibid., 402.

124. Ibid., 390.

125. Among his former students, James Michael Lee described Mary Boys, Thomas Groome, and Kieran Scott as his devoted disciples. See ibid., 387.

126. Refer to each reflective response of Michael Lee, Cully, and Browning to Huebner's thinking on curriculum. See ibid., 383–95, 411–19.

127. Ibid., 388.

128. Rationalism "regards reason as the chief source and test of knowledge. Holding that reality itself has an inherently logical structure, the rationalist asserts that

numbers and in spiritual vitality of the church today, so is intrinsically inappropriate as a curriculum philosophy for religious education.[129]

3. Aesthetic Approach

Maria Harris, one of Huebner's students, overcame a limitation of her teacher's cognition-centered curriculum theory by using Eisner's aesthetic curriculum model. Harris stresses different forms of representation, especially aesthetic experiences, and the role of imagination in the creating of religious education curriculum. Since she was influenced a lot by Eisner's curricular ideas, Eisner's aesthetic model will be dealt with briefly and then Harris's approach will be addressed.

Eisner starts building his curriculum theory, by criticizing the assumption that only propositional language and social science are able to contain and deliver meaning.[130] He argues that there should be multiple forms of data representations beyond the scientific pattern because he believes in *cognitive pluralism*:

> As a conception of knowledge, Cognitive Pluralism argues that one of the human being's distinctive features is the capacity to create and manipulate symbols. These symbols are powerful cultural resources that are employed in mathematics, music, literature, science, dance, the visual arts, indeed, in any area of human life in which action or form is used to give expression or to represent experience or intention.[131]

Eisner claims that a primary goal of schooling should be providing students with various forms of data representation so that they may

---

a class of truths exists that the intellect can grasp directly. There are, according to the rationalists, certain rational principles—especially in logic and mathematics, and even in ethics and metaphysics—that are so fundamental that to deny them is to fall into contradiction. The rationalist's confidence in reason and proof tends, therefore, to detract from his respect for other ways of knowing." See *Britannica.com*, s.v. "rationalism."

129. Michael Lee also criticizes the fact that Huebner had never been involved in any concrete curriculum design. He argues that it is a fatal limitation of Huebner's theory because he believes that "if curriculum theorizing is to have any genuine impact on religious education endeavour, then it must be joined by the theorist himself to concrete curriculum design and concrete instructional activity." Huebner et al., "From Theory to Practice," 388.

130. Eisner, "Promise and Perils," 4.

131. Eisner, *Educational Imagination*, 79–80.

interpret and recover meaning in a diverse range of cognitive forms.[132] He argues that there are two strong points of cognitive pluralism in terms of curriculum planning. First, cognitive pluralism seems to expand the concept of literacy: "Although the term *literacy* typically refers to the ability to read, it would be extended to include the encoding or decoding of information in any of the forms that humans use to convey meaning."[133] That is, under the concept of cognitive pluralism literacy means the ability to read various symbols containing meaning including language. Therefore, Eisner argues that educators should be concerned with the development of multiple forms of literacy, such as visual, musical, and theatrical forms.[134] He also emphasizes the role of imagination in accessing the experience of different forms of representation or symbol systems.[135] He argues that "knowing depends upon experience, either the kind of experience that emanates from the sentient being's contact with the qualities of the environment or from the experiences born of the imagination."[136] Second, Eisner maintains that the concept of various cognitive forms seems helpful for the teacher to take into account individual differences in the classroom:

> By creating a wider array of curricular tasks, those that require the use of different forms of intelligence, for example, or depend on different aptitudes, opportunities for success in school are expanded. These opportunities are expanded if success on this wider array of tasks is regarded as having equal intellectual merit. If, for example, high level ability in the arts is regarded as laudable, but non-intellectual in nature, and if the school gives its most highly prized awards to what it regards as intellectual achievement, children who shine in the arts will never shine as brightly as those who are excellent in mathematics; the arts, like the children attracted to them, will remain second-class citizens in the hierarchy of curricular values.[137]

As such, Eisner provides a broader understanding of knowledge and curriculum by accepting the concept of cognitive pluralism. Among alternative forms of research representation, he focuses particularly on

132. Ibid., 80.
133. Ibid., 81.
134. Eisner, "Artistry in Education," 382.
135. Eisner, *Cognition and Curriculum Reconsidered*, x.
136. Ibid., 31.
137. Eisner, *Educational Imagination*, 82.

aesthetic experiences. Eisner views the development of curriculum as the process of artwork as he thinks of teaching as an art. In *The Educational Imagination*, he provides four reasons for his understanding of teaching as an art: (1) teaching is an art because the teaching experience can be described as aesthetic; (2) teaching is an art because it is performed with classroom qualities, like "tempo, tone, climate, pace of discussion, and forward movement"; (3) teaching is an art because it is an unpredicted and heuristic action; and (4) teaching is an art because it discovers ends through action, especially through interaction with students.[138] Thus, Eisner considers the teacher to be an artist in that he/she creates a work of art in the classroom.

Influenced by Eisner's aesthetic approach to curriculum, Harris views teaching as an art and considers imagination to be *the heart of teaching*.[139] For her, teaching is a work of religious imagination. Distinguishing religious imagination from imagination, Harris argues that religious imagination consists of four forms of imagination: *contemplative, ascetic, creative,* and *sacramental* imagination. Contemplative imagination is for being in the presence of God; ascetic imagination is for being in the context of daily life; creative imagination is for creating new possibilities in educational practices; and sacramental imagination views all of human work including teaching as a holy sacrament.[140] She argues that religious imagination provides another lens through which human actions are examined.[141] In addition, religious imagination enables teachers to provide students with various ways of learning.

> The teacher is one who embodies—gives flesh to—form. . . . Form is not only the intention of content; it is the actual embodiment of content. . . . Because of the variegated possibilities in subject matter, the teacher must learn not just one form, but a repertoire of forms in order to teach. If the teacher hopes to make subject matter available, or in the more illuminating term, "accessible," the teacher must bring to bear a variety of incarnational possibilities on and in the teaching act. . . . The knowing subject possesses a broad range or variety of ways of learning: through concrete experience; through reflective observation;

---

138. Ibid., 154–56.

139. Harris, *Teaching and Religious Imagination*, 3; Harris and Moran, *Reshaping Religious Education*, 20.

140. Harris, *Teaching and Religious Imagination*, 4–23.

141. Ibid., 21–23.

through abstract conceptualization; and through active experimentation. We call these "ways" different aspects of the learning act. And we can call the learning act a learning circle.[142]

The five steps that Harris suggests as the process of teaching as a work of religious imagination are quite similar to the processes of pottery making: *contemplation, engagement, formgiving, emergence,* and *release.* The first movement is contemplation, in which the subject matter is considered as a Thou. In contemplation, the teacher and students can communicate with the subject matter as a partner, not regarding it as knowledge out there to be interpreted. Then, engagement follows. "Engagement means diving in, wrestling with, and rolling around in subject matter."[143] She argues that the teacher must love and respect the subject matter to become genuinely engaged. The third movement is formgiving, in which the teacher and students cooperate to produce something together out of the subject matter. From her perspective, formgiving is the central work of teaching, but it is a paradoxical process because from time to time something unexpected emerges. After the collaborative process of formgiving, something new is born. This is the fourth step, emergence. This "eureka" moment does not happen all the time; Harris claims that it happens in divine time. The final moment is release. This is the point where the teacher removes his/her hands from the subject matter and lets it go. It is also the point where new contemplation begins.[144]

In relation to these teaching steps, Harris asserts that "they are like steps in dance, where movement is both backward and forward, around and through, and where turns, returns, rhythm and movement are essential. . . . Each one of the steps, in its own way, draws on the four forms of imagination as the ways, forms, or paths of religious imagination."[145]

Harris's understanding of teaching is closely connected to her conception of curriculum. Harris applies the five steps of teaching directly to curriculum planning. For her, the construction of curriculum is "artistic educational work,"[146] so it should follow "the steps of artistic process."[147] Thus, the five steps of curriculum designing proposed by Harris are the

142. Ibid., 42–43.
143. Ibid., 30.
144. Ibid., 26–39.
145. Ibid., 25–26.
146. Harris, *Fashion Me a People*, 16.
147. Ibid., 172.

same as the steps of teaching discussed above: *contemplation, engagement, formgiving, emergence,* and *release*.[148] As in teaching steps, curricularists should bear in mind each step's tempo, rhythm, tone, and climate in the course of designing curriculum rather than leading the process like the steps of a staircase.[149]

In addition, Harris maintains that religious education curriculum should include all aspects of church life, such as, community (*koinonia*), prayer (*leiturgia*), teaching (*didache*), proclamation (*kerygma*), and service (*diakonia*).[150] She believes that fashioning learners to be God's people, a primary purpose of curriculum, should take place in all fields of church life.[151] Harris insists that planning a religious education curriculum is an educational ministry for a church congregation, and these five forms of church life are the contents of the educational ministry. Among these contents, she thinks that community, prayer, and service are the most basic components of the church's life, and when these three things are in place, teaching and proclamation will be possible.[152] Harris argues that "the fashioning and refashioning of the set of forms is the core of the educational ministry of the church. . . . In fashioning these forms we fashion the church. And because *we* are the church, the fashioning of the church becomes the fashioning of us" as a people with a pastoral vocation.[153] In this respect, she concludes that the curriculum is the pastoral work of fashioning and refashioning of koinonia, leiturgia, didache, kerygma, and diakonia.[154]

Necessity of Digital-Based Curriculum

I will employ the key curricular concepts of Harris in developing a new religious education curriculum for second-generation Korean Australian (SGKA) teenagers because her church-centered approach promoting five forms of church life is appropriate for this work focusing on religious

148. Ibid., 172–81.
149. Ibid., 172.
150. Ibid., 75–156; Harris and Moran, *Reshaping Religious Education*, 19–22.
151. Harris, *Fashion Me a People*, 16–17.
152. Harris and Moran, *Reshaping Religious Education*, 21.
153. Harris, *Fashion Me a People*, 17. Harris claims that religious educators should have three components of the pastoral vocation, priestly, prophetic, and kingly. See ibid., 26.
154. Ibid., 64.

education in the context of the Korean Australian (KA) churches. In addition, Harris's model of curriculum as artistic educational work based on cognitive pluralism and religious imagination is a good alternative to the Tylerian scientific-standardized paradigm on which the current curriculum paradigm of most KA churches, transmitting knowledge-out-of-context, is based. However, her approach has inherent curricular limitations particularly in the current digital world, because her model is an analog-based curriculum like most of the current curriculum.[155] Analog-based curriculum means a curriculum established for analog ways of learning, thinking and communicating, such as offline-centered communication, mass communication via mass media, paper-based culture, and hardware-centered manufacturing paradigm, which do not accord with today's students' ways of living and learning.

In order to highlight features of the analog-based and the digital-based curriculum, two forms of culture—analog and digital—will be contrasted in detail: (1) component based vs. service centered and (2) mass communication vs. mass self-communication.

Component Based vs. Service Centered

First of all, analog-based curriculum is based on a deep-rooted manufacturing paradigm. Since Bobbitt introduced Frederick Taylor's scientific management theory into the field of curriculum, the production orientation based on scientific management has long been embedded into curriculum planning.[156] Influenced by Tyler's scientific rationale, curriculum has been regarded as a product manufactured according to a blueprint.[157] Eisner criticizes this long-standing factory image in relation to education as follows: "*The dominant image of schooling in America has been the factory and the dominant image of teaching and learning the assembly line. These images misconceive and underestimate the complexities of teaching and neglect the difference between education and training.*"[158]

However, it seems difficult to conclude that Eisner fully overcame the manufacturing paradigm because his concepts of curriculum

---

155. Since her curriculum theory was developed in the 1970s and 1980s, it did not consider the nature and advantages of digitization.
156. Eisner, "Artistry in Education," 374.
157. Mitchell, "What Is 'Curriculum'?," 362.
158. Eisner, *Educational Imagination*, 361, italics in original.

planning are still rooted in *component-based modularity*. Fredrik Svahn argues that component-based modularity is an essential feature of the modern manufacturing paradigm that has been effective in the design of analog products.[159] He maintains that component-based modularity "has proved useful in the design of complex systems, such as cars or airplanes, by establishing interdependence within and independence across product components. It facilitates control over complex systems, allowing for concurrent design, and accommodates uncertainty."[160] He argues that "manufacturing firms have used component-based modularity to establish horizontal loose coupling between components and vertical tight integration of the design hierarchy. While components, and their inherent functionality, are managed autonomously by suppliers, integration into a system is strictly controlled by the manufacturer."[161]

As such, in component-based modularity, it is essential that each component should be integrated into the whole system by interacting with each other component. At this point, a party should control the process of integration of each part with a certain philosophy and direction. Most curriculum constructions in the twentieth century from Bobbitt and Tyler to Eisner and Harris have been done within component-based modularity. There seem few exceptions even nowadays. Regardless of whether they are traditionalists or reconceptualists, most curricularists have developed their own curriculum models and insights within component-based modularity, focusing on how to organize curricular components such as goals, learning experiences, and evaluation into a well-integrated educational program.[162]

While Eisner criticizes the Tylerian teacher-centered instructional paradigm, he emphasizes the teacher-centered selection of content and organization of components to enable students to gain a better educational outcome.[163] He refers to the authority of teachers in the process of integration of each component where the role of teachers is similar to

---

159. Svahn, "Sociomateriality," 23.

160. Ibid., 25.

161. Ibid.

162. For Eisner's thinking in curriculum planning, see Eisner, *Educational Imagination*, 125–53.

163. At this time, Eisner emphasizes the role of educational imagination. Ibid., 138.

that of a company that controls the production process in component-based modularity.[164]

According to the collaboration model presented by Gary Pisano and Roberto Verganti, component-based modularity seems closely related to a closed and hierarchical network mode.[165] It is *closed* in that a select group of participants are chosen by the authorities, and it is *hierarchical* in that the authorities control the direction of innovation. Pisano and Verganti describe the closed and hierarchical network paradigm using the term *Elite Circle*.[166] The elite-centered innovation might well be found in the process of curriculum planning rooted in component-oriented modularity.

On the other hand, Svahn argues that in the digital society a new modularity is emerging: service-based modularity. It is notable that the new mode is software service centered in which software logic dominates rather than being hardware component centered.[167] He explains the meaning of service as follows: "Within a service-oriented paradigm services are under continuous reassessment within a polyarchic, non-linear and relatively open innovation network, making offers evolve over time. Quality and customer satisfaction are addressed in terms of multiplicity and competition, eventually providing value to more users."[168]

Analyzing Svahn's reference to service-based modularity, two essential features emerge in relation to software services.

First of all, software services offer continuous updates of the software's quality, multiplicity, security, and competition. For this, a service provider should be closely connected to users so that it can receive continual and accurate feedback from them. If bugs are found in a software program, service providers distribute a patch to be downloaded so that users can fix them. Later, they normally provide a service pack to completely solve such problems or they address them in an updated version

---

164. Ibid., 126.

165. Pisano and Verganti present four collaboration options: closed/hierarchical (Elite Circle), open/hierarchical (Innovation Mall), open/flat (Innovation Community), and closed/flat (Consortium). For detailed accounts of the four models, see Pisano and Verganti, "Which Kind of Collaboration," 1–9.

166. Ibid., 4–7.

167. Svahn, "Sociomateriality," 23.

168. Ibid., 26.

of the software.[169] In this regard, software services are totally different from after service on a hardware product.

Hardware services are component based in the sense that they mainly focus on the replacement of broken components, while software services are *solution oriented* in that they pursue the continual upgrade of the software's functionality beyond finding bugs and fixing them. Component-centered hardware services tend to be rather passive in that services occur when customers need them or sometimes when massive products are recalled with technical faults, whereas solution-oriented software services are very active in that they are provided to users anytime when updates are necessary and anywhere through the Internet. As a result, in the case of hardware companies, customer relationships seem much less connected than software developers. These characteristics of hardware services are found in almost all analog-based curriculum materials. For example, when a textbook based on the hardware paradigm is published, customer services are usually very limited to the extent that defective books can be exchanged or extra materials subsequently released. In most cases, there is little connection between curriculum developers and ordinary users.

It is remarkable that the concept of solution-oriented software service is rapidly expanding into the recent development of a diverse range of customized IT (Information Technology) solutions for various areas like business, company systems, hardware products, educational institutions, and government agencies in order to resolve their problems and maximize their outcomes by integrating hardware, software, and service. In most cases, IT-based software plays a pivotal role in the integration of previously unconnected activities and artifacts.[170] A representative form of IT-based solution is *cloud computing*. It is building a software based virtual infrastructure online for the free flow of information-integrating hardware, software, server, database, and web-based storage. For example, in a cloud environment users can do their work using virtual software, virtual hardware devices, and web storage anywhere and anytime if the Internet is accessible. These software-led combined services are cutting-edge technology and lead into the future.[171] This is the reason why many

---

169. Gupta, "Practitioner-Oriented," 228–29.
170. Tuli et al., "Rethinking Customer Solutions," 1–2.
171. Armbrust et al., "View of Cloud Computing," 50–54.

Religious Education Curriculum 49

hardware manufacturers like IBM, HP, and Dell have been transforming into IT solution–centered companies.

Second, software services are based on a polyarchic, nonlinear and open network mode. As discussed above, component-based modularity is based on a closed and hierarchical network mode, while service-oriented modularity is rooted in an open and flat form of network. Pisano and Verganti call the open and flat network mode an *Innovation Community*. In an Innovation Community, anyone can propose problems, suggest solutions, and decide which one to select.[172] They argue that this form of Innovation Community seems appropriate for software services. They present the Linux open-source software community as an example of the open and flat network for software services. They maintain that "such open collaboration has been made easier by information platforms that allow participants to make contributions, share work, and observe the solutions of others."[173]

The open and nonlinear software service is currently in the limelight as an effective network approach in various areas beyond software-related companies. Referred to earlier, as hardware-software combined services are emphasized nowadays, an open and flat network model for collaboration with various third parties is being broadly accepted instead of the traditional model of closed and hierarchical network which is limited to a few professionals.[174] However, it is not easy to change to the new orientation. As Svahn argues, there is a lot of work involved in adopting a service-oriented modularity in organizations accustomed to the component-based approach.[175]

Svahn further claims that in digital innovation there is a clash between the two forms of modularity in which "continuing dialectic of *resistance* and *accommodation*" develops between the material agency and the human agency.[176] He argues that the dialectics between resistance and accommodation is an essential part of digital civilization:

> A key challenge in digital innovation is how to introduce a new form of materiality in an established mangling of sociomateriality.

172. Pisano and Verganti, "Which Kind of Collaboration," 5.

173. Ibid., 7.

174. Ibid., 8.

175. For example, people should learn new knowledge, should adapt to an open/flat networking style, and should create a service-oriented architecture. See Svahn, "Sociomateriality of Competing Technological Regimes in Digital Innovation," 30–35.

176. Ibid., 24.

> Here, the idea of mangling is somewhat stretched, when using it to describe how one form of material agency subjects itself to human agencies as it competes with another form of material agency. Digital innovation emerges out of this extended dialectical dance of agency, defined by resistance and accommodation between two distinct forms of material agency and human agency.[177]

The concept of a dialectic between resistance and accommodation seems to provide curricularists with an implication for curriculum innovation that moves from deep-rooted component-centered logic to a new software service-oriented paradigm.

Mass Communication vs. Mass Self-Communication

The second feature of the analog-based curriculum is that it is suitable for mass communication. Mass communication refers to transferring or transmitting a message to a large group of people, using mass media such as newspapers, books, radio, and television.[178]

In the mass communication era, ordinary people tend to be passive receivers of content. This phenomenon has been found in educational environments as well. In the classroom, students have been mass audiences for teacher-centered transmitting knowledge-out-of-context. Recently many teachers have often used multimedia like films, videos, or the Internet in order to help students easily understand what they intend to deliver, but even with audio-visual education students are likely to be passive receivers. Since John Dewey advocated progressive education, many scholars have continually emphasized student-centered education, but under the mass communication paradigm it is not easy to shift from a teacher-centered mode to a student-centered one with the traditional class structure. Curriculum models such as those of Eisner and Harris also take root in the form of mass communication.

In mass communication, physical contiguity is the basis of communication. Offline face-to-face communication has long been a dominant form of social interaction and decision-making. In such a paradigm, education tends to be considered as a face-to-face interaction in a physical classroom. Likewise, traditional educational practice is completely based

---

177. Ibid., 28.
178. Chaffee and Metzger, "End of Mass Communication?," 365–66.

on *the space of contiguity*.[179] However, in the digital era, the major form of communication is shifting from mass communication to mass self-communication. Mass self-communication is a by-product of digitization. Cees Hamelink explains digitization as follows:

> Digitization is the process through which information (whether relayed through sound, text, voice or image) is converted into the digital, binary language computers use. Computers cannot understand information in the form of pictures or words, but only when it is broken down into binary digits or bits: "zero" or "one," "yes" or "no," "on" or "off." The conversion of information into this form makes it possible to transmit information from different sources through one channel and to reduce the risks of distortion. Thus the use of the digital language facilitates the convergence of computers, telecommunications, office technologies and assorted audio-visual consumer electronics. Their integration, in turn, allows information to be handled at higher speed, with more flexibility, improved reliability and lower costs.
>
> Through digitization, the capacity of communications channels is greatly expanded, there is more scope for consumer choice, and more possibilities for interactive systems are created.[180]

Likewise, digitization has recently caused a daily revolution of information and communication. In the center of the revolution there are innovations of internet-based smart technologies like the smartphone or the tablet computer, and wireless communication technologies. Such wireless digital smart technologies are multifunctional: the Internet, the telephone, the television, games, and the personal computer became integrated into a smartphone or a tablet computer. People can connect to the Internet everywhere, which has brought a communication revolution—*mass self-communication.*[181]

Mass self-communication is building one's own systems of mass communication, "via SMS, blogs, vlogs, podcasts, wikis, and the like. File sharing and peer-to-peer (p2p) networks make the circulation, mixing, and reformatting of any digitized content possible."[182] Mass self-commu-

---

179. Castells describes a new form of spatiality in the digital era as the space of flows in which information can flow through the Internet channels regardless of the physical contiguity of the actors. See Castells, *Rise of the Network Society*, x-xvi.

180. Hamelink, "New Information and Communication," 4.

181. Castells, *Rise of the Network Society*, viii.

182. Ibid. Castells explains mass self-communication further, "Horizontal

nication is different from traditional mass communication in that it is "*self-generated in content, self-directed in emission,* and *self-selected in reception* by many who communicate with many."[183] In the mass self-communication era, people are no longer passive receivers allowed limited resources, but interactive agents who select, create, transform, receive, send, and post information on their own authority with a wide range of data and various tools.

In addition, various web-based social networking services like Facebook, Twitter, MySpace and Cyworld are providing people with great opportunities to expand their social relations, which is another recent transformation of communication. Danah Boyd and Nicole Ellison explain Social Networking Service (SNS) as a web-based site that allows people to build social networks in order to interact or share their lives through articulating their social links.[184] Sonia Livingstone and David Brake argue that web-based social networking has expedited transformations in the quantity and the quality of communication. SNSs have been rapidly adopted especially by young people because the key feature of SNSs is consistent with their wish to keep in contact with peers anywhere, anytime.[185] Livingstone and Brake analyze that "social networking disembeds communication from its traditional anchoring in the face-to-face situation of physical co-location where conventions of trust, authenticity and reciprocity are well understood, re-embedding it in more flexible, complex and ambiguous networks."[186] The decrease of face-to-face communication caused by online social networking tends to weaken people's communication ability offline. For example, since SNS users are accustomed to informal, relaxed, and playful interaction online, they tend to

---

networks of communication built around people's initiatives, interests, and desires are multimodal and incorporate many kinds of documents from photographs (hosted by sites such as Photobucket.com) and large-scale cooperative projects such as Wikipedia (the open source encyclopedia) to music and films (p2p networks based on free software programs such as Kazaa) and social political/religious activist networks that combine web-based forums of debate with global feeding of video, audio, and text. Thus, as analyst Jeffrey Cole reported to me, to teenagers who have the ability to generate content and distribute it over the net, it 'is not 15 minutes of fame they care about, it is about 15 megabytes of fame.'" See ibid.

183. Ibid., x.
184. Boyd and Ellison, "Social Network Sites," 211.
185. Livingstone and Brake, "On the Rapid Rise," 76.
186. Ibid., 77.

have difficulty in the management of formal and conventional relationships offline.[187]

Livingstone and Brake insist that the young people's desire to express themselves is another critical reason for the explosion in online communication via SNSs. Researchers say that young people quite enjoy creating an online representation of themselves and being recognized in the peer network.[188] Alexander Richter and Michael Koch also claim that *Identity Management* is a key function of SNSs: "Because people are constantly analyzed by others they construct consciously a social identity which they present to their counterpart. In SNS the profile people construct is this staging of oneself—for a particular audience, for a particular task to be achieved."[189]

Steven Chaffee and Miriam Metzger argue that although the traditional forms of mass communication have been changing rapidly because of the emergence of new web-based media, it is not yet ready to proclaim the end of mass communication. From their perspectives, mass communication still plays an important and unique role even in the digital society.[190] Manuel Castells also argues that "there is a growing interpenetration between traditional mass media and the Internet-based communication networks. Mainstream media are using blogs and interactive networks to distribute their content and interact with their audiences mixing vertical and horizontal communication modes."[191] André Mottart, Ronald Soetaert, and Bart Bonamie use the term *contact zone* in order to describe the coexistence of the two forms of communication.[192] Most SGKA teenagers are also living in the contact zone between the web-based mass self-communication and the offline-centered mass communication: *online-offline hybrid communication*.

As such, analog-based curriculum is based on the hardware component–centered and the mass communication–oriented paradigm. These two features reveal the four sub-characteristics of analog curriculum models: (1) a closed and hierarchical collaboration network; (2) component replacement–based passive service; (3) teacher-centered

---

187. Ibid.
188. Ibid., 76.
189. Richter and Koch, "Functions of Social Networking Services," 3.
190. Chaffee and Metzger, "End of Mass Communication?," 377–78.
191. Castells, *Rise of the Network Society*, ix-x.
192. Mottart et al., "Digitization and Culture," 30.

instruction-based mass communication; and (4) offline-bound learning space. It is not surprising that the analog-oriented curriculum based on these characteristics is no longer appropriate for a younger generation who are growing up digital. In the field of general education, in the last decade, there has been active and vibrant research on digital curricula suitable for a digital generation growing up with the new technology. However, in religious education, there has been a comparatively small amount of curricular research focusing on the digital ways of learning and communicating. Such ignorance regarding contemporary young people living in the digital society might result in the failure of curriculum reformation and innovation.[193] Thus, the development of a religious education curriculum for the digital generation is urgently needed.

---

193. Macdonald, "Curriculum Change," 139–47.

3
Understanding of Faith

SINCE THE FIRST SPECIALITY publication in the field of curriculum was launched by Franklin Bobbitt in 1918, various curriculum groups have emerged and have variously interpreted the meaning of curriculum. Recently, the spread of digital technology and Internet connectivity is throwing the spotlight on digital curriculum focusing on digital ways of learning, thinking, and communicating.

However, Tyler's technocratic curriculum for schooling still dominates the field of religious education in spite of the reconceptualist movement and the digitization of society. For it is still believed, in many circles, that faith can be effectively nurtured through transmitting a preexisting and objective Christian knowledge to students.[1] The case of religious education in the Korean Australian (KA) church is not exceptional, considering that its main curriculum approach is transmitting knowledge-out-of-context. At this point, a long-standing question arises again: *Is it really true that faith can be formulated through schooling?*

In this section, I will examine *what faith is* and *how faith is developed* by investigating an understanding of faith,[2] focusing on John Calvin (1509–1564) and Karl Barth (1886–1968).[3] After critically exploring the

1. Park, "Curriculum Model," 57–66.

2. The definition of Christian faith is varied depending on diverse Christian traditions. Primary theological concepts related to faith are also different according to various theological positions. Thus, it is noted that the understanding of faith described here is one of various Christian traditions understandings of faith. However, it is beyond of the scope of this book and the purpose of this chapter to attend to various faith definitions and compare them in order to analyze their strengths and weaknesses.

3. It is noted that when I discuss the two great theologians' understanding of faith, I will preserve their initial terminology as much as possible in order not to change the original meaning of their thinking. However, from a contemporary theological sensitivity to not gendering God, their original terms, especially personal pronouns for God such as *He*, *Him*, and *Himself*, have something to do with the masculinization of God. I am concerned about the exclusive language, but also recognize the historical situations of their age. Thus, I will use their original terminology in most cases, but will

understanding of faith of these two great theologians, noting the ways in which they agree and disagree with each other, I will propose several key dimensions of faith that may be described broadly in the Protestant tradition. I will then suggest some implications for the religious education curriculum for faith based on the key features of faith. This discussion will function as a theological and epistemological foundation for the establishment of a new religious education curriculum for second-generation Korean Australian (SGKA) adolescents in the KA church.

Calvin's Understanding of Faith

In the *Institutes of the Christian Religion*, Calvin refers to faith as the knowledge of God.[4] For Calvin, the first and foremost interest in faith is *who God is to human beings* and *what does His salvation mean to us*. His understanding of faith is closely connected to soteriology.[5] Thus, he defines faith as the certain knowledge of God's grace for our salvation, and argues that this knowledge is based on Jesus Christ and revealed through the Holy Spirit.[6]

The key point of Calvin's doctrine of faith as knowledge of God is that God is the subject who invites human beings into knowledge for salvation. The subjectivity of God means that God's self-revelation through Jesus Christ is the only foundation for human faith. Since God reveals Godself through Jesus Christ, a person can know God only through Christ, can be healed and restored only through Christ, and achieve God's will only through Christ. As such, Calvin's understanding of faith is God centered with a strong emphasis on Christology.[7] In stressing the subjectivity of God in terms of faith, Calvin emphasizes the concept of *accommodation* throughout his theology.

---

try to use inclusive terms as much as I can in this book.

4. Calvin, *Institutes*, trans. Battles, 1.1.1.

5. Kooi, *As in a Mirror*, 21.

6. Calvin argues that "we shall possess a right definition of faith if we call it a firm and certain knowledge of God's benevolence toward us, founded upon the truth of the freely given promise in Christ, both revealed to our minds and sealed upon our hearts through the Holy Spirit." Calvin, *Institutes*, trans. Battles, 3.2.7.

7. Ibid., 2.9.1.

God's Accommodation

With the concept of God's accommodation, Calvin argues that God accommodates God's self to human measure and human capacity by revealing himself, so that human beings may understand him.[8] For Calvin, God's stooping act is God's accommodation which makes it possible for a person to understand and know him. Thus, in this respect, God's accommodation is the only starting point for human beings to have faith as a form of knowing God. Without God's adjustment to human feebleness people cannot know him because of the ontological and existential gulf between God and human beings which resulted from the fall. Calvin views the fall as a hereditary corruption passed from one person to another, so claims that the results of Adam's guilt are passed down to all his descendants.[9] Stanton Norman interprets that for Calvin, the depravity results in total destruction in that it affects every part of the person: "Although the primary result of the Fall is spiritual death, other aspects of human existence are also affected. The natural endowments of the sinner, such as intelligence, will, and emotions, are corrupted by sin. Spiritual endowments, such as faith, love of God, holiness, etc., are lost."[10]

For human beings to approach God, this enormous gulf needs to be overcome. However, no human has the capacity to overcome such qualitative difference. Thus, for human beings to know him God bridges the gulf. This is God's accommodation. Cornelis van der Kooi places this concept at the center of Calvin's theological epistemology and focuses on the double action of God's accommodation as follows:

> One of the most important words that Calvin uses to describe God's action is *descendere*, coming (or going) down. God's act is a movement from above to below. We also find the word *ascendere*, to ascend or mount, directly linked with this. In other words, Calvin describes God's acts as movements in space, a movement from high to low and from low to high. Because by this movement God comes closer to man, to be within the reach of the human capacity to know, knowledge of God arises.[11]

Calvin believes that God invites human beings to have faith as knowledge of God through various means adjusted to human capacity.

---

8. Ibid., 1.13.1.
9. Ibid., 2.1.8.
10. Norman, "Human Sinfulness," 440.
11. Kooi, *As in a Mirror*, 41.

Among them, Calvin emphasizes three ways provided by God: (1) creation and nature; (2) human inward capacities; and (3) Holy Scripture as special revelation.

Various Means for Knowing God

1. Creation and Nature

Calvin believes that God reveals Godself in creation. He argues that humans can feel and acknowledge the presence of God by seeing the order and the majesty revealed in nature. He claims that while the mediation of nature is not the major proof, it should be regarded as the first proof for the presence of God.[12] As people see themselves in a mirror, so they might see God using nature as a mirror.[13] Calvin asserts the certainty of knowledge of God revealed in nature as follows:

> Lest anyone, then, be excluded from access to happiness, he . . . revealed himself and daily discloses himself in the whole workmanship of the universe. As a consequence, men cannot open their eyes without being compelled to see him. Indeed, his essence is incomprehensible; hence, his divineness far escapes all human perception. But upon his individual works he has engraved unmistakable marks of his glory, so clear and so prominent that even unlettered and stupid folk cannot plead the excuse of ignorance.[14]

In this way, Calvin argues that God reveals himself objectively within creation so that every human being can acknowledge him clearly. However, at the same time, he distinguishes God's objective revelation in nature from human acceptance. That is, although he admits the reality of general revelation in nature, he thinks that human beings because of their fallen nature cannot properly see God who is mirrored in creation. He argues that blind human beings are most likely to distort God's image reflected in nature and make various idols to serve: "While he sweetly attracts men to the knowledge of himself with many and varied kindness,

---

12. Calvin, *Institutes*, trans. Battles, 1.14.20.

13. Calvin calls all means provided by God for knowing him as mirrors reflecting him. Ibid., 2.2.11.

14. Ibid., 1.5.1.

they do not cease on this account to follow their own ways, that is, their fatal errors."[15]

2. Human Inward Capacities

Calvin thinks that God reveals Godself not only by using the external created world, but also by using inward human capacities. In relation to knowing God, Calvin has an interest in the *sensus divinitatis* (a sense of divinity) and the *sensus conscientiae* (the sense of conscience).

Calvin believes that God planted a sense of divinity in human hearts so that people can acknowledge him. For Calvin, revelation found in nature is outward revelation, while an awareness of divinity in the human mind is a form of inward revelation. Calvin thinks that the *sensus divinitatis* is an inward realization of the presence of God, and it is like "some seed of religion" planted in the human heart by God.[16] He argues that God not only put the sense of divinity in the human mind, but also renews it so it is not lost:

> There is within the human mind, and indeed by natural instinct, an awareness of divinity. This we take to be beyond controversy. To prevent anyone from taking refuge in the pretence of ignorance, God himself has implanted in all men a certain understanding of his divine majesty. Ever renewing its memory, he repeatedly sheds fresh drops. Since, therefore, men one and all perceive that there is a God and that he is their Maker, they are condemned by their own testimony because they have failed to honor him and to consecrate their lives to his will.[17]

Note that as with the general revelation found in nature, for Calvin, sinful human beings cannot know God relying only upon the *sensus divinitatis*. Since human beings have misused their inward capacity, distorting God into figures of their own imaging, various idols found in nature have taken the place of God. For Calvin, the *sensus divinitatis* without faith can encourage, rather than discourage, sin; few people are able to keep the divine feeling throughout their lives, because they are affected by sin.[18] He claims that "because most people, immersed in their own er-

15. Ibid., 1.5.14.
16. Ibid., 1.3.1.
17. Ibid.
18. Ibid., 1.4.1.

rors, are struck blind in such a dazzling theater, he exclaims that to weigh these works of God wisely is a matter of rare and singular wisdom."[19] According to Calvin, only those people who have faith as knowledge of God might be able to see the majesty of God through nature, by making proper use of the *sensus divinitatis*.[20]

Together with the *sensus divinitatis*, another human inward capacity provided by God for knowing him is the *sensus conscientiae*. The *sensus divinitatis* is closely related to seeing the majesty of God through God's created works, while the *sensus conscientiae* is connected to the capacity for judging good and evil.[21] Calvin claims that "our conscience does not allow us to sleep a perpetual insensible sleep without being an inner witness and monitor of what we owe God, without holding before us the difference between good and evil and thus accusing us when we fail in our duty."[22] For Calvin, a pure conscience could be a way for human beings to realize the fear of God's judgement, to confess their sins before God and to obey him. He argues that "conscience presses us within and shows in our sin just cause for his disowning us and not regarding or recognizing us as his sons."[23]

Calvin assesses the role of the *sensus conscientiae* more positively than that of the *sensus divinitatis*. However, even a good conscience can easily be defiled because of human sin, for degraded human beings tend to intentionally reject their inward faculty to judge good and evil.[24] In addition, Calvin argues that sinful people are most likely to suppress their conscience to commit sin without a sense of guilt.[25] For Calvin, human conscience is not, therefore, an exclusively reliable way to know God.

Calvin admits the reality of general revelation found in nature and human inward faculties, but rejects the possibility of an unmarred knowledge of God through "natural" means because of the fall.[26] Calvin's

---

19. Ibid., 1.5.8.
20. Ibid., 1.5.14.
21. Kooi, *As in a Mirror*, 73.
22. Calvin, *Institutes*, trans. Battles, 2.8.1.
23. Ibid., 2.6.1.
24. Ibid., 2.2.22.
25. Ibid., 2.2.23.

26. Kooi argues that "in the introduction to his commentary on Genesis Calvin makes it clear in an impressive way that Christian knowledge of God does not have its central source in the construction of the world, but in the Gospel, where Christ on the cross is proclaimed to us." See Kooi, *As in a Mirror*, 83.

theology of general revelation and of human inward capacities has not been uncontroversial; so a long theological debate on the possibility of a "natural" theology has ensued, especially among Reformed theologians.

A representative theologian who argued for the possibility of natural theology based on Calvin's theological reflections is Emil Brunner. Brunner acknowledges, like Calvin, the validity of general revelation. He also admits that general revelation in creation is insufficient for people to know God unless they also encounter God's revelation in Jesus Christ: "It is important to know . . . that from the very beginning God has revealed Himself in His creation, but that we can only know what this means through His revelation in Jesus Christ."[27] However, Brunner argues for the possibility of knowing God through divine revelation in creation because he believes that human beings still have a contact point with God. For this argument, he divides *the formal imago Dei* from *the material imago Dei* and argues that although the latter was impaired by the fall, the former is still active and serves as the point of contact for God's revelation.[28]

On the other hand, Barth is a representative theologian who rejects the possibility of any kind of natural theology. He argues that there is no *natural point of contact* between God and human beings, focusing on Calvin's argument that no one can know God by means of general revelation because of the sinfulness of human beings.[29] For Barth, humans can know God only through revelation in Jesus Christ witnessed through Scripture.[30] I will discuss Barth's idea of natural theology in more detail later.

---

27. Brunner, *Dogmatics I*, 21.

28. William Power understands these two concepts as follows: "In the dramatic narrative of Genesis, the author affirms that human beings, male and female alike, are created in the image (*selem*) and likeness (*demuth*) of God. Every Adam and every Eve is endowed with a unique personal nature and a capacity to pattern their lives on the model of the living God. That is, each of us is created in God's image in a unique sense (*eikon, imago*) and given and called to exist in God's likeness (*homoiosis, similitudo*). The former similarity between God and individual human beings constitutes the formal image of God in us, the latter similarity constitutes the material image of God in us." Power also argues that the material image of God was broken by human beings' sinful nature. Brunner, "Nature and Grace," 24; Power, "*Imago Dei—Imitatio Dei*," 131.

29. However, Barth's thinking about the fall is different from Calvin's. Barth understood the fall as an existential event rather than as a historical or hereditary one. Barth, *Church Dogmatics*, IV/1:508.

30. Ibid., II/1:168.

3. Scripture and Inspiration

Calvin argued that people cannot know God only through nature and reason because of the fall. Thus, he asserts the necessity of special revelation. For Calvin, Scripture is God's special revelation. He believes that the Bible is the Word of God.[31] For him, the key point of the Scripture is Jesus Christ through whom God reveals Godself. Humans become aware of God only through Jesus Christ, who is encountered through reading the Bible.[32] Unlike other means discussed above, the witness of special revelation cannot be defiled by sin because the Holy Spirit wrote it and God continually speaks through it.[33] Calvin argues that the Word is a guide and a teacher for humans to approach and know God.

> That brightness which is borne in upon the eyes of all men both in heaven and on earth is more than enough to withdraw all support from men's ingratitude—just as God, to involve the human race in the same guilt, sets forth to all without exception his presence portrayed in his creatures. Despite this, it is needful that another and better help be added to direct us aright to the very Creator of the universe. It was not in vain, then, that he added the light of his Word by which to become known unto salvation . . . Scripture, gathering up the otherwise confused knowledge of God in our minds, having dispersed our dullness, clearly shows us the truth of God. This, therefore, is a special gift, where God, to instruct the church, not merely uses mute teachers but also opens his own most hallowed lips.[34]

For Calvin, faith as knowledge of God is the fruit of Holy Scripture. At the same time, no one can understand the contents of Scripture without faith as a form of knowing God. Thus he argues that "it is foolish to attempt to prove to infidels that the Scripture is the Word of God. This cannot be known to be, except by faith."[35] Along with faith, Calvin emphasizes the importance of the role of the Holy Spirit in interpreting and understanding Holy Scripture. He argues that without the inner illumination of the Spirit it is impossible for human beings to appropri-

---

31. Calvin, *Institutes*, trans. Battles, 1.8.13.

32. Thus, he interprets the contents of the Old Testament Christologically. For Calvin, the Old Testament contains prophecies of Jesus Christ, and the New Testament testifies the achievement of the prophecy from the Old Testament. Ibid., 2.7.1.

33. Ibid., 1.9.2.

34. Ibid., 1.6.1.

35. Ibid., 1.8.13.

ately comprehend the contents of Holy Scripture. For he believes that the Spirit of God is *the author* of the Bible.[36] Throughout his writings, Calvin strongly argues that the authority of Holy Scripture is based on its divine authorship. For example, Calvin's commentary on 2 Timothy 3:16 is a representative statement of this view:

> In order to uphold the authority of the Scripture, he [Paul] declares that *it is divinely inspired;* for, if it be so, it is beyond all controversy that men ought to receive it with reverence. This is a principle which distinguishes our religion from all others, that we know that God hath spoken to us, and are fully convinced that the prophets did not speak at their own suggestion, but that, being organs of the Holy Spirit, they only uttered what they had been commissioned from heaven to declare. Whoever then wishes to profit in the Scriptures, let him first of all, lay down this as a settled point, that the Law and the Prophets are not a doctrine delivered according to the will and pleasure of men, but dictated by the Holy Spirit.[37]

This quotation demonstrates Calvin's idea of the verbal inspiration of the Bible. While he did not use the term *verbal inspiration* directly, he consistently insisted in his writings that the Bible was inspired and even dictated by the Holy Spirit.[38] Henry Beveridge interprets Calvin's use of the term *dictated* as follows: "Although Calvin uses the term 'dictated' in connection with this explanation of the manner in which the body of Old Testament Scripture was formed, this should not be taken to express the mode of Inspiration, but rather to call attention to the result of Inspiration."[39] Roger Nichole also claims that the meaning of the word *dictated* in Calvin's works is related not to God's special method for communicating with human beings, but to the result of Inspiration.[40]

His strong emphasis on the verbal inspiration of Scripture naturally results in the contention that he believed in the inerrancy of the Bible, the view that Scripture is correct and free from any kind of error. Many theologians have claimed that Calvin retained the doctrine of inerrancy.[41]

36. Ibid., 1.9.2.
37. Calvin, *Commentaries on the Epistles*, 248–49.
38. For example, see Calvin, *Institutes*, trans. Battles, 1.13.15, 1.18.3, 4.8.6.
39. Calvin, *Institutes*, trans. Beveridge, 918.
40. Nicole, "John Calvin and Inerrancy," 426.
41. For lists of scholars who maintain that Calvin held to biblical inerrancy, see ibid., 427.

However, Calvin's doctrine of inerrancy has long been debated and many scholars have argued that Calvin denied inerrancy, because Calvin also acknowledged, in some of his writings, that there are mistakes and discrepancies in the Bible.[42] For example, in his commentary on Acts 7:14 Calvin commented as follows:

> Whereas he [Stephen] saith that Jacob came into Egypt with seventy-five souls, it agreeth not with the words of Moses; for Moses maketh mention of seventy only. . . . Therefore, I think that this difference came through the error of the writers which wrote out the books. And it was a matter of no such weight, for which Luke ought to have troubled the Gentiles which were accustomed with the Greek reading. And it may be that he himself did put down the true number; and that some man did correct the same amiss out of that place of Moses. For we know that those which had the New Testament in hand were ignorant of the Hebrew tongue, yet skilful in the Greek.[43]

Some critics argue that these errors in the Bible are natural results of God's accommodation to human ways of knowing because of human words and concepts.[44] In this matter, theologians advocating Calvin's doctrine of inerrancy tend to insist that Calvin's indication of faults found in the Bible are about copyist mistakes rather than about original autographic text. Ralph Gore argues that "Calvin makes no allowances for error, either on the part of the apostles, or on the part of the prophets. There can be no errors in the original text, although allowances must be made for corruptions in transmission."[45] Similarly, Nicole contends that Calvin's references to errors in Scripture should be "interpreted as emendations in textual criticism rather than a correction by Calvin of the original message."[46] Jamin Hubner claims that the inerrancy of the original biblical text cannot be impaired in the process of God's accommodation by quoting Richard Muller's explanation of God's accommodation: "This *accommodatio* . . . in no way implies the loss of truth or the lessening of scriptural authority. The *accommodatio* . . . refers to the

---

42. For information of theologians claiming that Calvin rejected the doctrine of inerrancy, see ibid.

43. Calvin, *Commentary on the Acts of the Apostles*, 263–64.

44. Hubner, "Biblical Inerrancy."

45. Gore, "Calvin's Doctrine of Inspiration," 101–6.

46. Nicole, "John Calvin and Inerrancy," 430.

manner or mode of revelation . . . not to the quality of the revelation or to the matter revealed."[47]

In addition to the controversy regarding the doctrine of inerrancy, Calvin's idea that the Bible should be regarded as God's revelation in and of itself has also been criticized. Brunner, for example, rejects this allegedly Calvinist belief. For Brunner, Scripture is a secondary testimony and witness to God's revelation and is the means of faith.[48] He argues that the Bible is "a 'word' inspired by the Spirit of God; yet at the same time it is a human message; its 'human character' means that it is coloured by the frailty and imperfection of all that is human."[49] Barth also considers Scripture as a witness to God's revelation inspired by the Holy Spirit rather than the revelation itself. However, for him, when we read the Bible with the inner testimony of the Holy Spirit, it then *becomes* for us the Word of God.[50] Barth's idea of Holy Scripture will be discussed in more detail later. So far, I have examined Calvin's thought about the various means for knowing God such as creation and nature, human inward capacities, and Holy Scripture as special revelation.

Pietas (Piety): Obedience

Calvin believes that obedience is an inevitable dimension of faith, for without obedience it is hard to know God. Only through obedience to God, can human beings build an intimate relationship with God which is critical for knowing God. Thus, he argues that all right knowledge of God is born of obedience.[51] His emphasis on obedience in faith is closely related to his thinking about *pietas* (piety). He defines piety as "reverence joined with love of God which the knowledge of his benefits induces."[52] Calvin argues that piety is a precondition for knowing God, but also a fruit of faith. He claims that those who are pious will love, trust, praise, and obey God.[53]

47. Hubner, "Biblical Inerrancy," 19.

48. For more information of Brunner's doctrine of the Bible, see chapter 4, "Revelation as the Word of God," in prolegomena of his *Dogmatics* vol. 1, *Christian Doctrine of God*. Brunner, *Dogmatics I*, 22–34.

49. Ibid., 34.

50. Barth, *Church Dogmatics*, I/2:457.

51. Calvin, *Institutes*, trans. Battles, 1.6.2.

52. Ibid., 1.2.1.

53. Ibid., 1.6.2.

For, to begin with, the pious mind does not dream up for itself any god it pleases, but contemplates the one and only true God. And it does not attach to him whatever it pleases, but is content to hold him to be as he manifests himself; furthermore, the mind always exercises the utmost diligence and care not to wander astray, or rashly and boldly to go beyond his will. It thus recognizes God because it knows that he governs all things; and trusts that he is its guide and protector, therefore giving itself over completely to trust in him. Because it understands him to be the Author of every good, if anything oppresses, if anything is lacking, immediately it betakes itself to his protection, waiting for help from him.[54]

The ultimate purpose of piety is to unite with God, which is completed through unification with Jesus Christ. Calvin maintains that "now we see how Christ is the most perfect image of God; if we are conformed to it, we are so restored that with true piety, righteousness, purity, and intelligence we bear God's image."[55] In Calvin's concept of *pietas*, it is also noted that piety involves love of neighbor along with love of God. While the first meaning of *pietas* is unification with God, Calvin argues that the pious should go further to love, respect, and unite with others whom God uses as vessels of His blessing for them.[56]

Church as Nurturing Mother

Calvin regards the achievement of *pietas* as a life-long process rather than a one-off event.[57] He thinks that even those who come to know and worship God with their hearts might leave him because every human being is a sinner. At this point, he emphasizes the role of the church in helping members love God. For Calvin, the church is an outward means provided by God for nurturing people and encouraging them to lead a pious life. Calvin claims that proclamation of the gospel and the sacrament[58] are two representative external aids for achieving the purpose of the church,

---

54. Ibid., 1.2.2.
55. Ibid., 1.15.4.
56. Ibid., 1.17.9.
57. Ibid., 2.2.25.
58. Calvin claims that only baptism and the Eucharist are true sacraments found in Jesus Christ. See ibid., 4.4.22.

and fashioning from church members God's people.[59] He emphasizes the inner relation between the Bible and the sacrament, indicating that the sacrament is the visible Word of God showing us God's promises before our eyes.[60] Thus, he argues that "in order to prevent religion from either perishing or declining among us, we should diligently frequent the sacred meetings, and make use of those external aids which can promote the worship of God."[61] In this regard, Calvin describes the church as *the mother of all the godly*: the educational and nurturing function of the church is critical in developing faith.[62]

As such, Calvin argues that the purpose of faith as knowledge of God is unification with God, which is completed in Jesus Christ. For him, faith as knowing God is wholly God's grace and gift because without God's self-revelation people cannot know him and be saved. We human beings are able to know God only because God accommodates himself to humanity. Calvin argues that God invites people into knowledge of God, utilizing various means and ways for knowing him: (1) through general revelation in God's creation and inward human capacities such as the *sensus divinitatis* and the *sensus conscientiae*, and (2) through Holy Scripture as special revelation. While he admits the reality of general revelation in creation and human inward capacities, he argues that fallen people can know God clearly and wholly through special revelation in Scripture.

Holy Scripture is a kind of lens that assists the blind in knowing God. Note that the inner testimony of the Spirit is essential for people to understand the Bible and to have faith as knowledge of God. After people get faith as knowledge of God for salvation, they can enter the circular movement of *pietas* through obedience to God and intimacy with him. For Calvin, piety is not only the result of faith, but also a starting point for faith. Through this circular movement and through leading a pious and obedient Christian life, people can know God more deeply and intimately. For this, in Calvin's theology, the nurturing and teaching function of the church through preaching and the sacrament is indispensable for people to keep believing in God and loving God and neighbor.

---

59. Ibid., 4.1.9. For more information on Calvin's idea of faith education in the church, see book 4, chapter 1, "Of the True Church," in *Institutes of the Christian Religion*.

60. Ibid., 4.14.7.

61. Ibid., 2.8.34.

62. Ibid., 4.1.1.

Calvin's understanding of faith still strongly influences many Protestant theologians, but there have been long-standing debates in relation to his theological reflection, for example on the possibility of natural theology, on the verbal inspiration of the Scripture, and on the doctrine of inerrancy.

Barth's Understanding of Faith

As an interpreter of Calvin, Karl Barth's understanding of faith was understandably influenced by Calvin.[63] However, due to the fact that they lived four hundred years apart, there is both continuity and discontinuity between the two scholars' understanding of faith.[64] In this section, I will examine Barth's understanding of faith, focusing primarily on the doctrine of the Word of God (I/1 and I/2), the doctrine of God (II/1 and II/2) and the doctrine of reconciliation (IV/1) in his *Church Dogmatics*. Then, I will investigate the similarities and differences between the two scholars' understanding of faith.

God as the Subject of Revelation

Liberal theology in the nineteenth century, based on René Descartes's proposition, *cogito ergo sum* (I think, therefore I am) tended to regard faith as human religious experience. As a result, God was reduced to one of the objects which a human being may acknowledge. With the *1914 Manifesto of the Ninety-Three German Intellectuals to the Civilized World*, Barth gave up Liberal theology's anthropocentric methodology for knowing God and developed a God-centered theological approach.[65]

Barth's theocentric approach for knowing God starts from his emphasis on the ontological and existential difference between God and human. He argues that only God's revelation can bridge the qualitative gulf, not human thinking.[66] For him, God's self-revelation is the only foun-

---

63. See Kang, "Karl Barth," 193–221.

64. Since Kant criticized traditional theism with the concept of practical reason, divine beings have been regarded not to be proved by theoretical reason. Thus, Kooi argues that "Kant's philosophy serves as the hinge between the two panels of Calvin and Barth." See Kooi, *As in a Mirror*, 225–48.

65. See Park, "Kalbareut sinhakeseo ihaereul chuguhaneun sinangui wichiwa uiui," 175–81.

66. Barth, *Church Dogmatics*, II/1:31.

dation and principle for knowledge of God. No one can acknowledge God without God's self-revelation.[67] Barth claims that God has already revealed Godself in the incarnation of Jesus Christ, who is God's revelation.[68] He explains the revelation of God with the concept of three forms: the revelation of God consists of the revelation of Father as the subject, of Son as the objective reality, and of the Holy Spirit as the achiever of the revelation who helps human beings accept it subjectively.[69]

Since God has already been revealed through Jesus Christ, Barth does not begin his thinking about knowing God by asking, "Is it possible for human beings to know God?" Rather, he starts from the reality of the knowledge of God.[70]

> God's freedom for us men is a fact in Jesus Christ, according to the witness of Holy Scripture. The first and the last thing to be said about the bearer of this name is that He is very God and very Man. In this unity He is the objective reality of divine revelation. His existence is God's freedom for man. Or *vice versa* God's freedom for man is the existence of Jesus Christ. And now we continue by saying that in this objective reality of the divine revelation there is presupposed and grounded and brought within our knowledge its objective possibility.[71]

Therefore, for Barth, a theologically suitable question is not about the possibility of knowing God, but about the extent to which we can know him. Barth argues that the extent of human understanding of God depends on the extent of God's revelation to human beings.[72]

Faith as the Only Way of Knowing God

For Barth, like Calvin, faith is knowledge of the God who has revealed himself through Jesus Christ. Barth further considers faith as the only way of knowing the reality of God. Although God has already revealed Godself through Jesus Christ, Barth argues that human beings cannot

---

67. Ibid., II/1:4.
68. Ibid., I/2:1.
69. Ibid., I/1:98–140.
70. Ibid., II/1:64.
71. Ibid., I/2:25.
72. Ibid., II/1:63.

know him without faith.[73] Thus, Barth defines faith as "man's orientation to God as an object"[74] He explains it further:

> The turning, the self-opening, the surrender in faith, the Yes of faith, faith as obligation, love, trust and obedience in faith—all this presupposes and includes within itself the union and the distinction which man fulfils between himself and the God whose existence and nature make it all possible and necessary. This orientation which unites and distinguishes is the knowledge of God in faith.[75]

As such, for Barth, faith is *the knowledge of God as knowledge of faith*.[76] There are three critical concepts of Barth's idea of faith as the only way of knowing God: faith as an acknowledgement, faith as an act of knowing and church as a place for faith.

1. Faith as an Acknowledgement

In the *Church Dogmatics*, Barth explains faith as examining the *human before God* and *God before the human*. This is a big picture disclosing Barth's understanding of faith. In order for a person to know God, there should be two dimensions to this knowledge: the human side and God's side. From the anthropological side humans should stand before God to acknowledge him; from the divine side, God should objectify himself enough for human beings to know him. Note that the human action to stand before God is meaningless apart from God's prior decision to stand before human beings. That God stands before humanity means that God accommodates Godself to human capacities in order to be an acknowledgeable object.[77] God's objectification can be completed through Jesus Christ. A person standing before God is able to know God and be united with him through Jesus Christ.[78]

---

73. With the concept of "the *circulus veritatis Dei*" (the circle of the truth of God), Barth reveals the significance of faith in knowing God within the human's limits of the knowledge of God. Ibid., II/1:204–54. Ibid., II/1:14–15.

74. Ibid., II/1:13.

75. Ibid.

76. Ibid., II/1:21.

77. Ibid., II/1:3–62.

78. Ibid., II/1:67–68.

In this way, only when humans stand before God, and God stands before them, can humans know God. Barth argues that human readiness to acknowledge this rule and accept it with gratitude is the function of faith. For him, faith is acknowledging that knowing God becomes possible only through the grace of God in choosing to stand before human beings in a self-revelation suitable for human measure.[79] That is, faith is an acknowledgement enabling knowledge of God by human beings.

> Christian faith is an acknowledgement. . . . The recognition is certainly included in the acknowledgement, but it can only follow it. Acknowledging is a taking cognisance which is obedient and compliant, which yields and subordinates itself. This obedience and compliance is not an incidental and subsequent characteristic of the act of faith, but primary, basic and decisive.[80]

Furthermore, faith is a kind of opening-up before this gracious act.[81]

> The knowledge of God is wholly and utterly His own readiness to be known by us, grounded in His being and activity. Real man is the man who stands before God because God stands before him. The question of the readiness of this real man will arise later. Yet no final independence can be ascribed to the readiness of this real man, but only the character of a capacity and willingness for gratitude and obedience communicated by God to man and returning to its source.[82]

It is necessary to note, however, that for Barth knowledge of God through faith remains only an indirect knowledge of him. Barth distinguishes the *primary objectivity* of God from the *secondary objectivity* because of the qualitative difference between God and human beings. He argues that God is *immediately* objective to himself (the primary), while God is *mediately* objective to human beings in His revelation to people (the secondary).[83] Sinful human beings are only able to acknowledge God "in His clothed, not in His naked objectivity" through faith.[84] This does

---

79. Barth claims that "faith is nothing but the acknowledgement of this rule . . . of the limits and the veracity of our knowledge of God." Ibid., II/1:254.

80. Ibid., IV/1:758.

81. Barth also argues that "in the Bible faith means the opening-up of human subjectivity by and for the objectivity of the divine He, and in this opening-up the re-establishment and re-determination." Ibid., II/1:14.

82. Ibid., II/1:66.

83. Ibid., II/1:16–17.

84. Ibid., II/1:16.

not however mean that human knowledge of God by faith is imperfect or untrue. Barth argues that "his secondary objectivity is fully true, for it has its correspondence and basis in His primary objectivity."[85] At this point, Barth follows Calvin in emphasizing the grace of God in accommodating himself to humanity.[86]

Barth's understanding of faith as an acknowledgement is largely grounded in the ontological proof of God's existence of Anselm of Canterbury: *credo ut intelligam* (I believe so that I may understand). Barth asserts that for Anselm faith, expressed in prayer, is the only way of really knowing God. Only through the acknowledgement of faith can human beings open the door for meeting God.[87] Barth believes, like Anselm, that the certainty of faith is not the result of a long journey of speculation, but a starting point leading to the truth.[88] Barth considers Anselm's *fides quaerens intellectum* (faith seeking understanding) a Christian alternative to Descartes's anthropocentric methodology[89] and uses it as the main theological methodology for his theological masterpiece, *Church Dogmatics*.[90] Based on Anselm's *credo ut intelligam*, Barth restores the subjectivity of God in terms of the revelation of God.[91]

---

85. Ibid.

86. Ibid., II/1:17–18.

87. Barth, *Anselm*, 102.

88. Barth argues that "in faith we can only again believe, beginning at the beginning and continuing to believe." Barth, *Church Dogmatics*, II/1:247.

89. Garry Deverell argues that some theologians and philosophers who are sympathetic to Barth's perspective now read Descartes rather differently than Barth did. For them, Descartes's method is actually very similar to Barth's, beginning with a God who presents God's self to human consciousness before that consciousness has an opportunity to imagine God its own image. Deverell says that Emmanuel Lévinas's *Of God Who Comes to Mind* is an outstanding example. Deverell, *Bonds of Freedom*, 33–34.

90. Especially, in the preface of the doctrine of God, Barth admitted that he owed his theological attitude about knowledge of God to Anselm as follows: "I believe I learned the fundamental attitude to the problem of the knowledge and existence of God which is adopted in this section—and indeed in the whole chapter—at the feet of Anselm of Canterbury, and in particular from his proofs of God set out in *Prosl.* 2–4. May I therefore ask the reader to keep that text in mind, and to allow me to refer to my book *Fides quaerens intellectum: Anselms Beweis der Existenz Gottes* (1931), for an understanding of it." Barth, *Church Dogmatics*, II/1:4.

91. Park, "Kalbareut sinhakeseo ihaereul chuguhaneun sinangui wichiwa uiui," 191–93.

2. Faith as an Act of Knowing: Obedience and Prayer

It is important to recognize that Barth does not regard faith only as an acknowledgement. He goes further to see faith as an act of knowing God. He argues: "Faith is the act of *the* Christian life to the extent that in all the activity and individual acts of a man it is the most inward and central and decisive act of his heart, the one which—if it takes place—characterises them all as Christian, as expressions and confirmations of his Christian freedom, his Christian responsibility, his Christian obedience."[92]

For Barth, obedience to God is one of the human responses to God's grace in revealing himself to human beings.[93] Through obedience to God, human beings become able to build an intimate relationship with God, which might open the door to knowledge of God more widely, so that people may know God really and clearly. Thus, for him, faith without obedience is imperfect.

> In this act God posits Himself as our object and ourselves as those who know Him. But the fact that He does so means that our knowing God can consist only in our following this act, in ourselves becoming a correspondence of this act, in ourselves and our whole existence and therefore our considering and conceiving becoming the human act corresponding to the divine act. This is obedience, the obedience of faith. Precisely—and only—as this act of obedience, is the knowledge of God as knowledge of faith and therefore real knowledge of God.[94]

Together with obedience, Barth concentrates on the importance of prayer in the knowing of God. As we noted above, Barth accepted Anselm's concept of faith as a praying acknowledgement of the God already revealed in Jesus Christ. Barth believes that people can realize their weakness and hopelessness through speaking to God in prayer and thus desperately seek God's help. In the course of praying, human beings are able to know God intimately. In this respect, Barth says that "Anselm speaks about God while speaking to him."[95]

In addition, in relation to the temptation to objectify God like other objects and possess him within human faculties, Barth argues that

---

92. Barth, *Church Dogmatics*, IV/1:757–58.

93. Barth argues that "knowledge of God as knowledge of faith is in itself and of essential necessity obedience." Ibid., II/1:26.

94. Ibid.

95. Barth, *Anselm*, 102.

prayer is crucial for human beings to want to keep loving, trusting, and obeying God.

> Since it is the prayer that God will posit Himself as our object and ourselves as those who know Him, it must obviously run concretely: "Lead us not into temptation—into the temptation of an objectivistic consideration of God's secondary and primary objectivity; a disinterested non-obedient consideration which holds back in a place which it thinks secure. Lead us not into the temptation of the false opinion that Thou art an object like other objects which we can undertake to know or not just as we wish, which we are free to know in this way, or even in that. Lead us not into the temptation of wanting to know Thee in Thy objectivity as if we were spectators, as if we could know, speak and hear about Thee in the slightest degree without at once taking part, without at once making that correspondence actual, without at once beginning with obedience."[96]

As such, Barth understands faith as active and participatory knowledge of God rather than as passive and speculative knowledge of him. Barth's obedience-centered concept of faith corresponds to Calvin's piety-centered understanding of faith.

3. Church as a Place for Faith

For Barth, faith as the only way of knowing God can be objective and realistic in the church. It is, in the church of Jesus Christ, Barth argues, that God speaks to people, and they speak and hear about God. God is present in the church, speaking and listening. Thus, for Barth, the church of Jesus Christ is the place in which God is known through His revelation.[97] In this regard, Barth stresses the proclamation and teaching of the church. He argues that it is in the proclamation and teaching of the church that God himself speaks to human beings, which becomes the foundation of human faith: "The Word of God is God himself in the proclamation of the Church of Jesus Christ. In so far as God gives the Church the commission to speak about him, and the Church discharges this commission, it is God himself who declares His revelation in His witnesses."[98] In realizing

---

96. Barth, *Church Dogmatics*, II/1:26.
97. Ibid., II/1:3–4.
98. Ibid., I/2:743.

the commission to proclaim God, Barth argues, the church should be not only the teaching church, but also the hearing church.[99]

Barth insists that there are two forms of the proclamation of the church: preaching and the sacrament. The sacrament is another primary form of the proclamation along with preaching, but it must exist for the sake of preaching, not vice versa.[100] While Calvin considers the sacrament as an external means for containing and conferring grace, Barth thinks that the sacrament is the symbolic act that only shows the divine revelation and reconciliation because the church does not possess or cause grace.[101] In addition, unlike Calvin, it is noted that Barth considers only the Eucharist as the sacrament and views baptism with water as a Christian ethical decision or response to the effects of baptism with the Holy Spirit.[102] Barth argues that "Christian baptism is the first form of the human decision which in the foundation of the Christian life corresponds to the divine change [through baptism with the Holy Spirit]."[103] That is, for Barth, baptism with water is a faithful obedience corresponding to God's grace, the divine transformation. Although Barth's understanding of the sacrament is different from that of Calvin, Barth's emphasis on the nurturing function of the church through the proclamation by virtue of preaching and the sacrament is similar to Calvin.

The Role of the Holy Spirit: Inspiration of the Bible

For Barth, faith is the only way of knowing God. However, without the help of the Spirit, human beings cannot know God. The Father is the subject of revelation and the Son is the content of the revelation, while the Holy Spirit is the helper who enables revelation to be accepted by human beings.

> The Spirit of God is God in His freedom to be present to the creature, and so to create this relation, and thereby to be the life of the creature. And God's Spirit, the Holy Spirit, particularly

---

99. Ibid., I/2:797–884. Kooi relates Barth's emphasis on the role of the church in terms of faith with his soteriological understanding of faith. See Kooi, *As in a Mirror*, 288.

100. Barth, *Church Dogmatics*, I/1:70.

101. Ibid., I/1:47–70.

102. For accounts of baptism with the Holy Spirit and baptism with water, see respectively ibid., IV/4:3–40, 41–213.

103. Ibid., IV/4:44.

in revelation, is God Himself, so far as He can not only come to man, but be in man, and so open up man for Himself, make him ready and capable, and so achieve His revelation in him.... It is reality, therefore, by God not only coming to man, but meeting Himself from man's end. God's freedom to be thus present to man and hence to introduce this meeting—that is the Spirit of God, the Holy Spirit in God's revelation.[104]

Likewise, the role of the Spirit is essential for human beings to know God. Kooi proposes that for Barth, "to the extent that through the work of the Spirit man is made a participant in this movement, one can speak of real knowledge of God."[105] This is because of the *hiddenness* of God's revelation. In explaining this hiddenness, Barth refers to it in two dimensions. First, God's revelation is fundamentally concealed from human beings because of the qualitative difference between God and humans. Barth claims that sinful human beings cannot see God clearly because of the fall as Calvin thought. However, Barth, unlike Calvin, understands the fall as an existential symbol or saga for every human being.[106] Norman says that "Barth repudiated the doctrine of original sin as hereditary corruption. Original sin is not a disease passed from one person to another but rather is the radical, prideful departure of every person from the will of God."[107]

Second, the hiddenness of God's revelation is closely related to God's accommodation of the human in order to overcome this gulf. God accommodates God's self to human capacity in order for human beings to understand and know God through Scripture written with human words and concepts. Since human words, concepts, and symbols cannot describe God's revelation fully, these human methods hide God's revelation at least as much as they reveal it.[108] There seems to be a paradox, here, in that God is both revealed and concealed. However, the concept of the hiddenness of God's revelation indicates the qualitative gulf between God and human beings and human inability to know God completely—as God knows himself—in spite of God's revelation through Jesus Christ witnessed in the Bible. Therefore, the inner illumination of the Spirit is indispensable for human beings to know God through divine revelation.

104. Ibid., I/1:516.
105. Kooi, *As in a Mirror*, 293–94.
106. Barth, *Church Dogmatics*, IV/1:508.
107. Norman, "Human Sinfulness," 442–43.
108. Barth, *Church Dogmatics*, II/1:187.

Calvin also argues that people cannot understand Scripture without the help of the Holy Spirit. However, Calvin and Barth differ on the function of the Spirit in relation to the Bible. For Calvin, the Spirit is the author of the Scripture, so there is no error or limitation in it. Here, the role of the Spirit is like a teacher who writes a textbook. People should do their best in learning from the Spirit as students try not to miss a single word from the teacher.[109]

Barth, on the other hand, insists that although Scripture was inspired by the Holy Spirit, there are human errors in it derived from human language or human speech.[110] There is a big difference between Calvin's verbal inspiration of the Bible and Barth's idea of inspiration. Barth does not believe that the Bible was verbally inspired by the Spirit. Rather, for him, "inspiration is not a state but the free act of the Holy Spirit."[111] The human testimony of the prophets and the apostles became a witness of God's revelation by the free act of the Spirit. In the same way, the Bible as a human witness of God's revelation becomes for us the Word of God by an act of the Spirit. As such, Barth emphasizes the relationship between the Holy Spirit and the Bible—the writer as well as the reader—in his understanding of the inspiration of the Scripture.[112] The next quotation demonstrates this well:

> But in His eternal presence as the Word of God He [Jesus] is concealed from us who now live on earth and in time. He is revealed only in the sign of His humanity, and especially in the witness of His prophets and apostles. But by nature these signs are not heavenly-human, but earthly- and temporal-human. Therefore the act of their institution as signs requires repetition and confirmation. Their being as the Word of God requires promise and faith—just because they are signs of the eternal presence of Christ. For if they are to act as signs, if the eternal presence of Christ is to be revealed to us in time, there is a constant need of that continuing work of the Holy Spirit in the Church and to its members which is always taking place in new acts.[113]

Geoffrey Bromiley interprets Barth's doctrine of inspiration as a means to "safeguard the uniqueness of God Himself and especially of the

---

109. Calvin, *Institutes*, trans. Battles, 1.11.5.
110. Barth, *Church Dogmatics*, repr., I/2:463–72.
111. Bromiley, "Karl Barth's Doctrine of Inspiration," 74.
112. Barth, *Church Dogmatics*, repr., I/2:513–17.
113. Ibid., repr., I/2:513.

Incarnation of the divine Son."[114] However, he criticizes Barth for rejecting the objectivity of the work of the Holy Spirit. Bromiley argues that "if inspiration is not complete until it takes place in the individual, then God does not speak unless He speaks to me, and this means in practice that the only real or important act of 'inspiration' takes place subjectively in the recipient."[115]

Opposition to Natural Theology

Barth, who argues that a person can know God only through the inner illumination of the Holy Spirit, decisively rejects the general knowability of God in natural theology. The general knowability of God means that humans can know God through human inner capacities or the order and majesty of nature. For Barth, nature and reason without God's revelation cannot be ways for knowing God. Russell Moore understands Barth's position on natural revelation as follows:

> Barth articulated in his response to [Emil] Brunner and in his *Church Dogmatics* a view of revelation that located all of God's disclosure of himself to humanity in Jesus Christ. This Christomonism led Barth to deny, for instance, that Psalm 19 teaches a universal revelation in nature or that Romans 1 teaches that fallen humans can "reason" from the visible things to the invisible. Barth saw any attempt at a "point of contact" with fallen humanity . . . as a dangerous repudiation of the gospel.[116]

To decisively reject the possibility of natural theology, Barth criticizes the *analogia entis* (the analogy of being).[117] The *analogia entis* focuses on the similarity between God as Creator and human beings as creatures. Those who emphasize the ontological similarity between God and humans tend to argue that human beings can know God through general revelation in creation and human inner capacities because the ontological similarity opens an epistemological way for people to know God. However, according to Barth, the assertion of the natural knowability of God is to commit an error, ignoring the qualitative difference between God and humans and furthermore identifying the human being

---

114. Bromiley, "Karl Barth's Doctrine of Inspiration," 73.
115. Ibid., 80.
116. Moore, "Natural Revelation," 101.
117. See Barth, *Church Dogmatics*, I/1:260–83.

with God.[118] Barth argues that without the readiness of God revealing himself to people humanity will never be able to know God.[119]

Barth's alternative to the *analogia entis* is the role of the *analogia fidei* (the analogy of faith). The analogy of faith means that human beings can overcome the gulf between God and humans only by faith in Jesus Christ, who is God's revelation.[120] Barth strongly argues that there is no anthropological contact point for knowing God on the human side. Jesus Christ is the only contact point given to human beings for knowing God. He claims that this contact point is available only in faith.[121] Only in faith can people notice God's revelation in their lives and know God clearly and definitely.[122]

> The image of God in man of which we have to speak here and which constitutes the real point of contact for the Word of God is the one awakened through Christ from real death to life and so "restored," the newly-created *rectitude* now real as man's possibility for the Word of God. This point of contact is, therefore, not real outside faith but only in faith. In faith a man is created by the Word of God for the Word of God, existing in the Word of God, not in himself, not in virtue of his humanity and personality, nor from the standpoint of creation, for what is possible from the standpoint of creation from man to God had actually been lost through the Fall.[123]

---

118. Ibid., II/1:182.

119. Following Barth, Eberhard Jüngel also criticizes the concept of *analogia entis*. For Jüngel, the theory of *analogia entis* seems to reinforce a belief that God's being is static and unchangeable, which raises a question, how such God can exist in the temporal world. Jüngel criticizes the *analogia entis* with two Aristotelian definitions of analogy, an *analogy of proportion* and an *analogy of attribution*. Deverell analyzes Jüngel's criticism as follows: "These doctrines of analogy were used by Dionysius, Aquinas and Kant to claim some kind of relation between God and the world: in the first case by claiming that God is to the world as the soul is to the body; and in the second by claiming that God is the unconditioned condition for everything that exists. Jüngel points out, however, that neither strategy actually *works* unless one is first able to demonstrate either that the God is knowable in Godself, or that the precise proportionality between God and the world is already known. Thus, the traditional doctrines of analogy succeed only to underline and reinforce the belief that while we might know something of God's 'effects' in the world, we can know nothing of the essence of God in Godself." Deverell, *Bonds of Freedom*, 36–37.

120. Barth, *Church Dogmatics*, I/1:280–83.

121. Ibid., II/1:249.

122. Ibid., II/1:227.

123. Ibid., I/1:273.

However, for Barth, the overcoming of the gulf in faith does not mean the ontological identification of God and humans.[124] Barth interprets Calvin's argument about the reality of general revelation for knowing God, on which Brunner developed his natural theology, as a possibility before the fall, not after the fall. For Barth, since the first Adam sinned against God, there is no human contribution to knowledge of God for salvation. The knowledge of God as knowledge of faith is totally the result of God's grace alone (*sola gratia*).[125] Influenced by Barth, Eberhard Jüngel also emphasizes the ontological difference between God and humans, and considers the humanity of God, especially the death of God on the cross, the only way for human beings to know God. Jüngel thinks that God has been already revealed through the *human* Jesus Christ.[126] Jüngel takes Barth's work a step further by focusing on "the difference of a still greater similarity between God and man in the midst of a great dissimilarity" rather than on the difference of a still greater dissimilarity.[127]

Rodney Holder criticizes Barth's extreme position rejecting even the objectivity of general revelation in nature.[128] Holder claims that we should consider the historical background of Barth's days such as the Nazi regime and liberalism in order to understand Barth's thought on natural theology. He explains that Barth definitely rejected the possibility of natural theology because for Barth the general knowability of God could validate the Nazi regime and strengthen the anthropocentric theological methodology ignoring God's initiative in revelation.[129] Holder, however, denies the radical change to the later Barth's thinking of natural theology even after the Nazi era. He argues that "the key text is Barth's 1956 lecture 'The Humanity of God.' . . . Here he is more generous to his opponents. . . . Nevertheless it was clear that that theology [natural theology] could no longer continue as it was."[130]

As such, Barth's understanding of faith is wholly based on his theocentric and Christocentric understanding of God's revelation. Barth underlines the subjectivity of God in the event of God's self-revelation,

---

124. See ibid., II/1:225–29.
125. Ibid., II/1:170.
126. Webster, "Eberhad Jüngel," 5.
127. Deverell, *Bonds of Freedom*, 43; Jüngel, *God as the Mystery of the World*, 288.
128. Holder, "Karl Barth," 34.
129. Ibid., 30–33.
130. Ibid., 32.

rejecting an anthropocentric theological methodology. He rejects the general knowability of God without Jesus Christ as God's revelation. Along with the reality of God's revelation, the qualitative gulf between God and humans is an essential concept in his doctrine of God's revelation. Because of the qualitative difference human beings cannot know God, although God reveals Godself objectively by accommodating himself to human measure and capacity. God's revelation is concealed because of the fall.

Thus, Barth considers faith as the only way of knowing God. Without faith, one cannot understand God's revelation. For Barth, faith is an acknowledgement of the subjectivity of God in the event of God's revelation and an acceptance of God's revealing grace with gratitude. Faith is like standing before God with reverence and expectation, but if God does not stand before humans, faith becomes meaningless. Barth considers faith not only as an acknowledgement, but also as an act of knowing God. Barth underlines the active aspect of faith throughout his doctrine of faith.[131] Especially, he emphasizes obedience and prayer. Through obedience humans can participate in God's works for salvation as His partners, and through prayer one seeks the help of the Spirit in overcoming the temptation to objectify God. Barth argues that this faith is possible and can be developed in the church of Jesus Christ, in which God speaks and listens to the congregation, and people can speak and hear about God's revelation.

We also noted that in Barth's understanding of faith the role of the Spirit is essential because of the qualitative difference between God and humans. To overcome the gulf, God accommodates himself to human understanding, using Scripture written with human words, concepts, and symbols. However, this results in another hiddenness of God's revelation because human language and speech cannot fully describe God. Thus, without the inner illumination of the Holy Spirit no one can understand the Bible. At this point, in terms of Scripture Barth highlights the free act of the Spirit influencing the writer of the Bible as well as the reader.

Key Characteristics of Faith

In the course of discussing Calvin and Barth's ideas of faith, it was found that there is both continuity and discontinuity between Calvin and Barth in their understanding of faith. Considering that Calvin lived in

---

131. See. Barth, *Church Dogmatics*, IV/1:757–79.

pre-modern society dominated by traditional theism, and Barth lived in modern society dominated by the anthropocentric Western Enlightenment, their correspondence to key concepts in terms of faith is amazing in spite of the many differences caused by their different life contexts. Rather than driving the reader to confusion, such differences can help us understand faith more deeply and widely. Since the purpose of this chapter is to find key characteristics of faith to be considered in developing the religious education curriculum for faith, not to analyze some controversial issues related to faith, I will outline some of the key characteristics of faith by appraising, in turn, the similarities and differences between Calvin and Barth.

Personal Knowledge: God's Invitation

For Calvin and Barth, God's revelation is the starting point of faith as knowledge of God. God is the subject in the event of God's revelation, so knowledge of God is not the result of human thinking, but God's grace. If God does not reveal Godself to human beings, no one can know God. In God's revelation, Calvin and Barth commonly underline God's accommodation. Although their ideas of revelation are different in many respects in terms of the reality of general revelation and the understanding of Scripture as special revelation, both of them agree that God accommodates himself to human measure and capacity in order for humans to understand and know him overcoming the qualitative gulf between God and humans.

For them, God's accommodation is *God's invitation* into loving relationship with him and the essence of God's accommodation is the Incarnation of Jesus Christ as God's revelation. They both argue that God became a human being to be fully revealed to people through the event of the Incarnation of Jesus Christ. With the concept of God's accommodation, we can see God encouraging us and opening new opportunities for knowing him. We can feel God's passion for building a personal relationship with us. God is not out there, but here, among us. To know God means not to observe God out there objectively, but to communicate with him personally. Thus, we can say that faith is personal knowledge of God.

Spiritual Knowledge: Inner Testimony of the Spirit

We found big differences between the two scholars in their understanding of Scripture. While Calvin considers the Bible as the Word of God verbally inspired by the Holy Spirit, Barth thinks that Scripture is a human witness to the Word of God inspired by the Spirit which comes to people as the Word of God through the inner testimony of the Spirit. For Calvin, in Scripture there is no error, whereas for Barth there are errors and limitations in the Bible derived from human language and speech. Our theologians are in agreement, however, that the Bible provides the only reliable way for knowing God clearly, since they both see the fall as the core problem undermining "natural" forms of knowledge and they both regard the action of the Spirit as essential to understanding Scripture. For them, knowledge of God can be obtained only through reading the Bible under the inner illumination of the Spirit. Without the help of the Spirit, we cannot understand Scripture and consequently cannot know God. In this respect, faith is spiritual knowledge of God.

For Calvin and Barth, the term *spiritual* denoted a God-centered life focusing on living in the divine mystery. In relation to spirituality, Calvin emphasized living in the divine presence with the term *pietas*, while Barth underlined the importance of corresponding to the divine act through prayer and obedience in knowing God. It is notable that their understanding of spirituality does not accord with contemporary spirituality developed by *the desire for a unifying idea* in modern society.[132] Gabriel Moran argues that "there is a deeply felt need for something that would overcome the fragmentary character of contemporary life. The spiritual holds out the promise of healing our world's splits."[133] Thus, new spirituality being used in public institutions, such as schools, hospitals, and welfare centers, is primarily interested in helping people fulfil their potential as individuals and human beings. This kind of spirituality is closely related to spiritual well-being—generic spirituality—which is an essential part of people's overall health along with the physical, mental, emotional, and social wellness.[134] Such contemporary understanding of spirituality is totally distant from what Calvin and Barth thought as *spiritual*. Harris's definition of spirituality corresponds to what spirituality

---

132. Harris and Moran, *Reshaping Religious Education*, 105–8.
133. Ibid., 106.
134. Byrne, "Embracing Life at Its Fullest," 184–93.

means in this book. She defines spirituality as "our way of being in the world . . . in the light of the Mystery at the core of the universe."[135]

Participatory Knowledge: Obedience to God

Calvin and Barth have different ideas about the role of humans in obtaining faith as knowledge of God. While Calvin relatively understates the role of a person in the process of knowing God, Barth focuses on the importance of the active response of the human being although he consistently stresses the initiative of God's revelation in humans knowing God. In the same way, in the process of salvation Barth focuses on God's mercy and human freedom for answering *yes* or *no* to God's invitation, whereas Calvin emphasizes God's freedom and human predestination.[136]

However, we should be aware of the fact that *in relation to the relationship with God* rather than to the qualitative difference between God and human beings, Calvin highlights the importance of human participation and response to God's work—obedience—with the concept of piety. For Calvin, obedience to God is essential in obtaining faith as it enables people to build a personal relationship with God. So, he underlines piety which produces love, trust, and obedience to God. Similarly, Barth underscores the role of obedience in the process of knowing God. For Barth, without obedience no one knows God. Obedience is crucial in establishing a loving relation with God along with prayer. Thus, for both of them, faith is participatory knowledge of God.

Communal Knowledge: Church as Faith Community

Calvin and Barth both agree that faith as knowledge of God can be developed in the church as a faith community. For Calvin, the church is an outward means provided by God for nurturing faith. He even calls the church a nurturing mother. He also argues that a primary duty of the church is to educate people to know God so he has a keen interest in faith education in the church. In the same way, Barth underlines the importance of proclamation and teaching in the church for developing faith. For him, the church is the place in which God reveals Godself to people. They also agree that the sacrament in the church is critical in

---

135. Harris and Moran, *Reshaping Religious Education*, 109.
136. Gibson, *Reading the Decree*, 114–19.

developing Christians' faith, although their opinion of the sacrament is very different. Calvin views the sacrament as the visible Word of God conferring grace, while for Barth the sacrament is a form of proclamation of God, the symbolic act that proves the divine revelation proclaimed in preaching. Unlike Calvin who considers baptism and the Eucharist as the sacrament, Barth views baptism with water as a human response to God's gift through baptism with the Holy Spirit and acknowledges Eucharist as the only sacrament. However, both of them emphasize the role of sacrament practiced in the church in the process of faith development.

In this respect, faith is communal knowledge of God. However, it should be noted that church-centered education does not mean an anthropocentric education. For both Calvin and Barth, the teaching of the church is God centered because both of them underline God's commission to the church in terms of faith education.[137] As such, Calvin and Barth agree that faith is personal, spiritual, participatory, and communal knowledge of God.

Implications for the Religious Education Curriculum

The purpose of religious education is to nurture faith as knowledge of God, so faith should be at the center of religious education. Thus, the religious education curriculum should be a planned series of educational activities for faith development. In this respect, religious education curricularists must understand *what faith is*, *how people get faith*, and *how faith is communicated*. This is the reason why I have investigated the characteristics of faith in this chapter, appraising the understanding of faith according to Calvin and Barth. In spite of a time difference of nearly four hundred years between Calvin and Barth, I found that they both stand in the Reformed tradition of *sola fide*, *sola gratia*, and *sola scriptura* in terms of faith as knowledge of God. Although there are still some controversial issues about their ideas of faith due to their different life-contexts, I think that Calvin and Barth are in agreement about key characteristics of faith. For them, faith is personal, spiritual, participatory, and communal knowledge of God.

---

137. Calvin argues that God has committed to the church the educational duty for developing faith. Calvin, *Institutes*, trans. Battles, 4.1.5. Barth also insists that God has given the church the commission to educate people to know God. Barth, *Church Dogmatics*, I/2:743.

Through investigating what faith is, I found that Tyler's schooling paradigm based on modern objectivistic epistemology is not appropriate for developing faith because the truth which it pursues is objectivistic, positivistic, and individualistic knowledge which is totally different from faith as personal, spiritual, participatory, and communal knowledge of God. Based on the four characteristics of faith, I now suggest some implications for a religious education curriculum suitable for nurturing faith.

Above all, religious education for faith should be God's education, *pedagogia Dei*. Pedagogia Dei means that God is the subject of religious education, and the purpose of religious education is to achieve God's will toward people.[138] The core of Calvin and Barth's understanding of faith is that God is the subject in the event of his revelation so God's self-revelation is the starting point for human knowledge of God. For Calvin and Barth, human beings will never be able to know God through their own power and ability. Humans can understand and know God only in his grace and only by his grace. Thus, religious education for faith should be God's education. The purpose of all educators should be helping people realize God's vision for them and how to achieve it by seeking God's guidance. In pedagogia Dei, pastors, teachers, and the whole congregation should not be the subject of religious education. Rather, they should remember that they are just partners taking part in God's education.

Pedagogia Dei is inherently Trinitarian education because God is a Trinity. Calvin and Barth both believe that God has revealed Godself through Jesus Christ as witnessed in the Bible. For them, Jesus Christ is the essence of God's revelation, the content, and the way. And the Holy Spirit is the helper for humans to realize God's will revealed through Jesus Christ. In this respect, religious education for faith should focus on the incarnation, death, and resurrection of Jesus Christ and the works of the Spirit. Moral education apart from Jesus Christ and the Holy Spirit cannot be religious education for faith. Thus, the religious education curriculum should be designed suitably for pedagogia Dei promoting a Trinitarian education.

Second, religious education for faith should be faith community education. Calvin and Barth agree that faith can be obtained and nurtured in the church as a faith community. Calvin defines the church as an external means and aid for human faith provided by God. Barth also emphasizes the importance of proclamation and teaching by the church

---

138. Yang, "Gyoyukui gwanjeomeseo ikneun kalbinui gyohoeron," 471–75.

in terms of knowledge of God. In this respect, the educational mission of the church should not be restricted to Sunday School ministry. Rather, the educational commission of the church should be achieved through all dimensions of the church's life, for example, teaching (didache), worship (leiturgia), community (koinonia), proclamation (kerygma), and outreach (diakonia).[139]

Faith community education means that not only teachers in Sunday School, but every member of the congregation of the church should take responsibility for the educational mission given by God. The religious education curriculum for faith should include all dimensions of the church as educational contexts and develop various educational activities around the whole of church life.

Third, religious education for faith should be prayer-centered spiritual education. Spiritual education stressing prayer, contemplation, and fasting can be a significant way for meeting God personally. For Barth, prayer is an act of knowing God. Through prayer, people can build a loving relationship with God, confess their sinful nature and helplessness, and seek the help of the Spirit. For Calvin, prayer is also stressed in *pietas*. Calvin sees piety as attending to the only, true God who enables humans to love, trust, and worship him. Given that Calvin and Barth consider faith as personal relationship with God, not as intellectual knowledge, one cannot expect the development of faith without prayer. In this respect, religious education for faith should help people approach God through prayer so that they may meet God personally. If religious education is not prayer-centered spiritual education, but focuses on transmitting knowledge about God, such education may strengthen intellectual belief, but not holistic faith. At this point, the role of corporate prayer and public liturgy should be also stressed in the development of faith. If confined to personal prayer alone, faith would skew knowledge of God in individualistic and ahistorical ways.[140] The religious education curriculum for faith should strengthen the spiritual dimension of its educational activities, personally and communally.

Finally, religious education for faith should be participation focused education. Calvin and Barth both underline the importance of people's participation and involvement in education for faith. Their emphasis

---

139. See Harris, *Fashion Me a People*, 75–156.

140. Harris also emphasizes the corporate dimension of spirituality and advocates the necessity of group disciplines for developing spirituality. Harris and Moran, *Reshaping Religious Education*, 118.

on obedience is a representative example. For Calvin and Barth, obedience is one of the key points in developing faith. They argue that faith as knowledge of God is possible only in obedience and can develop only through obedience. Without obedience, it is impossible to unite with God. It accords with Jesus' saying, "You are my friends if you do what I command."[141] Their arguments about the role of prayer and the sacrament in faith development also show well their concern for participation driven education. Thus, in the process of religious education it is very important to provide students with a variety of opportunities to participate in God's works through obedience, prayer, and liturgy. At this point, it is significant that teachers should help students understand, interpret and reinterpret the meaning of their participation in practices of Christian events. Otherwise, their participation could easily be meaningless, which would result in the failure of faith education.[142]

---

141. John 15:14 NIV.

142. From the same vein, Thomas Groome stresses the process of reinterpretation of Christian tradition in faith education. Groome argues that for this the teacher should fully understand his/her students' real situations and needs so that the teacher may provide appropriate opportunities for students to reinterpret faith tradition and to discover meanings from it for their lives. Groome, *Sharing Faith*, 138–42; Huebner et al., "From Theory to Practice," 367.

4
Socio-Historical Background of the Korean Australian Church

History of Korean Immigration into Australia

According to the *1958 Australian Year Book*, a Korean was naturalised in Australia in 1957. This is the first official record of Korean immigration to Australia.[1] Based on this date, *50-Year History of Koreans in Australia* was published in the Korean language in 2008. To date, however, there has been a lack of reliable information on the history of Korean immigration to Australia.[2] To overview the history of Korean immigration into Australia effectively, I divide the history into four parts: early migration, the first wave of immigration, the second wave of immigration, and new trends of immigration.

Early Migration

The beginning of relationships between Australians and Koreans seems to go back to the mission of the Victorian Presbyterian Church of Australia in Korea at the end of the nineteenth century. Joseph H. Davies, the first Australian missionary in Korea, arrived in Seoul, Korea, on October 5, 1889, with his sister, Mary and died of small pox and pneumonia on April 5, 1890, at Busan after a survey walking tour to Busan from Seoul.[3] Since

---

1. Yang, "Hanho gan chogi injeok gyoryuwa hanin sahoeui hyeongseong," 28.
2. James Coughlan argues that "the dearth of easily accessible material concerning the Korean community in Australia is due in part to the short history of critical mass emigration from Korea to Australia, and because there has been almost no scholastic interest directed towards the Korean community in Australia." Coughlan and McNamara, *Asians in Australia*, 172.
3. Chung, "Beyond Dichotomy," 25–33.

then, more than a hundred Australian missionaries mostly commissioned by the Victorian Presbyterian Church of Australia have served Koreans mainly in the Busan-Gyeongnam area in the southern part of Korea.[4]

With the help and support of Australian missionaries, between 1921 and 1941, a number of Koreans came to Australia for study or training.[5] According to confirmed documents, these Koreans were the first Koreans who temporarily stayed in Australia. Ho Yol Kim was the first Korean to come to Australia, arriving on September 9, 1921, for study at the University of Melbourne.[6]

The official relationship between the two countries began in earnest with the decision of the Australian government to dispatch Australian troops to Korea during the Korean War from 1950 to 1953. James Coughlan describes the effect of the Australian entry into the Korean War in terms of Korean immigration to Australia as follows:

> The presence of Australian troops in southern Korea during and after the Korean War led to a number of Australian soldiers establishing permanent relationships with Korean women, many of whom were later to immigrate to Australia as "war brides." In addition, in the wake of the war, a number of Korean War orphans were adopted into Australian families....
>
> The post-Korean War immigration of several hundred Korean orphans marked the first wave of Korean immigration into Australia.[7]

Myung Duk Yang searched for concrete figures about Korean War brides and Korean War orphans in the 1961 *Census of Population and Housing of Australia*, but there was no reference to Korean-born migrants in the document. He asked the Australian Bureau of Statistics, the Australian Department of Immigration, the National Library of Australia, the Australian Museum Archives, the Returned and Services League of Australia, and the Australian Adoption Association for some information on Korean War brides and orphans, but he could not find appropriate data. Yang assumes that there may be documents somewhere or that

---

4. Yang, "Hanho gan chogi injeok gyoryuwa hanin sahoeui hyeongseong," 19–21.
5. Kim, "Koreans," 659.
6. Yang, "Hanho gan chogi injeok gyoryuwa hanin sahoeui hyeongseong," 21–22.
7. Coughlan and McNamara, *Asians in Australia*, 173–74.

such data may not exist because the number of Korean War brides and orphans who entered Australia was very few.[8]

In addition, according to statistics of Global Overseas Adoptees' Link, there is no record of the Australian adoption of Korean orphans between 1958 and 1975. The adoption program began with five Korean orphans who came to Australia in 1976.[9] Therefore, Coughlan's argument that "the post-Korean War immigration of several hundred Korean orphans marked the first wave of Korean immigration into Australia"[10] seems unverifiable—at least at the moment.

In the 1960s, a number of Korean scholars and students came to Australia for study supported by the *Colombo Plan* which was established to assist developing Asian countries in their technical and economic development. Among those scholars or students, some settled in Australia after finishing study and started to form the Korean community in Australia.[11]

The First Wave of Korean Immigration into Australia

In 1968, a significant event happened in terms of the history of Korean immigration to Australia. On June 20, 1968, the first Korean migrant family to go through the official Australian immigration procedure arrived in Sydney.[12]

After that, between 1968 and 1969, a few engineers came to Australia as migrants with their families under the Skilled Migration Program.[13] During the early 1970s, a small number of professionals, such as helicopter pilots, taekwondo masters, and geography scholars, migrated to Australia legally.[14] According to the 1971 Australian census, 468 Koreans resided in Australia, mainly in Sydney.[15]

---

8. Yang, "Hanho gan chogi injeok gyoryuwa hanin sahoeui hyeongseong," 28.

9. Kim, "Hanin dongpo sahoeui seongjanggwa geu jiljeok byeonhwa 2000 nyeon ihu," 110.

10. Coughlan and McNamara, *Asians in Australia*, 174.

11. Yang, "Hanho gan chogi injeok gyoryuwa hanin sahoeui hyeongseong," 30–31.

12. Park, "Hanin dongpo sahoeui jeongchak," 39–42.

13. Richmond, "Becoming a Multicultural Nation," 452.

14. Park, "Hanin dongpo sahoeui jeongchak," 44–47.

15. Seol, "Sydney Korean Community," 24.

The mass immigration of Koreans to Australia started in earnest with the entry of Korean engineers who had worked in Vietnam until the end of the Vietnam War. Many of these workers did not return to Korea. Instead, they sought new opportunities in other places such as: America, Canada, and Australia. Since three Vietnam War engineers arrived in Australia on June 25, 1972, a few thousand Korean workers, mostly men, have come to Australia from Vietnam with temporary visas for work. Up until 1975 most of them came to Sydney because there were more available workplaces and fellow Koreans than in other areas. Many overstayed their visa conditions and then sought a way to settle in this new land legally and permanently.[16] Some of them succeeded in getting permanent visas with the support of the company or institution employing them, but there were still many who stayed illegally.

At this time, a few Koreans led by Da Yul Choi helped illegal Korean immigrants apply for permanent residency with the support of an Australian lawyer, Morgan Ryan. As many as 486 people applied for permanent visas in this way, and in September 1975, all of them personally received conditional approval letters stating that if they passed the physical examination and the Korean police check, they would be granted permanent residency. After four months, all of them were able to obtain permanent residency along with other illegal immigrants because of the Federal government's amnesty provisions of January 26, 1976. As a result of the amnesty, more than five hundred Koreans were freed from illegal immigrant status.[17]

These amnesty migrants invited their families in Korea to join them and significant family immigration to Australia followed soon after. According to the 2007 "Statistics of Korean Migrants to Overseas" issued by the Korean Ministry of Foreign Affairs and Trades, 728 people in 1976, 454 in 1977, and 476 in 1978 migrated to Australia.[18] Compared to the fact that the total number of Korean migrants to Australia departing

---

16. Han and Han, "Koreans in Sydney," 26.

17. Park, "Hanin dongpo sahoeui jeongchak," 60–65.

18. The statistics include only long-term residents. The numbers between 1962 and 2001 show only those who reported their emigration to the Ministry of Foreign Affairs and Trades before departure. Those who obtained permanent residency in Australia and reported it to the Korean Embassy were included in the 2002 statistics. The figures for those who moved to Australia from any third country other than Korea did not appear in the data.

from Korea between 1962 and 1975 was 359 people, the 1976 amnesty brought enormous changes to the Korean community in Australia.[19]

The first amnesty also triggered the migration of other Koreans to Australia. Many Koreans who worked in countries other than Korea, such as engineers in the Middle East, agricultural migrants in South American countries, and miners and nurses in West Germany, rushed to Australia for better economic and educational conditions during the period from 1976 to 1979. However, many of them overstayed their visas and became illegal immigrants, failing to obtain permanent residency. They suffered from acute stress which resulted from their unstable immigrant status and some of them were arrested by officers of the Immigration Department and deported to Korea.[20]

The second amnesty declared on June 19, 1980, saved more than two hundred illegal Korean immigrants from deportation. Those who were pardoned by the second amnesty invited their families to join them soon after, which paved the way for further growth of the Korean community in Australia. These two amnesties marked the first wave of Korean immigration into Australia.[21] This fact can easily be verified by the Australian census. According to the 1976 census, 1,460 Korean-born people resided in Australia, but through these two amnesties the Korean population in Australia increased sharply to 9,285 people in the 1986 census, which showed the Korean population had become about six times larger than the figure in the 1976 census.[22] Most Amnesty migrants and their families settled in Sydney, laying the foundation for Sydney to be the biggest place of residence for Koreans in Australia since that time. However, it is noted that the proportion of Koreans in Sydney in the whole Korean Australian population has continually decreased since the 2001 census: 69.5 percent of the whole Korean population in Australia lived in Sydney at the time of the 2001 census, 60.9 percent in the 2006 census and 53.9 percent in the 2011 census.[23]

---

19. The number of 359 people does not include Korean migrants departed from other regions than Korea. Park, "Hanin dongpo sahoeui jeongchak," 39.

20. Ibid., 65–72.

21. Park and Cho, "Hanin dongpo sahoeui yeokdongjeok baljeon," 74.

22. Richmond, "Becoming a Multicultural Nation," 452.

23. Australian Bureau of Statistics, "2006 Census of Population and Housing: Country of Birth of Person by Sex for Time Series, Australia"; Australian Bureau of Statistics, "2011 Census of Population and Housing: Country of Birth of Person (BPLP) by Greater Capital City Statistical Areas (UR)."

The Second Wave of Korean Immigration into Australia

After the family reunification program following the second amnesty in the early 1980s, significant numbers of Korean skilled or business migrants came to Australia, from the mid-1980s until the early 1990s, initiating the second substantial wave of Korean immigration into Australia. Joy Han and Gil-Soo Han argue that "the key reason for the growth of the Korean population in Australia in the 1980s was actually the arrival of skilled migrants in the mid-1980s, and business migrants, whose rates of arrival first jumped in the late 1980s."[24]

Han and Han describe skilled and business migrants in this period as "well-equipped container migrants" in comparison with "the empty-handed amnesty migrants."[25] However, although skilled or business migrants had better conditions than amnesty migrants in many respects, they also faced huge challenges in settling in this new land. Han and Han explain it further:

> The task of re-establishing their livelihoods in Australia would prove more challenging. Most of these professionally trained Korean migrants would disappointingly find themselves in manual labour for want of English language proficiency. Similar sets of challenges met those Koreans who had arrived under the federal government's business migration initiatives. . . .
>
> Korean business migrants arrived during the global economic downturn of the 1980s and the recession which Australia underwent through to the early 1990s. This may have made fine policy sense to the government; however the reality for business migrants and also skilled migrants was not as sensible. They have encountered language and cultural barriers which have hampered their employment and enterprise opportunities, and their aspirations and expectations have been profoundly frustrated, not least by economic conditions.[26]

According to the 2007 statistics of Korean migrants moving overseas, the number of migrants to Australia increased considerably from 619 people in 1985 to 1155 people in 1986. The number entering Australia continued at a high rate until the number dropped sharply to 536 in 1993: 1556 people in 1987, 1442 in 1988, 1333 in 1989, 1162 in 1990, 1113

---

24. Han and Han, "Koreans in Sydney," 26.
25. Ibid.
26. Ibid., 27.

Socio-Historical Background

in 1991, and 1093 in 1992.²⁷ During this time, over 40 percent of Korean migrants came to Australia under the business migration category.²⁸

This growth in the number of migrants entering Australia from Korea directly influenced the Korean population in Australia. According to the 1991 Australian census, there were 20,868 Korean-born residents.²⁹ This means that 11,583 Korean people were added to the Korean population in Australia in just five years, which was 2,298 more people than the whole Korean population in Australia until 1986.

New Trends in Korean Immigration to Australia

An interesting fact is that while the Korean Ministry of Foreign Affairs and Trades reported that since 1993 the number of migrants to Australia from Korea decreased progressively to 216 people in 1997, which was the lowest since 1984,³⁰ the 1996 Australian census showed that the Korean population, on the contrary, had risen to 30,091 people compared with 20,868 in the 1991 census.³¹

This phenomenon may have resulted from the fact that since the introduction of the point-based immigration system in 1992 those who obtained permanent residency after studying or working in Australia increased dramatically. In the case of Koreans, Standard Business Sponsorship (Subclass 457) visa holders, State/Territory Sponsored Business Owner (subclass 163) visa holders, and overseas students who study a certain subject in the Migration Occupation Demand List for Skilled-Independent Migration (Subclass 885) have been representative of those who study or work in Australia with temporary visas for a certain period of time and then apply for a permanent residency visa under certain conditions. They were also skilled or business migrants like most former Korean immigrants, but the average age of Korean migrants became younger than in the past because of the new point-based immigration system. Since the mid-1990s a considerable number of Korean youth

27. Park and Cho, "Hanin dongpo sahoeui yeokdongjeok baljeon," 75.
28. Han and Han, "Koreans in Sydney," 27.
29. Coughlan and McNamara, *Asians in Australia*, 175.
30. Ministry of Foreign Affairs and Trades, "Statistics of Korean Migrants to Overseas, 1962–2009."
31. Kim, "Hanin dongpo sahoeui seongjanggwa geu jiljeok byeonhwa 2000 nyeon ihu," 103.

have studied and obtained permanent residency through the Skilled-Independent Migration program before their marriage.

Through such channels, the number of Korean migrants to Australia has steadily increased and this growth can be seen in the Australian census. According to the 1996 census, there were 30,091 Korean-born residents in Australia, and the number grew to 38,745 people in the 2001 census, 52,763 in the 2006 census and 74,538 in the 2011 census.[32] If second-generations who were born in Australia with Korean ancestry are added, the result of the 2011 census shows that the number of Koreans in Australia rises to 84,633 people.[33]

Characteristics of the Korean Australian Community

As discussed above, with the exception of amnesty migrants and their families between the mid-1970s and the early 1980s, most of the Korean migrants to Australia have been skilled or business migrants. There were two significant waves of Korean immigration into Australia, and since the second wave between the mid-1980s and the early 1990s, the number of Korean migrants has considerably increased under the Australian Point Based Immigration System.

Based primarily on the results of the 2011 census, I provide five main characteristics of the Korean Australian community that make it easier to understand Koreans in Australia.

First, the Korean Australian community is relatively young. According to the 2011 census, the median age of Korean Australians is 31.2 years old. Considering the median age of the total Australian population is 37.8 years old, it is one of the young communities in Australia. Those aged less than thirty-nine years of age make up about 70.8 percent of the Korean population in Australia, while those aged 60+ years old make up only 6.3 percent. In addition, children aged less than eighteen years of age make up 23.7 percent of Korean migrants in Australia.[34] These

---

32. Australian Bureau of Statistics, "2006 Census of Population and Housing: Country of Birth of Person by Sex for Time Series, Australia"; Australian Bureau of Statistics, "2011 Census of Population and Housing: Country of Birth of Person (BPLP) by Greater Capital City Statistical Areas (UR)."

33. Australian Bureau of Statistics, "2011 Census of Population and Housing: Ancestry 1st Response (ANC1P) by Greater Capital City Statistical Areas (UR)."

34. Australian Bureau of Statistics, "2011 Census of Population and Housing: Age in Single Years (AGEP) by Ancestry 1st Response (ANC1P)."

statistics definitely show that the Korean community in Australia is quite young. Coughlan argues that "their youthfulness . . . signifies that this community is in a position to continue to participate in the economic advancement of Australia."[35]

Second, the Korean Australian community consists mainly of people who arrived in Australia in the last decade. Those who came to Australia from 2002 to the census date in 2011 make up 53.9 percent of the Korean Australian population, while those who came to Australia before 1979 make up just about 3.5 percent. If the number of those who arrived in the 1990s is considered, 78.2 percent of Korean Australians have arrived in Australia since 1990.[36] This relatively short history indicates that the majority of Korean Australians are first-generations and many of them are still struggling to settle in this new land.

Most of the first-generation Koreans tend to adhere strongly to Korean culture and value systems and want to teach their children to be Korean, which may cause intergenerational or intercultural conflicts at home and/or in the Korean community. This ethnicity-related trait is revealed in the rate of those speaking the Korean language at home. According to the 2011 census, 79,787 Korean Australians (94.3 percent) were using Korean at home, which indicates quite well the Korean Australians' tendency to retain their Korean culture and to teach their children to speak Korean.[37]

Third, Korean Australians are highly educated. According to the 2011 census, 79.1 percent of Korean-born Australians completed year twelve or its equivalent. Considering that only 38.4 percent of the total Australian population completed year twelve or its equivalent, the percentage of highest year of school completed in the Korean Australian community is quite remarkable.[38] These statistics show that Korean Australians are quite well educated, which is in line with Coughlan's analysis of educational characteristics of the Korean community in Australia: "The Korean-born community in Australia has a much greater propor-

---

35. Coughlan and McNamara, *Asians in Australia*, 176.

36. Australian Bureau of Statistics, "2011 Census of Population and Housing: Year of Arrival in Australia (ranges) (YARRP) by Country of Birth of Person (BPLP)."

37. Australian Bureau of Statistics, "2011 Census of Population and Housing: Language Spoken at Home (LANP) by Greater Capital City Statistical Areas (UR)."

38. Australian Bureau of Statistics, "2011 Census of Population and Housing: Highest Year of School Completed (HSCP) by Country of Birth of Person (BPLP) - 4 Digit Level."

tion of its population with post-secondary qualifications than the rest of the Asian-born community in Australia and Australia's population overall, and thus may be considered as a highly educated community."[39]

It is also noteworthy that the number of Korean Australian students attending Technical or Further Educational Institutions, University or other Tertiary Institutions is 13,296 according to the 2011 census. Given that the whole population of Korean Australian young adults aged nineteen to twenty-four who are potential students in tertiary institutions is 10,188, it appears that not only young adults, but many adults are undertaking further studies for various reasons such as beginning a new career or undergoing a period of adjustment to the new land.[40] These statistics indicate not only that the Korean Australian community is enthusiastic about children's education, but also that many Korean Australians are struggling to adjust to this new land and seeking new opportunities by obtaining an Australian certification.

This phenomenon is closely related to the fourth characteristic of the Korean Australian community: the high rate of occupational downgrade of Korean professionals due to their relatively poor English proficiency and different certification systems between Australia and Korea. For example, Han's case study of the occupational structure of a group of Korean professional migrants in Australia is a good illustration. He conducted research into 130 Korean migrants who specialized in computer engineering in 1999. He found that among them only thirty percent were employed in a computer-related company, while the rest worked as unskilled workers or ran small local shops.[41] Han argues that many Korean professionals or skilled engineers find it difficult to get a job related to their specialization and/or are not promoted according to their abilities because of their relatively poor proficiency in English.[42]

---

39. Coughlan and McNamara, *Asians in Australia*, 184.

40. Australian Bureau of Statistics, "2011 Census of Population and Housing: Type of Educational Institution Attending (TYPP) by Country of Birth of Person (BPLP) - 4 Digit Level."

41. Han, "Immigrant Life," 5–29, quoted in Lee, "Hanindeului jikeopgwa gajeong saenghwal," 222–23.

42. Han, "From Overt to Covert Racial Discrimination," 7–10. However, it is quite interesting to see that 59 percent of the Korean Australian migrants born in Korea answered in the 2011 census that their proficiency in spoken English is good or very good. This seems to show that there is a big gap between Koreans' personal confidence and the standard requirement expected by Australian society in terms of English proficiency. See Australian Bureau of Statistics, "2011 Census of Population and Housing:

It is also noted that different certification systems between the two countries have created a large barrier to professional Koreans continuing their careers in Australia. For example, Korean doctors or dentists must obtain certain certifications recognized by the government of Australia in order to treat patients in Australia regardless of their qualifications or careers in Korea. Gyung Sook Lee notes that Australian society has subtly discriminated against foreign professionals by not actively recognizing foreign certification. In the period when there is a shortage of jobs as a result of the economic depression, overseas-born professionals seem to be disadvantaged because of lack of recognition of their qualifications and careers.[43]

For these two reasons, many Korean professionals or skilled engineers in Australia have been working in blue-collar jobs or running small shops. According to the 2006 census, blue-collar jobs were the second largest occupation (about 16 percent) of Korean Australians after professionals (about 23 percent).[44] Data on Total Personal Income in the 2011 census also serves as an indicator of the matter. According to the statistics, the proportion of high-income people who earn more than $78,000 per year is only 5.5 percent of the employed or self-employed Korean-born Australians, which is twice as low as that of the whole Australian population (11.6 percent). The majority of Korean Australian workers (32.3 percent) earn from $20,888 to $64,999 per year.[45]

It is also interesting to see that according to the 2011 census 24 percent of Korean Australians are unemployed, which is much higher than the unemployment rate of the whole Australian population (6.1 percent).[46] This data seem closely related to two factors. First, the high proportion of Koreans attending educational institutions (26.5 percent) seems to be a major reason for the high rate of unemployment. As indicated above, many Korean adult migrants are studying to get a new opportunity by getting an Australian certification because they cannot

---

Proficiency in Spoken English (ENGP) by Country of Birth of Person (BPLP) - 4 Digit Level."

43. Lee, "Hanindeului jikeopgwa gajeong saenghwal," 221.

44. DIAC, "Community Information Summary: South-Korea-born."

45. Australian Bureau of Statistics, "2011 Census of Population and Housing: Total Personal Income, weekly (INCP) by Country of Birth of Person (BPLP) - 4 Digit Level."

46. Ibid.

get a job in their former careers.⁴⁷ Second, poor English proficiency and different certification systems between the two countries seem to make it especially hard for Korean women to find a job. Unlike men, it is not easy for women to work outside their careers in a foreign land, which causes many of them to be full-time housewives supporting their families. This high rate of unemployment influences the financial status of many Korean migrant families.

This social/occupational downward mobility may cause Korean migrants to feel disadvantaged and inferior to Australians. To overcome this kind of difficulty, they believe that they should work harder than Australians. This experience seems to have a marked impact consciously or unconsciously on the personal and family life of Korean migrants in Australia. Those who feel different from mainstream Australians may stick to the Korean ethnic community.

Sheena Choi, M. Elizabeth Cranley, and Joe Nichols describe this phenomenon as follows:

> Because of their inadequate ability to communicate effectively in English, first generation Korean immigrants are, in general, confined to the ethnic community and are unable to find jobs in their trained professions even with their high levels of educational attainment. Therefore, they experience social/occupational downward mobility, which becomes a source of individual and family tension. Most of these immigrants become self-employed entrepreneurs in alternative blue-collar jobs, and their activities are generally limited to the Korean communities.⁴⁸

Their argument is based on the Korean American experience, but there seems little difference between the two communities in respect of this matter. In addition, first-generation Korean Australians tend to push their children not only to succeed in the host society in place of them, but also to keep a Korean identity. Considering that the recent migration of Koreans to Australia is primarily for the education of their children rather than for economic betterment, it would be easily understood that parents' disappointment is likely to increase their expectation for the success of their children.⁴⁹

---

47. Australian Bureau of Statistics, "2011 Census of Population and Housing: Type of Educational Institution Attending (TYPP) by Country of Birth of Person (BPLP) - 4 Digit Level."

48. Choi et al., "Coming to America," 52.

49. Park and Cho, "Hanin dongpo sahoeui yeokdongjeok baljeon," 80.

Choi, Cranley, and Nichols refer to this matter like this:

> Unlike economic immigrants, education immigrants appear to pay greater costs for their opportunities. Unable to find a job in a trained profession due to language barriers, these middle class immigrants appear to experience greater anxiety in addition to the problems experienced by immigration. The extraordinary burden caused by the social/occupational downward mobility of immigrant families has an evident psychological impact. Furthermore, the sacrifices that parents make and their subsequent high expectations for their children both motivate and add stress to young immigrants' lives. Children want to live up to their parents' expectations, but at the same time they struggle with the desire to embrace the American ideal of independence and self-determination. These socio-cultural conflicts are at the center of these youths' efforts to forge a sense of identity and place.[50]

Finally, it is also remarkable that the rate of church affiliation of the Korean community in Australia is quite high. According to the 2011 census, 58,494 Korean Australians identified themselves as Christians and this figure is about 69.1 percent of the whole Korean population in Australia.[51] Compared to the 2006 census, the proportion of church affiliation decreased slightly from 70.9 percent to 69.1 percent, but the rate is still high.[52] Among various Christian traditions, the proportion of Koreans attending the Reformed church including the Uniting Church and the Presbyterian church is quite high, 48.5 percent, followed by those affiliated with the Catholic Church, 32.6 percent.[53] The main reason for the growth of the Korean ethnic church in Australia is that the Korean Australian church has been not only a religious institution, but also a Korean social community where much of the stress and hardship of settling in a foreign land is relieved. The importance of the Korean Australian church to the lives of Korean migrants in Australia will be further discussed in the following section with a description of its three major features.

50. Choi et al., "Coming to America," 58.

51. Australian Bureau of Statistics, "2011 Census of Population and Housing: Religious Affiliation (RELP) - 1 Digit Level by Ancestry 1st Response (ANC1P) - 4 Digit Level."

52. Australian Bureau of Statistics, "2006 Census of Population and Housing: Ethnic Media Package, Persons born in Korea, Republic of (South)."

53. Australian Bureau of Statistics, "2011 Census of Population and Housing: Religious Affiliation (RELP) - 3 Digit Level by Ancestry 1st Response (ANC1P) - 4 Digit Level."

The Korean Australian Church

The very high rate of church affiliation of Korean Australians is one of major features of the Korean Australian community. Since the period of early migration into Australia, Korean ethnic churches have strongly influenced Koreans in Australia in many respects. Yang argues that the Korean ethnic church has been a meeting place for non-Christians as well as Christians, where they can speak Korean freely, and can comfort and share with each other. Thus, from the early days of Korean immigration into Australia, Korean churches in Australia naturally became an important part of Korean migrants' lives, regardless of whether or not they had a Christian faith.[54] As Pyong Gap Min and Dae Young Kim analyzed Korean churchgoers in the United States, Korean Australian immigrants also "preserve Korean cultural traditions and ethnic networks through their active participation in ethnic congregations."[55]

Center for Korean Immigrants: Multidimensional Ministry

The first Korean Australian church is the Korean Church of Melbourne established in Melbourne on July 8, 1973, a Presbyterian church which became a Uniting Church in Australia in 1977. Twenty adults and thirteen children gathered to worship for the first time at the Burwood Presbyterian church with the Reverend Alan Stuart, their first pastor who could lead the Korean-speaking service because he was a former missionary in Korea.[56] Considering that the total number of Koreans in Melbourne in 1973 was only 69 people (47 adults and 22 children) according to the 1973 address book of the Korean Society of Melbourne established on December 31, 1972, it is remarkable that nearly 50 percent of Koreans in Melbourne participated in the first service.[57]

Stuart reminisces as follows:

> One of the great features of the Sundays was the cup of tea/coffee after the services and the opportunity this gave to the Koreans to have fellowship and swap news, all in their own language. I

---

54. Yang, "Hanindeului jonggyo hwaldong," 142.

55. Min and Kim, "Intergenerational Transmission," 265.

56. Melbon-haningyohoe Yeoksa-pyeonchan wiwonhoe, *Melbon-haningyohoe samsipnyeonsa*, 13.

57. Nahm, "Biktoria haninhoe (VIC)," 330.

realized, perhaps just a little, how necessary this was. Many of those working, or studying at the university, had to spend much of their time conversing in English, which, being the second language for all of them, meant there was always a measure of stress or tension as they strove to understand Australians who are not used to watching their language to avoid words not frequently used, and who frequently do not speak distinctly. For at least a short period in the week, these folk could relax without the conscious effort of ordering their language. Also wives and mothers who had little English and thus little opportunity for fellowship, particularly valued this hour.[58]

Gi Young Nahm, a founder of the church, also recalls that all members of the congregation of the Korean Church of Melbourne waited for the Sunday service because they were happy that they could sing Korean hymns and listen to Korean sermons.[59] These testimonies show well how important the Korean ethnic church was to Koreans in Australia.

Following news of the establishment of the first Korean Australian church in Melbourne, there was a movement to build a Korean church in Sydney. As a result, on September 9, 1974, about seventy people gathered at a Protestant church in Redfern for the first Korean service in Sydney with the Reverend Dr. John Brown, also a former missionary in Korea, as their first pastor. The church is the Sydney Korean Uniting Church today, the second oldest Korean Australian church. It was also a Presbyterian church and became a Uniting Church in 1977.[60] A remarkable thing is that when Rev. Brown was absent, two Korean Catholic priests who were studying in theological school used to lead the Sunday services, which shows that at first the church was not concerned about denominational differences.[61]

As discussed above, during the period between 1972 and 1975, many Korean workers who were employed in Vietnam during the Vietnam War came to Australia at the end of the war, seeking new opportunities. Most of them came to Sydney because compared to other Australian cities there was an abundance of work as well as other Korean migrants. The influx of these workers marked the first wave of Korean immigration into Australia bringing a huge change in many respects to Korean

---

58. Melbon-haningyohoe Yeoksa-pyeonchan wiwonhoe, *Melbon-haningyohoe samsipnyeonsa*, 15.

59. Nahm, "Biktoria haninhoe (VIC)," 338.

60. Brown, "Birth of Early Korean Churches," 265.

61. Ibid., 266.

society in Australia, as many of them obtained permanent residency not only through the sponsorship of companies or institutions that employed them, but also through the Federal Government's Amnesty Provisions in 1976.

At that time, members of the congregation of the Sydney Korean church made efforts to help these workers settle in this new land, providing comfortable settings in which they could enjoy fellowship and share their stories. Regardless of Christian faith, many Koreans came to the church to meet fellow Koreans and thus relieve the stresses of their immigrant experiences. Brown recalls the church of that period as follows:

> During late 1974 and 1975 some hundreds of Koreans who had worked in civilian support positions in Vietnam during the war began to come to Australia. For them the church became a focal point for fellowship, news and information. Many became Christians through that experience of "church." Others simply enjoyed the friendship and the weekly escape from loneliness. Most of these men and the few women who came had trades or professional skills. They were able to obtain employment. For many of them, this was an initial step towards setting up their own small business in Australia. Much time was taken up in assisting the people who had come in from Vietnam to obtain permanent residence permits, and then to bring their families from Korea to Australia.[62]

Naturally, the church became a central part of the lives of Korean migrants beyond the role of the religious institution. For example, the church ran a Korean language school on Saturday mornings to teach immigrant children Korean language and culture, a senior school that helped old people adjust to the new environment, and an English class to help immigrants improve English skills.[63] The Korean Church of Melbourne has also done similar things like supporting a Korean language school, running English classes for Korean migrants, assisting the Korean Society of Melbourne to do its tasks for Korean migrants and so on.[64]

Likewise, the first Korean churches in Melbourne and Sydney became centers of Korean society and have played multidimensional roles, assisting Korean immigrants to settle and adjust to the host society in positive and healthy ways. This multidimensional ministry for Korean

---

62. Ibid., 266–67.
63. Ibid., 274.
64. See Nahm, "Biktoria haninhoe (VIC)," 337–46.

migrants has been the most remarkable characteristic of the Korean Australian (KA) church.

As the Korean population in Australia steadily increased, the number of Korean Australian churches has grown as well, and their roles have changed with the expansion of the Korean Australian community. However, it is not difficult to see that Korean ethnic churches are still playing important roles in the well-being of Korean Australians, considering the current high rate of church affiliation.

Cultural Institutions for Second-Generation Young People

The Korean Australian churches have also become centers for preserving Korean cultural traditions, values, and language for second-generation Korean Australian (SGKA) young people. Not only the Christian gospel, but also Korean language, ethnic values, and culture have been actively taught especially in Sunday School sessions in order to help second-generations establish an ethnic identity. The tendency underlining the necessity of ethnicity promoting religious education in the church is still found in many KA churches. Although there are many people who point out the importance of English-speaking ministry in the Korean church for the faith development of SGKA young people, there are still a considerable number of first-generations who believe that passing on Korean culture and values to future generations should be a primary task of the KA church.[65]

S. Steve Kang also argues that the Korean ethnic church should play a key role in the construction of the ethnic identity of second-generation young people.[66] Like many other ethnicity-related scholars, he argues that ethnic identity development is a critical developmental task for ethnic minority adolescents as strong ethnic group membership is likely to give rise to a positive self-concept and a decrease in psychological stress in the lives of ethnic minority young people.[67] For him, the church for Korean migrants has been a place in which second-generation Korean young

---

65. Melbon-haningyohoe Yeoksa-pyeonchan wiwonhoe, *Melbon-haningyohoe samsipnyeonsa*, 28–29.

66. Kang, *Unveiling*, 199.

67. Ibid., 70–73. Also see Phinney, Horenczyk, et al., "Ethnic Identity," 496; Holcomb-McCoy, "Ethnic Identity Development," 122.

people are able to keep Korean culture and values alive. Although it is true that too much emphasis on the Korean way of thinking and living in the Korean ethnic church tends to draw from the younger generation a strong aversion to Koreanization, keeping Korean culture, language, and values in the church seems essential for second-generation young adults to establish a well-balanced identity between the two cultures and to develop reconciliation with their parent's generation.[68]

George Knight et al. also argue that ethnic identity might be fostered in a specific context in which ethnic language or values are accepted and utilized. They call it *immediate contextual influences*.[69] In this regard, the KA church seems to be an important place for activating ethnic factors such as language and etiquette. This insight shows that the KA church and its religious education practice provide indispensable opportunities for SGKA adolescents to encounter ethnic values and develop an ethnic identity. In addition, the KA church can be "a place for the mutual validation of ethnic identity" for SGKA young people.[70] In the Korean immigrant church, they can meet fellow Korean second-generations and share their life stories and experiences with one another, feeling understood, accepted, and welcomed, which is essential for second-generation Korean young adults to build a healthy identity in the host society.[71]

Extreme Schism

There are not only advantages of the Korean ethnic church for Korean Australians and their families, but also negative dimensions. One of the negative factors is the extreme schism in the KA churches, especially among the Protestant churches.

The fact that there are currently more than 255 Korean churches of different denominations throughout Australia especially in the Sydney area with a Korean population of just over 80,000 reveals the seriousness of schism in KA churches.[72] Most of those churches are reported to be

68. Kang, *Unveiling*, 203–4.
69. Knight et al., "Social Cognitive Model," 225.
70. Kang, *Unveiling*, 199.
71. Ibid.
72. According to *Christian Review* (September 2014), a monthly Korean Christian magazine, there are more than 255 Korean Australian churches recorded in the phone directory. Among them, more than 165 churches are located in the metropolitan area of Sydney. See *Christian Review*, "Classified Phone Directory," 86–88.

small and are not able to afford their ministers. These divisions in KA churches have not only led to clashes in the Korean community, but have also been a significant barrier to spreading the gospel. Brown criticizes this extreme church schism as follows: "Are the churches merely religious clubs competing for members? The establishment of so many small congregations is an embarrassment to the Church, creates a more difficult atmosphere in which to bear witness to the Gospel of reconciliation, and has a negative effect within the whole Korean Australian community."[73]

Why have Korean Australian churches undergone these severe divisions? There may be a few major reasons, but the sociocultural and psychosocial circumstances of Korean migrants in Australia should be considered as the major factor.

As discussed earlier, many first-generation Koreans in Australia have experienced difficulties in keeping their careers because of the language barrier and/or the different certification system, and even discrimination and prejudice from the host society. Considering that a majority of Korean Australians are skilled and business migrants who were the well-educated, middle class in Korea, and they are from an extreme monocultural and monolingual society, the sense of status inconsistency of Korean Australians seems more severe than might be thought.

As a result, many Korean migrants tend to be confined to the ethnic community and are ghettoized from mainstream society. In this situation, Korean Australians tend to show off competitively to other Koreans who they were in the past in Korea or what they have achieved in Australia, even at the Korean church, in order to compensate for their loss of status in mainstream society. This competition is likely to become a source of individual and community tension and to turn into a conflict for power or hegemony in the Korean Australian society. In this respect, the Korean ethnic church has naturally become a unique and major political forum because churches have been at the core of Korean Australian communities.

From the same perspective, Sung Pyo Jun and Gordon Armstrong, who researched conflicts within Korean American churches, suggest *the sense of relative deprivation of Korean migrants resulting from status inconsistency* as a major factor for the conflict and schism of Korean ethnic churches because the sense of relative deprivation is likely to induce power competition in a church. Through mail surveys of 366 members

---

73. Brown, "Birth of Early Korean Churches," 273.

of two Anglo churches and two Korean ethnic churches in America, they proved a relationship between the sense of relative deprivation and the political behavior of immigrants.[74]

They argue that Korean migrants who perceive relative deprivation regarding their current occupation tend to feel a need to seek power in a church more strongly than those who are satisfied with their jobs. In addition, Koreans who experience relative deprivation with their current income tend to make efforts to gain power in a church, while income-satisfied counterparts are inclined to be indifferent to church affairs or politics. A remarkable finding in their research is that non-immigrants who feel relative deprivation in regard to their occupation or income do not show any tendency to seek power in a church.[75] Jun and Armstrong conclude that Korean migrants' status inconsistency causes this difference. They claim that since Korean migrants' relative deprivation is closely related to their sense of status discrepancy resulting from immigration and being a minority in the host society, when they feel relative deprivation about their job or income or anything else, they tend to seek power in a church to compensate for their marginalization in the larger society.[76]

Likewise, Korean migrants' negative immigrant experiences and status discrepancy between the past and the present are closely related to conflicts and divisions within KA churches.

The second major factor for the schism of Korean Australian churches is connected with the large number of Korean pastors. Since there is a surplus of Korean Protestant pastors in Korea, members separated from their former congregation have easily been able to find a new pastor and build a new church. Han refers to this abundant supply of church ministers in Korea as a major reason for the schism of the KA churches. He argues, "Some parts of the surplus of Korean theological graduates have been absorbed into countries such as Canada, the USA, and Argentina. Since 1974, Australia has become another destination for Korean ministers and theological graduates in search of a position."[77]

The fact that it is not difficult to find a new minister makes it easier for churches to split. On the other hand, in the case of the Korean Catholic church in Australia, there have been few church divisions in spite of

---

74. Jun and Armstrong, "Status Inconsistency," 103.
75. Ibid., 114–16.
76. Ibid., 103–7.
77. Han, "Expansion and Schism," 282–84.

various conflicts within it as it is difficult to find an available priest not only because of the centralist control of priests in the Catholic Church, but also because of its institutional structure which is not a Congregationalist church.[78]

Finally, pastors' limited understanding of Korean migrants and their life contexts have resulted in severe disparities and conflicts between pastors and church members, which have sometimes developed into church divisions. When members who separated from their churches start a new church by themselves, they tend to find a new pastor in Korea and call them into Australia. At this time, most of the newly inducted pastors from Korea begin their ministries without enough understanding of the unique sociocultural contexts of migrants and their experience of relative deprivation resulting from status diminishment.

As a result, their ministries tend to be distant from the real demands of church members, and their authoritarian and hierarchical leadership tend to cause tensions and clashes with church members who have been accustomed to an egalitarian approach to leadership in Australia. In addition, many ministers in the KA churches seem to have a keen interest in church growth and introduce various church growth programs from Korea, but in many cases their efforts are likely to fail because they overlook the unique features of KA churches. For example, many Korean migrants have come to church for social or psychological reasons rather than religious ones and thus, there are still many non-Christians among the members of the congregation regardless of their long period of attendance.[79]

These three main factors contributing to conflict and schism in Korean ethnic churches in Australia are not separate but are interrelated. In addition to these three principal factors, Korean traditional Confucian legalism and Korean fundamentalist Christianity which generate extreme formalism concerning dogmas also seem to be important issues related to church division. The divisions among KA churches have directly exerted negative influences on the harmony of Korean Australian communities. As a majority of Korean Australians have been affiliated with Korean ethnic churches since the early period of Korean immigration into Australia, conflicts and disagreements within Korean ethnic

---

78. Ibid., 285–86.

79. Yang, "Hanindeului jonggyo hwaldong," 152. Also see Han, "Expansion and Schism," 283.

churches have naturally been connected to tensions and hostilities within Korean society in Australia.[80]

Church schism has also eroded the authority and influence of KA churches. Many Koreans in Australia tend to see conflicts and divisions in Korean churches as "fighting for a bowl of rice or a piece of pie."[81] As a result, a considerable number of Korean Australians have grown tired of constant news of church divisions and new churches, and close their minds even to the gospel. Many members of Korean Australian churches have stopped attending church activities or have even changed their religion. Many SGKAs have also been influenced by negative public opinion about the Korean ethnic church in Australia.

As such, the KA churches have served Korean migrants and their families not only as a religious institution, but also as a center of the Korean Australian community. In terms of Korean language and culture, the KA churches have played an important role in helping SGKA young people continue to speak the Korean language, to learn Korean values, and to build a healthy balanced identity. However, at the same time, due to the extreme church separation, the KA church has also had negative impacts on the harmony of the Korean community and on the Christian lives of many church members.

Four Korean Australian Churches Selected as Research Sites

According to the planned process I selected four KA church youth groups as research sites for analyzing current religious education curricula for SGKA adolescents and implementing semi-structured interviews with SGKA teenagers, teachers, and youth pastors

The first church, to be called the Southeast church, is a Uniting Church located in a southeastern suburb of Melbourne. It is the oldest Korean immigrant church in Australia established in 1973 and is the biggest one in the state of Victoria. About eight hundred people including young children attend the church. Among the church population, the rate of old immigrants who came to Australia more than twenty years ago is very high compared to other Korean Australian churches in Melbourne. Consequently, the church is very stable and conservative.

---

80. Yang, "Hanindeului jonggyo hwaldong," 151.
81. Han, "Expansion and Schism," 299.

After many years of effort, in 2008 a full-time SGKA pastor was called, for the first time in the church's history, to start an English ministry for SGKA young people. Being responsible for ministry for 1.5- or second-generation young adults, the current SGKA pastor in the Southeast church is in charge of English language ministry for adolescents aged thirteen to eighteen. The youth group for secondary school students is the primary site for the current research in the Southeast church. The department is, in size, about sixty students and fifteen teachers.

An interesting aspect is that unlike the ministry for young adults in the church which is divided into two congregations with different pastors, Korean and English, the youth group ministry has been done solely by an English-speaking pastor since 2008 although there are a considerable number of overseas students from South Korea coming to the church. Financial difficulties, personnel problems, limited church space etc. seem to make it hard for the church to divide the secondary students' department into two groups. It is also noted that children from two years old to the sixth grade of primary school are cared for in the Korean-speaking preschooler group and primary school student group.

There are four full-time ministers (a senior minister, two associate ministers for the Korean ministry, and a SGKA minister for the English ministry) and three part-time pastors for the Sunday School in the Southeast church. The senior minister, a first-generation, came to the church in 2010 from the United States.

The second church, the Northeast church, is a Uniting Church located in a northeastern suburb of Melbourne and the second biggest Korean Australian church in Melbourne consisting of about three hundred people including children. It was established in the 1991 following a split from the Southeast church. Although its financial status is weak and its history is short compared to the Southeast church, when compared with other Korean churches in Melbourne, the Northeast church is relatively stable in terms of numbers and finances. Church membership consists mainly of people who came to Australia less than fifteen years ago. In addition, it is noted that over the last decade many business migrants have settled in this church for various reasons such as its location, atmosphere, and similar age bracket which seem to contribute to them feeling at home in the church.

There is no English ministry for 1.5- or second-generation children, adolescents, or young adults, who feel more comfortable communicating in English. There are four departments in the Korean-speaking Sunday

School: preschool, primary, secondary, and young adults. Among them, this research focuses on ministry for adolescents in the church. About forty students attend the secondary department, and a part-time Korean-speaking pastor is in charge of this ministry in cooperation with ten teachers. As with the case of the Southeast church, SGKA teenagers are mixed with overseas students from South Korea in the youth group.

In the Northeast church, there are two full-time ministers (a senior minister and an associate minister who is in charge of the ministry for young adults as well as general Korean ministries) and two part-time pastors (one of whom serves the educational department for children and the other, secondary students). Preschoolers at the church are taken care of by volunteer teachers and parents without the pastor being in charge. The senior minister, a first-generation, replaced his predecessor in 2010 and came directly from South Korea.

The third church, the East church, is a Presbyterian church located in an Eastern suburb of Melbourne and consists of more than two hundred people including children. It was founded in 2004, also splitting from the Southeast church. Since the history is short compared to the Southeast church and the Northeast church, this congregation consists mainly of new arrivals who came to Australia less than five years ago. The church has grown steadily, and recently purchased a new worship place large enough for its congregation. As a result, the members of the East church are struggling in terms of finance, which has adversely affected its educational environment.

There are four departments in its Sunday School divided according to age level into: preschool, primary, secondary, and young adults group. Among such departments, adolescents and young adults are cared for by a full-time pastor and primary school children have been guided by a part-time pastor. The group for preschoolers is operated by volunteer teachers. In the case of the youth group for teenagers, seven teachers are leading about twenty students. Like the Southeast church and Northeast church, SGKA adolescents and overseas Korean students are studying together. In the church, there are three pastors: two full-time and one part-time. The senior minister came to Melbourne from Sydney to start the church in 2004 and has served it since that time.

The fourth church is called the Central church. The church is a Presbyterian church established in 2003 located in an Eastern suburb of Melbourne. It has about 150 members including young children and most members are relatively new arrivals with young children. The Central church was started by a Korean pastor, but he left a year after it began for personal reasons. The current senior pastor came to the church in 2004 after finishing a theological degree in Melbourne and has served the congregation for seven years. Due to financial issues, the church could then afford only a part-time youth pastor, but in 2011 it was able to afford to hire another full-time pastor. The associate full-time pastor is now in charge of all the Sunday School departments except preschoolers from primary school students to young adults. In the case of the youth group for adolescents, there was a part-time youth pastor, but when he suddenly had to return to Korea, the associate pastor became responsible for the youth group. Preschoolers are cared for by volunteer teachers and parents.

5
The Lives of Second-Generation Korean Australian Adolescents

IN THIS CHAPTER, I will investigate the lives of second-generation Korean Australian (SGKA) adolescents based on semi-structured interviews with fourteen SGKA teenagers, ten teachers, and four youth pastors.[1] Four major characteristics in relation to their lives as an ethnic minority in Australia will be discussed in detail: growing up in an ethnicity promoting family environment, the high rate of church affiliation, the complexities of identity formation, and growing up as the digital generation. This analysis will provide significant knowledge of SGKA youth. The content of this chapter is critical in establishing a religious education curriculum for SGKA teenagers growing up in the Korean Australian (KA) church, because the unique needs, issues, and situations of the individuals on whom the religious education programs focus should be noticed in order to create an appropriate curriculum for them.[2] Arthur Applebee similarly claims that without understanding the complexities of the student context the curriculum is likely to be meaningless monologue resulting in knowledge-out-of-context rather than significant dialogue which attends to their lives.[3]

Table 2, 3, and 4 provide information about those who were interviewed. All names of participants mentioned are pseudonyms. All the interviews except two were conducted face to face,[4] and when necessary, email or phone interviews were held to obtain further information. Some

---

1. Among a total of twenty-eight participants, nine informants (one pastor, four teachers and four SGKA students) were from the Southeast church, six (one pastor, two teachers and three SGKA students) from the Northeast church, seven (one pastor, three teachers and three SGKA students) from the East church, and six (one pastor, one teacher and four SGKA students) from the Central church.

2. Eisner, *Educational Imagination*, 6–7.

3. Applebee, *Curriculum as Conversation*, 101–3.

4. Two teacher informants, Henry and Andrew, were interviewed via email because of their personal circumstances.

interviews were held in English and others in Korean depending on the participants' preference.

Table 2. Information of SGKA Teenage Informants

Name	Sex/ Age	Grade	Church	Age at Immigration
Nick	M/ 18	Grade 11	Northeast	5 years old
Julia	F/ 16	Grade 10	Northeast	3 years old
Kris	F/ 15	Grade 9	Northeast	N.Z. born
Charlie	F/ 14	Grade 9	East	N.Z born
Molly	F/ 16	Grade 10	East	5 years old
Peter	M/ 15	Grade 9	East	5 years old
Luke	M/ 15	Grade 9	Southeast	Australian born
William	M/ 13	Grade 7	Southeast	18 months old
Ian	M/ 17	Grade 11	Central	2 years old
Abigail	F/ 13	Grade 7	Central	7 months old
Kate	F/ 14	Grade 8	Central	2 years old
Grace	F/ 17	Grade 11	Southeast	Australian born
Rose	F/ 16	Grade 10	Southeast	Australian born
Lily	F/ 15	Grade 9	Central	Australian born

Table 3. Information of Youth Group Teacher Informants

Name	Sex/ Age	Church	Length of Teaching at the Current Church	Length of Immigration
Judy	F/ 47	East	2 years	15 years
Jarvis	M/ 21	East	4 years	Australian born (2 generation)

Name	Sex/Age	Church	Length of Teaching at the Current Church	Length of Immigration
Sam	M/ 21	Northeast	4 years	10 years (1.5 generation)
Isabella	F/ 50	Northeast	1 year	10 years
Albert	M/ 38	East	4 years	6 years
Robert	M/ 55	Southeast	2 years	5 years
Karen	F/ 22	Southeast	2 years	9 years (1.5 generation)
Sophie	F/ 41	Central	1 year	17 years
Henry	M/ 26	Southeast	7 years	Australian born (2 generation)
Andrew	M/ 21	Southeast	1 year	19 years (2 generation)

Table 4. Information of Youth Group Pastor Informants

Name	Sex/Age	Church	Length of Service at the Current Church	Length of Immigration
Paul	M/ 32	Northeast	1 year	6 years
Mark	M/ 32	East	1 year	1 year
Ben	M/ 39	Southeast	5 years	Australian born
Ralph	M/ 38	Central	6 months	6 months

Growing Up in an Ethnicity Promoting Family

Strong Parental Authority

Most SGKA adolescents have grown up in an ethnically centered family climate in which traditional Korean values were strongly stressed. Traditional Korean values are primarily based on Confucianism that demands unconditional obedience to authority figures like parents, teachers or elders. This has resulted in authoritarian and hierarchical leadership in Korean families which has been a barrier to conversation between parents and children, and emphasizes the father's decision as representative of the family rather than any individual opinions.[5]

This hierarchical environment in Korean ethnic families is contrary to Australian values, such as mateship, egalitarianism, and individualism.[6] This clash of cultures tends to be problematic for SGKA young people since Korea is regarded as a highly collectivist society, while Australia is described as highly individualistic.[7] Geert Hofstede describes the difference between individualism and collectivism as follows:

> Individualistic societies emphasize "I" consciousness, autonomy, emotional independence, individual initiative, right to privacy, pleasure seeking, financial security, need for specific friendship, and universalism. . . . Collectivistic societies, on the other hand, stress "we" consciousness, collective identity, emotional dependence, group solidarity, sharing, duties and obligations, need for stable and predetermined friendship, group decision, and particularism.[8]

The extent of this clash of cultures tends to depend on the level of parents' adherence to Korean culture. As discussed in the previous chapter, many first-generation Korean parents in Australia adhere strongly to their Korean ethnic heritage because of their strong ethnic orientation and negative immigrant experiences. It is noted that the more parents adhere to Korean culture and values, the more their children feel the complexity and ambiguity between the two cultures. Janice Im argues that the Korean migrant parents' experience of the host culture is very

---

5. Swidler, "Confucianism for Modern Persons," 16.
6. Ashkanasy et al., "Leadership Attributes," 38.
7. Torres and Pérez-Nebra, "Influence of Human Values," 65.
8. Hofstede, *Culture's Consequences*, 330, quoted in Im, "Ecological Examination," 11–12.

influential not only for their children's adaptation to the mainstream society, but also for their ethnic identity development because Korean parental authority is powerful.[9] Her research with second-generation Korean American young adults shows that the most influential area affecting the participants is connected to parental authority and expectation.[10] Urie Bronfenbrenner's theory of ecology seems to strongly support Im's argument.

According to Bronfenbrenner's ecological theory of human development, there are four ecological realms that affect the process: microsystem, mesosystem, exosystem, and macrosystem. Among them, parental influence is closely related to microsystem and exosystem: *microsystem* means the innermost level of an individual's entire ecological system such as family, school, and peer group, while *exosystem* is "one or more settings that do not involve the developing person as an active participant, but in which events occur that affect, or are affected by, what happens in the setting containing the developing person."[11] From the perspective of microsystem, the relationship with parents is critical to SGKA children's identity formation. Positive relationships with parents may support and encourage identity exploration and minimize identity problems, while negative relationships may hinder the search for a balanced identity and thus cause an identity crisis.[12] In addition, among the various exosystems, parental experience of immigration may greatly affect SGKA adolescent's formation of cultural identity. If the migrant parental experience of the host culture is positive, the parents will generally support their children in adapting to the new land and actively receive new culture and values while trying to help them build a balanced identity. On the contrary, if the parental experience of immigration is negative, their children are likely to have problems in adapting to mainstream society and in establishing a healthy identity. Im insightfully describes the influence of negative parental experiences of immigration on their children's identity development as follows:

> Parents in this case, demand increased family enmeshment and nostalgic adherence to their traditional values, consequently,

9. Im, "Ecological Examination," 9.

10. See ibid., 18–49.

11. Bronfenbrenner, *Ecology of Human Development*, 25. Mesosystem is the relationship between two or more microsystems and macrosystem is about belief systems or ideology underlying a given culture or subculture. See ibid., 25–26.

12. Im, "Ecological Examination," 9.

which inevitably retards their children's social integration into American culture. Moreover, due to their nostalgia for their home country, parents may remind their children of the sacrifices they made in order to provide them with a better future. This in turn . . . leads the children to have feelings of guilt when they disappoint their parents. It is reasonable to speculate that the combination of both social isolation and sense of family obligation may decrease the child's willingness to exert autonomy in the future. Lastly, any future attempts by the child to become "Americanized" may be viewed negatively by their parents, leading to a decrease in parental support during identity exploration.[13]

Parents' High Expectation of Academic Achievement

This strong parental influence is closely related to SGKA teenagers' striving for excellence. Most SGKA adolescents are strongly oriented towards academic achievement. In the interview project, among fourteen SGKA student participants twelve students responded that their biggest current concern is academic achievement for future success. For example, in the case of Abigail, a thirteen-year-old attendee at the Central church, entering a selective school in Melbourne was the most important issue at the time of interview.[14] For William, a thirteen-year-old SGKA student attending the Southeast church, obtaining a musical scholarship provided by a private secondary college in Melbourne was critical. So, he said that he has devoted to practicing his musical instrument for a long time.[15] Upper grade students like Nick, Julia, Ian, Grace, and Rose also shared that their greatest current concern is to enter a good university for future success.[16]

This phenomenon is closely connected to Korean parents' high expectation of academic achievement resulting from their negative immigration experiences and their purpose for migrating. Many first-generation Korean Australians tend to be disappointed and depressed when they cannot find a job related to their specialities or careers because of their relatively poor English or unrecognized Korean qualifications or

13. Ibid., 11.
14. Abigail, interview.
15. William, interview.
16. Grace, interview; Ian, interview; Julia, interview; Nick, interview; Rose, interview.

licenses. Nevertheless, most of them accept such situations and sacrifice their careers for the success of their children in this new land because in most cases their primary purpose for migrating to Australia is for the education of their children rather than economic betterment.

The expectation of Korean Australian parents of their children in terms of upward mobility into mainstream society is linked to an emphasis on their children's academic achievements. It is also noted that the Korean culture's emphasis on working hard and obtaining perfection may influence SGKA adolescents' attitude to education.[17] However, this relatively strong desire for scholastic advancement in the Korean community in Australia tends to impose a heavy burden on SGKA teenagers, which may often cause guilt about not satisfying parents' expectations and/or bring about conflicts with parents because of different values or visions.

Grace, a seventeen-year-old attendee at the Southeast church, criticized Korean parents' attitude regarding competition in terms of children's academic achievement.

> They try to give you the best—what they couldn't have. They try to give you a better education. . . . In the Korean community, their children's education is the parent's gossip. I hate that. All the Korean parents know each other, what other children's scores are and what they do. They care about other kid's scores more. They compare all the kids. . . . I try to remind my mom that it's not a competition. Even if you do well, they always want better. They concentrate on the things you can't do, rather than the things you can do. They look at your bad marks, not your good marks.[18]

Lily, a fifteen-year-old student in the Central church, also shared some conflict with her mom in terms of her education. "In my school there are high achievers, where you have to sit a test to get in. I didn't try to get into it. I am in the normal class. My mom thinks you get into a class based on how smart you are. She judges me and my brother on which class we are in."[19]

In respect of this problem, S. Steve Kang argues that "one root problem of the cultural conflict between the two generations lies in the

---

17. Im, "Ecological Examination," 18–19.
18. Grace, interview.
19. Lily, interview.

unrealistic and insatiable expectations the first generation brings to bear on the second generation, as a way of repaying the sacrifice the parents made."[20]

High Rate of Attendance at the Korean Ethnic Church

The second main feature related to the lives of SGKA youth is their high church affiliation. According to the 2011 census 69.1 percent of the Korean population in Australia identified themselves as Christians.[21] Given most Koreans' strong monocultural orientation, their relatively poor English proficiency, their ethnic group–centered immigrant lives, and the extent of Korean ethnic churches' influence in the Korean Australian community, it is assumed that most Korean Australian Christians attend Korean ethnic churches. It is also noted that considering most young people go to church with their parents, a considerable number of SGKA adolescents have grown up with a close connection with the Korean Australian church.

Through the interviews with fourteen SGKA youth, I found that many SGKA participants enjoy their church life in the context of the KA church in spite of a number of difficulties. I will discuss three factors which attract them to the Korean immigrant church. And then, their difficulties in relation to their Korean churches will be investigated in detail. These problems are closely connected to their suggestions for the Korean ethnic church.

Attractive Factors

First, in the case of Nick, an eighteen-year-old SGKA student in the Northeast church, he found that attending church has been helpful for his faith development. Nick said that the atmosphere of the Korean church seems more spiritual than the Australian church. When he worshiped God at a local church, he felt a kind of emptiness as the worship was boring. In worship at the Northeast church, he said that he was very

---

20. Kang, *Unveiling*, 129.

21. Australian Bureau of Statistics, "2011 Census of Population and Housing: Religious Affiliation (RELP) - 1 Digit Level by Ancestry 1st Response (ANC1P) - 4 Digit Level."

impressed by the Korean style of worship, praise, and prayer although he could not fully understand the Korean sermon.

> Comparing that to youth programs in other Christian groups in Australia, it is a lot more spiritual. Some churches don't believe in speaking in tongues, but I found that kids here are a lot more serious, but some are just here to meet other people. They have a lot more awareness about the Bible.[22]

Charlie, a fourteen-year-old attendee at the East church, was also satisfied with the Korean way of believing in God. She liked the Korean worship and prayer style. Although she had no problem in understanding English sermons, she said that when she listens to Korean preaching, she tends to feel more touched and passionate. She feels a sense of intimacy when she speaks and listens to Korean because she feels it is as if she talks to parents and siblings. For her, English is a kind of official language, while Korean is private because she has used Korean at home with her parents and siblings since she was very young.[23]

Molly, a sixteen-year-old girl attending the East church, has the same experience and opinion as Charlie's in terms of faith style. She said that her faith has improved by attending a Korean church and listening to Korean sermons. She feels it is attractive, comfortable, and exciting in the Korean style of worship. She even argued that Koreans should worship God in the Korean language even if it is necessary to learn diverse faith traditions.[24]

A sense of intimacy within the Korean community is another factor calling them to the Korean ethnic church. It was remarkable that many SGKA students who feel comfortable in English answer that they prefer the Korean ethnic church to the local church because they want to communicate with people who have similar experiences of growing up and a similar cultural background.

Luke, a fifteen-year-old student attending the Southeast church, said that he had sometimes attended English-speaking local churches, but found it difficult to share his experience with local students even though he had no difficulties with English. Although he was born in Australia and feels more comfortable with Australian rather than Korean culture, he said that he feels more connected with SGKA adolescents like himself and feels a sense of belonging in the Korean church. Therefore, when he

22. Nick, interview.
23. Charlie, interview.
24. Molly, interview.

was asked which church, the Korean ethnic church or the Australian local church, he would choose after becoming independent from parents, he firmly answered that he would select the Korean ethnic church because of the sense of belonging and connection.[25]

Abigail also said that she prefers the Korean ethnic church to the English-speaking local church because she feels more connected with Korean people including SGKAs. Since Korean overseas students make up the majority of her youth group, she said that she sometimes feels isolated in the church especially when she cannot understand the subtle nuances of Korean expressions or the meaning of Korean humour. However, she claimed, she feels a sense of intimacy when she is with Koreans in the church.[26]

For Lily who had relatively poor Korean proficiency, English is much more comfortable than Korean. However, when it comes to relationships in the church, she also said that being with Korean people, especially SGKA students, is more comfortable. She said, "In the Korean church, it is good to easily understand one other because there are many similarities."[27]

Ben, the thirty-nine-year-old second-generation pastor in charge of the youth group in the Southeast church, analyzed this phenomenon as follows:

> There is an ingrained, inbuilt desire to be with people who are likeminded, not only in terms of profession, thinking or theological perspective. But there is something deep within every human being that wants to connect with people of the same background, upbringing, appearance and culture. I think the fundamental issue comes down to identity: "who am I?" That is why I think, ethnic churches have the importance of second gen ministries because there is always a need/desire for second generation to connect with people who share an identity. As the church begins to build that identity and as we begin to share that identity, the whole area of doing life together as a community, there is actually that desire. So English speakers can go to any church, but there is a certain cultural aspect that brings a great deal of comfort, that people want to be part of.[28]

25. Luke, interview.
26. Abigail, interview.
27. Lily, interview.
28. Ben, interview.

Andrew, a twenty-one-year-old second-generation teacher in the Southeast church, also shared that his experience of "being surrounded by people of similar positions and upbringings made church community a lot more relatable."[29] He claimed that this is the reason why Korean ethnic churches should run an English-speaking ministry for SGKA adolescents even though they can go to an English-speaking local church.[30]

Finally, feeling proud of their Korean background is an important aspect in making SGKA adolescents happy to attend a Korean ethnic church. In the interview, it was notable that the rate of those who expressed a sense of pride in their Koreanness was relatively high. Among fourteen SGKA teenage participants eleven students directly or indirectly showed that they are proud of their Korean background. They commonly mentioned Korea's high technology and economic success as a reason for their pride.

For instance, Kate, a fourteen-year-old girl who goes to the Central church, said that she is very proud of Korea because it has achieved great economic success in a relatively short period overcoming the tragedy of the Korean War. She knew that Korea is a member country of the G20 and the Organization for Economic Cooperation and Development (OECD), and its Gross National Income (GNI) per capita is higher than $20,000. Mentioning Korean international companies like Samsung, LG, Hyundai, and Kia, she said that sometimes she is annoyed when some Australians do not know that they are Korean corporations.[31]

Kris, a fifteen-year-old girl who goes to the Northeast church, said that she is also proud of Korea as it is one of the economically successful countries in Asia and is a leading country in the field of information technology and high-tech industry.[32]

In addition, the current wave of Korean pop culture seems to be a factor making many SGKA adolescents feel proud of their mother country. It has been a long time since Korean movies, dramas, and pop songs gained tremendous popularity in Asian regions. Nowadays, the wave is spreading to other regions like Europe, North America, and South America. In Australia, there are also many fans especially among Asian immigrants. Almost all SGKA participants in this interview project said

29. Andrew, interview.
30. Ibid.
31. Kate, interview.
32. Kris, interview.

that it is true that their school friends love K-pop and in some schools there are K-pop fan clubs. This trend became more remarkable since the massive global hit of Psy's *Gangnam Style* in 2012.

Ian and William said that it is delightful to see that their school friends love K-drama or K-pop. For them, it is amazing that the pop culture of a small country like Korea influences people of many other nationalities although there are also many people who are indifferent to it.[33]

Charlie said that some school peers tend to have a friendly feeling toward her only because she has a Korean background.[34] Rose shared a similar experience that some school peers were envious of her only because she is able to understand and speak Korean.[35]

The Korean Wave not only gives SGKA adolescents a sense of pride, but also provides them with opportunities to learn Korean culture and language. Regardless of a preference for the Korean pop culture, almost all SGKA participants in this research except Nick responded that they often watch Korean dramas or movies on the internet, or listen to Korean pop songs, which is very helpful in improving their Korean proficiency and knowledge of Korean culture.

Julia, Kris, Abigail, and Molly argued that their Korean language skills have improved by watching Korean dramas, movies or entertainment shows. Whenever they encountered difficult expressions or incomprehensible scenes, they would ask their parents, which has been good for family relationships.[36]

Even those who do not feel comfortable in the Korean language like Peter, Luke, and Lily said that they like watching Korean dramas, movies, comedies or entertainment shows although they often find it is hard to understand them. They agreed that watching Korean programs is fun and helpful in improving their Korean language skills.[37]

Ben argued that accessibility to Korean entertainment through the internet or various resources is one of the biggest differences between his generation and the present generation. He said that when he grew up in Australia in the 1970s and 1980s, it was difficult to experience Korean pop culture because there were only a small number of Koreans in

---

33. Ian, interview; William, interview.
34. Charlie, interview.
35. Rose, interview.
36. Abigail, interview; Julia, interview; Kris, interview; Molly, interview.
37. Lily, interview; Luke, interview; Peter, interview.

Australia, so there was not much Korean pop culture, which limited his Korean proficiency and pride in his Koreanness.[38]

Difficulties of Settlement

First, many SGKA interviewees shared that they hate the hierarchical and authoritarian atmosphere based on age in the Korean Australian church. They cannot understand why Korean culture is more dominant than Christian culture in the church. They think that the church should develop an egalitarian atmosphere in which the opinions of every church member are treated fairly regardless of age.

Grace said that she cannot understand the age-based hierarchical church structure. For her, it is not reasonable that adults are considered more important in making decisions in relation to church ministry simply because they are older than children or youth. She argued that she cannot accept that the opinions of the younger generation are undervalued compared to those of first-generation adults.[39]

Peter, a fifteen-year-old attendee at the East church, also said that the adults in his church are strong in maintaining the Korean style of church administration. He argued that they are authoritarian and hierarchical, so they tend to undervalue the opinions of the younger generation.[40]

In the case of Nick, he attended an English-speaking local church for a long time before coming to the current church a year ago. He said that he had long preferred the Australian church to the Korean one not only because of his lack of proficiency in Korean, but also because of his negative experience of the Korean ethnic church. He thought that the Korean church seems to be dominated by Korean culture rather than by Christian culture and faith. He also said that he hates the competitive spirit among Korean Australian churches.[41]

Most SGKA participants argued that Korean ethnic churches should change their church structure to be more egalitarian and Christian. They thought that Korean church leaders should treat SGKA young people as their partners in ministry, not only as their children to be educated by them. To do this, they argued, church leaders should better understand

---

38. Ben, interview.
39. Grace, interview.
40. Peter, interview.
41. Nick, interview.

the unique lives of SGKA young people, not guessing or judging them from their own perspectives and experiences.

Second, many SGKA participants also claimed that church pastors or teachers seem ignorant of the major issues of SGKA, such as identity problems, school life, family life, and peer relationships. As a result, they said that sometimes the topics or content of the pastor's sermon or group discussion were superficial and overlooked their real life-contexts. For example, Ian, a seventeen-year-old attendee at the Central church, argued that his Sunday School teaching is often irrelevant to his life.[42] Julia claimed that in many cases she learns about dogmas or Bible stories that do not relate to her current concerns.[43] William shared that when the content of a sermon is distant from his life-context, he finds it hard to actively participate in group discussion.[44]

Among the major issues of SGKA youth, school life, especially peer relationships in school, were often mentioned as the topics that are not appropriately addressed in their youth group.

Charlie argued that her church educators seem interested in the lives of SGKA young people, but do not understand how SGKA youth live outside the church context, especially in school. In her youth group, she said, the real concerns of SGKA adolescents and their school lives are hardly mentioned:

> Although we are still young, we have personal concerns, so I want church teachers to understand what they are and present a kind of guideline. For example, in the case of racial discrimination, it happens often in school, but they don't know. . . . School is very different from church. We should behave differently in both worlds. We should be different persons in church in terms of language, culture, and dialogue topics.[45]

She said that sometimes she finds relief through church worship especially when she is in trouble in school or at home. At that time, however, she shared that if she listens to a sermon unrelated to her situation, she is most likely to be disappointed.[46]

---

42. Ian, interview.
43. Julia, interview.
44. William, interview.
45. Charlie, interview, translated into English.
46. Ibid.

Molly also argued that if church educators learn about school life in Australia, they can understand SGKA teenagers, support them in their difficulties, and provide them with appropriate guidelines. She claimed that "school life influences us a lot, especially a life of faith. However, parents don't mention much about school life because they don't know it much. So, Haksengbu [youth group] should know about school life and present guidelines."[47]

For this, many SGKA students suggested that church teachers and pastors should spend time and energy to understand SGKA young people and build a closer relationship with them. SGKA participants in this research were interested in improving their relationship with their teachers/pastors in the church, but most of them said that the relationship was shallow, and they meet teachers/pastors only in the church and only on Sundays.

For example, Kate said that she does not meet and spend time with church teachers on weekdays because everyone's life is hectic. However, she wanted to build a more intimate relationship with teachers so that she might more easily consult them about those things she cannot ask her parents.[48]

Ian also wished to feel a more personal connection with church teachers. However, he said that he does not share private issues with them because he has little in-depth conversation with them. Therefore, he suggested church teachers should approach students first as it is hard for students to approach teachers.[49]

Many SGKA participants thought that the superficial relationship between teachers and students resulted in teachers' lack of appropriate understanding of SGKA. In addition, it was found that language barriers or different cultural preferences were a significant factor against building a close relationship between SGKA students and first-generation teachers. Many SGKA students shared the fact that they feel more connected to 1.5- or second-generation teachers than to first-generation educators.

Grace and Rose said that they feel more comfortable being with 1.5- or second-generation teachers in the church.[50] In this regard, Peter wished to have more second-generation teachers in his youth group be-

---

47. Molly, interview.
48. Kate, interview.
49. Ian, interview.
50. Grace, interview; Rose, interview.

cause he believed that second-generation teachers can understand SGKA students like him better and educate them more suitably.[51]

However, in reality, there seems to be little difference in terms of the degree of relationship with church teachers regardless of whether they are first-generation teachers or 1.5- or second-generation ones. This means that regardless of bilingual ability or cultural similarity, if teachers do not spend enough time with SGKA teenagers in the church or outside of church, it is very hard for them to create a close relationship with SGKA students.

Third, many SGKA informants said that the language barrier limits their participation in the activities of the Korean youth group. For the majority of SGKA teenagers English is the first language for study, social life, and faith development. Among the fourteen interviewees in this research, twelve students reported that they feel confident and comfortable using English rather than Korean. Thus, many SGKA teenage students attending a Korean-speaking youth group experienced slight or serious hardships in understanding Korean sermons and Bible teachings because of their lack of proficiency in Korean.

For Lily, it is very hard to understand Korean sermons and teachings in her youth group because of her lack of proficiency in Korean. Although her parents stress the importance of speaking Korean and push her to speak Korean at home with her three younger siblings, she said that it feels alien to talk to them in Korean, so she usually speaks to them in English. As a result, there is tension with her parents in terms of Korean language. Therefore, she said that she wants to go to an Australian church in order to understand the gospel.[52]

Peter said that his relatively poor proficiency in Korean is the biggest obstacle in adjusting to the church. His Korean ability is not good enough to listen to Korean sermons, as he said that he can understand only 20–30 percent of what his Korean pastor preached.

> In A-Dong-Bu [Children group], she lowered the standard of Korean language in the sermon, because there were preps to year six. When I got to high school, it was really different—the way they prayed and worshiped. It was hard to adjust. Then the sermon, I didn't really understand them, because the Korean they used was more difficult, and I am not really good at

---

51. Peter, interview.
52. Lily, interview.

Korean. In Bible study, I tried to resign because it is difficult to understand.[53]

He feels comfortable listening to English sermons and praying in English. As his church is strongly dominated by the Korean faith tradition and culture, he continually feels isolated and frustrated because of his preference for English. As a result, he failed to gain a sense of belonging to his church, so he wants to move to a local church. He said that in the English church he would be able to fully understand the sermons and teachings and pray in English without any feeling of alienation.

Nevertheless, Peter cannot move to an English-speaking church because his father is the senior minister in the East church. Thus, he really hopes that his church starts an English-speaking ministry, but he understands that it is very hard to realize his wish at the moment because the number of SGKAs in his youth group is low compared to Korean overseas students and the financial situation of the church is not good enough to launch a new English-speaking youth group. As a temporary remedy, the youth group of the East church formed an English Bible study group with those students who are not good in understanding Korean and provides them with an English-speaking Korean teacher.[54]

Most SGKA interviewees attending the three Korean-speaking youth groups said that a ministry for English speakers is necessary for their faith development. A remarkable thing is, however, that most of them stressed the need for a balance between Korean-speaking and English-speaking ministry rather than an English dominated environment.

Kate has studied the Bible stories with a bilingual teacher. She said that as she has some difficulty in understanding Korean sermons, she is satisfied with the small English-speaking group. Therefore, she needs an English-speaking ministry in order to fully understand the meaning of the gospel. However, she emphasized the need to keep a balance in using English and Korean in the church as follows: "I think it would be good to swap between the two. To do it, in English one time and Korean the next so that the people are more comfortable with English and Korean."[55]

Abigail also stressed the need for a balance between Korean-speaking and English-speaking ministry in the church. She argued that the

---

53. Peter, interview.
54. Ibid.
55. Kate, interview.

Korean Australian church should have Korean and English preaching and teaching together because SGKAs should keep both languages.[56]

Likewise, many SGKA teenagers attending a Korean-speaking youth group agree with the importance of a Korean-speaking ministry for SGKAs, although they are struggling in understanding the Korean teaching and thus are asking for an English-speaking ministry. They stress the need for balance in the use of Korean and English in the church. This phenomenon seems to relate to their positive thinking and pride in Korean culture.

On the other hand, SGKA interviewees attending the Southeast church were generally satisfied with their church's English-speaking youth group largely because they are able to comprehend their pastor's sermon.[57] Since all four SGKA participants of the Southeast church grew up in the Korean-speaking children's group of the church, they knew the difference between Korean-speaking and English-speaking ministry. All of them shared some difficulties in comprehending Korean sermons and teachings in the children's group.

Luke was born in Australia and has attended the Southeast church since his birth. When entering primary school, he began to experience some difficulty in speaking and listening to Korean, so in the children's group, he said that he could not fully understand what teachers taught in Korean. He felt isolated and alienated, so did not want to come to the church. However, in his English-speaking youth group, he found the gospel meaningful for his life. Luke argued that understanding the Bible is critical in developing one's faith.[58]

Grace was also satisfied with her church's English-speaking youth group. She said that joining in the youth group has been helpful in improving her faith because the gospel is proclaimed in English. She is happy to listen to English sermons on Sundays and share what she felt with her teacher and friends in English. Grace argued that other Korean Australian churches should start an English-speaking ministry for SGKA adolescents like her church because the number of SGKAs is increasing rapidly and will continue to increase. She said that if her church does not run an English-speaking youth group, she will move to a local church

---

56. Abigail, interview.

57. At the time of the interview project, the Southeast church was the only Korean ethnic church in Melbourne that provided an English-speaking ministry for SGKA young people.

58. Luke, interview.

because she cannot understand Korean sermons, so attending the Korean ethnic church will be meaningless for her.[59]

Therefore, compared to SGKA students in Korean-speaking youth groups, SGKA members in the Southeast church youth group seem not to feel the necessity for Korean-speaking ministry for SGKA young people. Considering many other SGKA teenagers who are struggling to understand Korean sermons on Sundays in a Korean-speaking youth group, it is certainly advantageous for developing faith to be able to fully understand the pastor's preaching and to be involved in activities without language-related stress. However, at the same time, I found that many Korean-speaking students left the group after it changed into an English-speaking ministry in 2008 because they did not like an English dominated atmosphere in the Korean ethnic church.

Furthermore, it was remarkable to hear that not only those Korean-speaking students, but also many English-speaking SGKA teenagers, especially older students, have not been actively involved in the group and have even left the church for other reasons like faith, friendship or personal issues. For example, Rose argued that in spite of providing an English-speaking ministry, there are many SGKA friends who have been absent from the church for a long time. The rate of absenteeism of older students is high, so the majority of the youth group is, at the moment, comprised of year seven and eight students. She suggested that the pastor and teachers in the youth group should be concerned about long-term absentees.[60]

Karen, a twenty-two-year-old 1.5-generation teacher in the Southeast church, said that since the English-speaking ministry for SGKA teenagers started, many SGKA adolescents who had not come to the church because of language problems began to attend the group, but a considerable number of those who returned left the church again because of reasons like their faith problems, their relationship with other students, and the lack of the teachers' care and concern.[61]

Likewise, although it is necessary to provide SGKA adolescents with various opportunities to listen to English sermons and teachings, it is also critical that pastors and teachers in charge of them should be concerned about their students' personal issues in order to involve them

---

59. Grace, interview.
60. Ibid.
61. Karen, interview.

more actively and satisfactorily in the group. Starting an English-speaking ministry is a very important step, but building an appropriate model suitable for their church situation is more essential.

Finally, there is another big issue in terms of SGKA teenagers' church life: relationship with Korean international students.

Relationship with Korean international students at the Korean ethnic church is a critical issue for most SGKA adolescents who are not confident in the Korean language in terms of adjusting to the church and youth group. As many teenage Korean students are coming to Australia to study and the number of SGKA adolescents is not high because of the short history of Korean immigration to Australia, Korean overseas students are in the majority in the youth groups in most of the Korean Australian churches except for a few large churches which run an English ministry for SGKAs.

Except for the Southeast church, the only church in the Melbourne area with an English-speaking youth group at the time of the interviews, the other three churches researched have a larger proportion of Korean overseas students compared to SGKA teenagers. For example, in the case of the Northeast church and the East church, more than 70 percent of high school students are Korean international students. In the Central church, the population of Korean students is about 60 percent. In the youth group of the Southeast church, on the contrary, SGKA students comprise about 60 percent of the whole population. However, even in the Southeast church SGKA adolescents feel uncomfortable connecting with Korean overseas students, which tends to cause a problem in regard to enjoyment of church life.

The difficulties between the two parties are largely based on issues related to language. Most SGKA interviewees reported that the Korean proficiency of Korean overseas students is the biggest difference for them. SGKA participants feel that they are poor at speaking Korean compared to Korean students, so they tend to be reluctant to use the Korean language when talking to them. This phenomenon seems stronger among those who are not confident in the Korean language. The Korean-speaking atmosphere of the church makes SGKA adolescents step back from relationships with Korean overseas friends. In addition, the difference in culture and value systems resulting from different experiences of growing up tends to make it harder to build good friendships. Consequently, although most Korean overseas students are bilingual and many of them are long-term students who plan to go to an Australian university, many KA churches have not been able to successfully resolve this matter.

Kris said that she never uses Korean language with Korean students at the church although she has little problem in understanding Korean sermons. She does not want to speak Korean in front of them because her Korean proficiency is not as good as theirs. In addition, she is aware of some cultural differences among Korean students, but she cannot recognize what those differences really are. Consequently, she did not try to actively communicate with them because she did not feel her language skills were adequate, but also because she felt uncomfortable associating with them.[62]

Nick is very poor at communicating in Korean. His lack of proficiency in Korean directly affected his relationship with Korean-speaking students. Since the majority of the current youth group in Nick's church, the Northeast church, are Korean overseas students, Nick has been struggling to settle into the youth group. He said that he really wants to make friends at the church, but he has difficulty in communicating with church friends because of the language gap and cultural differences.[63]

Likewise, many SGKA interviewees shared the fact that their poor Korean proficiency and cultural differences are the biggest obstacles preventing them from approaching Korean overseas students. However, among SGKA interviewees, there were some students who liked to communicate with Korean overseas students.

For example, Charlie was influenced a lot by her church environment which encouraged using Korean language in the church. She was born in New Zealand, so English is her first language, but in the course of being involved in the church her Korean has improved. Charlie said that although she is still more comfortable with English, she feels a sense of intimacy when she talks to church friends in Korean. Charlie shared her feelings about the Korean language as follows:

> I like school peers as well, but feel more comfortable in hanging around with Korean church peers. I feel like talking my words in Korean rather than in English. English is more comfortable, but Korean feels mine. My Korean vocabulary is limited, but when I speak Korean I feel like speaking at home. English is my first tongue, but is inferior in intimacy.[64]

62. Kris, interview.
63. Nick, interview.
64. Charlie, interview; translated into English.

Second-Generation Korean Australian Adolescents

Ian also had little problem in making Korean friends in the church. He said that he is an outgoing person, so he always tries talking to Korean international students in Korean. As a result, he has built good relationships, not only with Korean high school students, but also with young Korean adults in his church. Ian said that it is exciting to learn Korean culture and values from Korean church friends and Korean young adults.[65]

The common features of SGKA adolescents like Charlie and Ian who have little problem in communicating with Korean overseas students are that they feel confident in speaking Korean, that they like to share Korean culture with Korean friends, and that they are rather outgoing and sociable. In addition, their churches' Korean environment encouraged them to speak Korean rather than English, which improved their Korean. On the contrary, those who are not confident about their Korean proficiency are likely to step back from Korean international students even if they want to keep company with them and are interested in Korean culture because they do not want to make mistakes. In this case, their churches' Korean atmosphere tended to cause them to feel isolated and discouraged.

The case of SGKA attendees at the Southeast church, however, was different from those attending the Korean-speaking youth group. In the case of the Southeast church, English is the main language in the youth group and SGKA students are the majority. In the youth group, the Korean overseas students, rather than the SGKA students, have been struggling to settle into the group, making efforts to speak English and become accustomed to Australian ways of living. However, from sharing with SGKA interviewees attending the Southeast church, I found that even in an English-speaking environment, SGKA adolescents felt uncomfortable in approaching Korean overseas students because they thought that Korean students were culturally different from them.

Rose highlighted that the hierarchical Korean culture is the biggest obstacle to making friends with Korean people. In Korean culture, Koreans do not use a person's name except when they are friends, close younger persons, or children. When they talk to older persons or people in a public relationship, they use a suitable honorific title instead of their name. For example, children never name their father, mother or older siblings. In the case of a boy, he should call his older brother *hyeong* and his older sister *nu-na*. On the other hand, in the case of a girl, she should call her older brother *o-ppa* and her older sister *eon-ni*. In the youth group,

---

65. Ian, interview.

Korean students use a suitable title for older students such as *hyeong, nu-na, o-ppa,* or *eon-ni*. Rose was accustomed to using people's names, so she disliked the situation in which she should call older students with a certain title instead of using their names. She said that she does not call her older sister *eon-ni* at home. This cultural difference made her feel confused or in conflict with Korean students.[66]

Grace agreed with Rose's opinion about Korean hierarchical culture. She said that she cannot understand why she should use an honorific title for people who are only one year older than her.[67]

The uncomfortable relationship between SGKA adolescents and Korean international students has been a slight or serious problem in most youth groups of Korean Australian churches regardless of their language preference. If such problems cannot be resolved appropriately, the youth group is most likely to separate into two groups. As a result, it cannot be a warm faith community for SGKA adolescents as well as for Korean overseas students. In such an environment they cannot feel a sense of belonging to their youth group, and consequently cannot be actively involved in the church. In order to create a warm relationship between the two parties in the KA church, realistic and appropriate solutions suitable for each church context are urgently needed.

Some SGKA students were aware of the seriousness of this matter and suggested church educators should help them develop closer relationships with each other. For them, it is important that teachers provide appropriate opportunities for the two groups to better understand each other.

For example, Grace and Rose proposed a combined class with both groups for improving the relationship between both parties. Their suggestion of such a combined class was impressive because they identified themselves as Australians and had few Asian peers in school. This shows that they are aware that they should overcome the distant relationship with Korean overseas students in order to develop their youth group into a faith community. Only then, will they feel a sense of belonging to the KA church.[68]

When Nick was asked if he had any suggestion for the religious education of his youth group, he promptly answered that he wants church teachers to provide opportunities for making friends with Korean

---

66. Rose, interview.
67. Grace, interview.
68. Ibid.; Rose, interview.

international students. He said that he wants to keep company with them, but it is very hard because of their different life-contexts, cultural disparity and the language barrier. The reason why Nick wants to make friends with Korean students and keeps attending the Korean church in spite of his lack of proficiency in the Korean language was that he wants to find a place where he feels a sense of attachment.[69]

Twofold Identity Formation

The twofold identity formation is another major characteristic of SGKA young people. Most SGKA youth are simultaneously undergoing, consciously or unconsciously, two processes for achieving a stable identity: personal and ethnic identity formation.

Erik Erikson argues that personal identity formation is a critical task for the adolescence period.[70] Stressing the importance of a moratorium stage in the identity formation process of adolescents, he claims that moratorium is a turning point and without it adolescents cannot appropriately resolve the issue of identity crisis.[71] Jean Phinney and Anthony Ong explain Erikson's concept of identity development as follows:

> For Erikson, identity refers to a subjective feeling of sameness and continuity that provides individuals with a stable sense of self and serves as a guide to choices in key areas of one's life. Identity is not something that individuals automatically have. Rather, an identity develops over time, beginning in childhood, through a process of "reflection and observation" that is particularly salient during adolescence and young adulthood but may continue through adulthood and is expected to lead to a resolution or an achieved identity. An achieved identity combines childhood identifications, individual interests and talents, and the opportunities afforded by the context in a unified self-structure. It is associated with numerous indicators of psychological wellbeing. Not all individuals achieve a stable identity, however, and the failure to do so results in role confusion and the inability to make progress toward meaningful commitments.[72]

---

69. Nick, interview.
70. Erikson, *Identity: Youth and Crisis*, 17.
71. Ibid., 128.
72. Phinney and Ong, "Conceptualization and Measurement," 274.

It should be noted that Erikson underscores collective aspects of identity as well as personal facets. For him, one cannot achieve identity tasks appropriately by focusing only on the personal dimension. Rather, people should be supported by their own group which is significant to them in order to achieve a stable, healthy identity.[73] In this respect, especially for ethnic minority young people living between the host society and their ethnic community, building a positive ethnic identity is critical in achieving a healthy personal identity. Cheryl Holcomb-McCoy also claims that in many cases obtaining solid ethnic group membership is likely to establish a healthy personal identity between the two cultures.[74] From the same perspective, Jean Phinney, Gabriel Horenczyk, Karmela Liebkind, and Paul Vedder emphasize the importance of ethnicity in the lives of ethnic minority young people. They argue that ethnic identity formation is a critical developmental task for ethnic minority adolescents.[75]

For Phinney and Ong, the process of exploration and commitment is essential in achieving an ethnic identity. Influenced by James Marica, Phinney and Ong claim that individuals tend to develop from ethnic identity *diffusion* (lack of a clear identity) or *foreclosure* (commitment to an identity without exploration) to ethnic identity *achievement* through the process of active exploration called *moratorium*.[76] They insist that although people reach adulthood, it is not true that every adult might be able to achieve an ethnic identity. Rather, many adults are continually going through the process of ethnic identity development across the life span.[77]

In case of ethnic minority adolescents like SGKAs, establishing a secure ethnic identity seems to be very complicated. They have to deal with various challenges in building a balanced identity between traditional and new cultures, preserving strong ethnic identification and high

---

73. Erikson, *Identity*, 22–24.

74. Holcomb-McCoy, "Ethnic Identity Development," 122.

75. Phinney, Horenczyk, et al., "Ethnic Identity," 496.

76. Marcia provided four types of ego-identity: achieved identity, moratorium, foreclosed identity and identity diffusion. "By interviewing 20 male college students, I found exceptions to the original dichotomy of identity versus identity diffusion. Two types of identity were formed—Identity Achievement, exhibited by those who had made their own choices, and Foreclosure, exhibited by those who had merely followed parental dictates. Similarly, two types of identity diffusion were seen—Moratoriums, shown by those who were struggling and concerned, and Identity Diffusion, shown by those who were floundering and unconcerned." Marcia, "Development and Validation," 22.

77. Phinney and Ong, "Conceptualization and Measurement," 275.

self-esteem related to their ethnic group amidst prejudice and discrimination from the host society. Some of them need also to resolve tensions with the parental generation which are caused by culture and value differences. At the same time, they undergo the personal process of ego identity development through exploration of identity issues and commitment to relevant identity domains.[78] These two aspects, *ethnic and personal*, are closely intertwined and form the *twofold identity development* of SGKA adolescents. Many SGKA participants in the interviews were also slightly or seriously undergoing the twofold identity development.

Recognizing Racial Difference

According to many scholars like Erikson, Marcia, and Phinney, a moratorium period of identity exploration precedes identity achievement. When people are in a moratorium, they tend to feel confused or uncomfortable because they do not make their own choices. When it comes to ethnic identity, such a moratorium tends to begin when people notice for the first time that they are racially different from the mainstream. William Cross names such realization as *Encounter* in his research of the process of *Nigrescence*, a five-stage model for African American youth to achieve a black identity.[79] He argues that "from the Encounter stage, the person enters an intense transition phase (*Immersion-Emersion*), during which the existing and emergent identities battle for psychological dominance."[80]

In the interview project with SGKA adolescents, it also turned out that realizing their Asian appearance is a critical starting point for seeking their identity.

Nick said that when he was a child, he thought he was an Australian, but he found that he is technically a Korean because of his racial appearance. Although his Korean language ability is poor and his knowledge of

78. "Exploration is the process of examining and experimenting with alternative directions and beliefs and commitment is the strength or clarity of goals, beliefs, and standards that one holds regarding the self." Holcomb-McCoy, "Ethnic Identity Development," 120.

79. The five stages for *Nigrescence* suggested by Cross are as follows: Pre-encounter, Encounter, Immersion-Emersion, Internalization, and Internalization-Commitment. See Vandiver et al., "Cross's Negrescence Model," 175–82.

80. Cross, Strauss, and Fhagen-Smith, "African American Identity Development," 38.

Korean culture limited, he decided that he should belong to the Korean community. In Nick's case, considering that he felt much more comfortable with English and the Australian culture than with the Korean language and culture and showed considerable antipathy towards parts of Korean culture in the interview, realizing the racial gap in his perceived Australian identity was a turning point for his identity conversion. This is the reason why he expressed a desire to learn more Korean things and to participate in the Korean ethnic church even after graduating from secondary school.[81]

Jarvis, a twenty-one-year-old second-generation teacher in the East church, shared a similar experience in relation to his Asian appearance. He said that when he was a child, he thought that he was a pure Australian, so he did not want to learn Korean culture and language, and hated going to the Korean ethnic church with his parents. He disliked his parents and other Korean adults in the church because they pressed him to respect and keep traditional Korean values and norms. He argued that recognizing his Korean appearance resulted in a big change in his identity.

> I always used to speak English and I never understood my mom and dad's cultures. So we always used to fight because I was like "we are in Australia, why are you following Korean culture." Now that has all been cleared up, it is just about making sure you get all your thoughts out and make sure you experience stuff. That is what adolescent stuff is—experiencing as many things as you can (cultures, languages) and not staying in your shell. Once you are an adult you will be in your shell. Kids should act like kids. Physically I am a Korean person. Mentally and emotionally I was an Australian. The thing that changed my mind, was that I realized it doesn't matter how Australian I want to be, I am not going to be completely Australian because my blood is Korean.[82]

On the other hand, Grace identified herself as an Australian because she was born in Australia and does not feel connected to Korean people. In school, she mostly associates with white peers rather than Asian friends. She said that all her best friends are Caucasians. Nevertheless, she was concerned about the attitude of Australian society which tends to judge people by their skin colour. She said that she is very annoyed whenever she is treated as an overseas student because of her Asian

81. Nick, interview.
82. Jarvis, interview.

appearance. Although she said that she is a pure Australian regardless of categorization, she selected this issue as one of the deepest concerns of most SGKA young people.[83]

Ben argued that many SGKA adolescents, especially those who consider themselves as Australian rather than Korean, are struggling with such racial categorization. In terms of this issue, Ben thought that to be concerned about their appearance shows that they are not satisfied with what they currently are and are still searching for what they truly are. He said that it will take great time and energy, sometimes huge stress and deep anger, to discover where they stand between the two cultures.[84]

Hybrid Identity: A Third Culture

From his experience of growing up as a SGKA and his ministry experience with other SGKA young people, Ben argued that almost every SGKA child and young person is consciously or unconsciously undergoing some degree of confusion between the two cultures. He claimed as follows:

> There is within every second generation person, there is a hyphen, standing (a bridge) between two cultures. For me, I have Korean parents, I am Korean, but I am brought up in Australia. So there is a hyphen between Korean and Australian. So within every second generation, there is a bridge between two cultures. Within that bridge (a large line), there is a third culture, Korean Australians—almost tricultural. A hyphen is a short line. We have a chasm in the middle ground. One side we have Korean culture, and the other side we have Australian culture. There is a hyphen that bridges the two, and in that hyphen we have a third culture, which is Korean Australian culture. So a second generation's identity is really "how do you find yourself and who am I within this hyphen (third culture)—Korean Australians." I don't think the hyphen means integration. The way I have seen it, is that we take the best of Korean and Australian cultures and we mix them together to create a new culture.[85]

Nick suggested a hybrid identity as a healthy identity for SGKA people. He argued that a hybrid identity seems appropriate for SGKAs

83. Grace, interview.
84. Ben, interview.
85. Ibid.

enabling them to accept two cultures and values. In creating such a hybrid identity, Nick said, it is important to provide SGKA children with many opportunities to understand the two cultures and decide their identity for themselves. He claimed that those who create a hybrid identity would have few problems in keeping company with Korean or Australian friends.

> I think the healthiest thing would be for them to make the choice, but you have to give them that opportunity. So, at the early ages, I think you should send them to schools with a greater number of Australian children. It gives them the ability to be more open to Australians, and not be scared of them. I think that is important. I think taking them to Korean church might work to be more familiar with Korean church. Trying to get them to read English books, watch Australian TV, let them hang out with Australian friends. When they get to a certain age they have Korean friends and Australian friends. They can hang out with both very openly, very comfortable. They have a hybrid identity, but it is not biased in any way. I think that would be the healthiest.[86]

From the same perspective, Abigail argued that she is a hybrid. She argued that at school or home she can usually switch her cultural mode depending on the people with whom she gets along. That is, she said, she behaves like Koreans within the Korean community, while within the Australian context she changes her behavior and values to suit without great effort.[87]

Switching between two values and norms is a remarkable feature of a hybrid identity. William Cross, Linda Strauss, and Peony Fhagen-Smith explain such transference of cultural norms with a term, *codeswitching*, in their research on the identity of African Americans:

> The *codeswitching function* allows a person to temporarily accommodate to the norms and regulations of a group, organization, school, or workplace. Codeswitching, or *fronting*, may occur when an organization or group shows signs of discomfort with explicit expressions of difference, especially race. In situations that foster codeswitching, African Americans act, think, dress, and express themselves in ways that maximize

---

86. Nick, interview.

87. Abigail, interview.

the comfort level of the person, group, or organization toward which the communication is focused.[88]

That is, codeswitching means to "switch from his or her natural way of doing things to the way that is suggested or demanded by the situation."[89] Cross, Strauss, and Fhagen-Smith maintain that only those who have explored and obtained an achieved identity are able to perform the function of codeswitching appropriately and healthily.[90] On the contrary, codeswitching without identity exploration might cause a fluid identity. In the status of identity fluidity, it might be hard for young minority people to search for who they are or where they stand.

Im argues that foreclosed second-generation Korean American youth are most likely to be fluid in their identity although they can switch their way of living depending on the situation. She maintains that those who are in identity fluidity tend not only not to feel confused between the two cultures, but also not to feel a sense of belonging to both groups.[91] Only after achieving a stable identity through moratorium, might an individual be able to create a healthy hybrid identity. For when they begin to search for who they are or where they stand between the two cultures, they cannot easily switch between two cultural norms and regulations because *they try to choose rather than switch*.

In this respect, Ben shared his experience in terms of switching between the two worlds: "As a young child, there was no problem living in two worlds. As I grew up, and began to have an identity, I could not jump between the two and I had to go in the middle. That was the beginning of the identity crisis."[92]

Faith as an Alternative Identity

In the process of the identity development of SGKA adolescents, realizing racial difference might be a starting point for ethnic identity exploration and for creating a healthy hybrid identity as a third culture. However, simultaneously they would experience slight or serious racial discrimination and cultural prejudice in the host society. They need to overcome

88. Cross, Strauss, and Fhagen-Smith, "African American Identity," 32.
89. Cross, Smith, and Payne, "Black Identity," 97.
90. Cross, Strauss, and Fhagen-Smith, "African American Identity," 34.
91. Im, "Ecological Examination," 37–49.
92. Ben, interview.

a sense of marginalization in order to achieve a healthy identity. Otherwise, they are likely to be torn between the two worlds. I found that many SGKA participants have felt marginalized because of their racial difference.

In Charlie's case, she experienced direct discrimination from her white peers when she was in sixth grade. Since then, even after entering secondary school, she has been very cautious about friendship and was easily hurt by her peers. She said that when she behaves like her white peers, they do not discriminate or show dislike for her. Therefore, in school she has tried to act in the Australian way and follow her white peers' codes in order to be accepted by them, hiding her real likes and dislikes. She confessed that such efforts tend to cause feelings of stress and alienation. Although she keeps good company with her white peers at school, she shared that she does not feel any sense of belonging or of being one of the group. Therefore, she mainly gets along with other Asian peers because she can share a similar cultural background.[93]

Lily said that she has also experienced racial discrimination in school from time to time. She shared, "Sometimes I have negative experiences. People tend to tease Asians mostly about their eyes, and they try to speak Chinese in front of you, which is really rude. So it is annoying."[94] She argued that there is no way to overcome such discrimination so she tries to ignore it. She said that she tries to spend time with her white peers because white students are inclined to dislike Asian students going around together or speaking their national tongue at school.[95]

Even Peter, who thinks of himself as an Australian and associates only with white peers, said that racial discrimination is a fact of school life. Peter argued that Australia is still a white-centered country although it has become very multicultural, so it is natural that ethnic minorities like him sometimes feel a sense of discrimination or suffer disadvantages in some ways. He claimed that since he cannot change such an atmosphere in Australian society, he tries to downplay or ignore it in order not to be hurt whenever he experiences discrimination from his school friends.[96]

> There is a wall between me and my friends because their outer appearance is different to mine. When people see me, they see

---

93. Charlie, interview.
94. Lily, interview.
95. Ibid.
96. Peter, interview.

me as different people, different culture. Other than that, I have no other problems. I fit in really well. I try not to be emotional. I just see that as a joke. When I was younger, I was bullied, and I became a bully myself because I was insecure. In secondary school, they would make fun of me because of my heritage, but I move on and try not to get emotional. There is no point telling my parents about it. It will stop eventually.[97]

It is interesting to see that many SGKA participants argued that faith provides them not only with a bigger picture with a holistic perspective for examining where they stand, but also with a strong sense of belonging. Russell Jeung reports similar research findings. He argues that faith provides ethnic minority youth with "a chance to escape the undesirable aspects of their racial status by adopting an alternative identity, by making Christianity the locus of their identity."[98] Kelly Chong also argues that faith provides a kind of refuge from the sense of alienation or brokenness based on racial difference.[99]

For Charlie, faith is an important factor providing her with a significant sense of attachment. She confessed that the more her relationship with God deepens, the more her sense of alienation resulting from her experience of discrimination heals. She argued that intimacy with God generates peace in her mind and improves her psychological well-being.[100]

In Nick's case, faith provides him with an alternative identity enabling him to overcome a sense of marginalization. He confessed that he does not feel he belongs either to Australia or to Korea and said that racial discrimination or cultural prejudice is prevalent in varying degrees in Australian society. Simultaneously he thought that he could not be accepted as a Korean by Korean people. For him, faith presents an alternative identity to cultural identity, and is a hub connecting both cultures.[101]

Growing Up in the Digital Age: Digital Generation

Last but not least, growing up with digital technology is a significant feature of today's SGKA teenagers. All the SGKA teenage informants in this

97. Ibid.
98. Kim, "Second-Generation Korean American Evangelicals," 22.
99. Chong, "What It Means to Be Christian," 262.
100. Charlie, interview.
101. Nick, interview.

research project are the digital generation who are actively using a variety of technology, IT devices, and the Internet in their lives for communication with peers, entertainment, obtaining information, and homework. Most scholars writing about today's students agree that their ways of learning, thinking, and communicating are totally different from those of the analog generation. For example, today's young people are always accessing the Internet via mobile devices, connected to their friends via SNS like Facebook, good at multitasking, accustomed to learning with various multimedia, and comfortable in virtual space.[102]

These characteristics were found through the interviews with the fourteen SGKA adolescents. First of all, it is remarkable that all the SGKA participants except two students had their own smartphone. Using one's own smartphone means that they can always access the Internet and SNSs with their mobile phone anywhere if they use mobile telecommunication networks like 3G/4G or an accessible Wi-Fi service. This interview project showed that smartphone users connect to the Internet and SNSs more often than those who do not have a smartphone. For example, Abigail who did not own a smartphone said that she usually uses the Internet and SNSs about 1–2 hours a day, while all the smartphone users who shared their daily duration of internet usage, except Nick, said that they normally connect to the Internet and SNSs for more than three hours a day.[103]

Interestingly, all the SGKA participants except Nick had their own account of more than two SNSs, especially Facebook and KakaoTalk [a Korean mobile SNS]. It was found that the frequency in use of SNSs is closely related to the duration of internet usage. Active SNS users connected to the Internet much longer than those who do not use SNSs often. Julia shared her story in relation to SNS as follows:

> I spend a lot of time on SNS. I carry my phone with me everywhere and constantly check things on Facebook and KakaoTalk. Especially with KakaoTalk I spend hours on it, about 3–4 hours. But it's not 3–4 hours non-stop. It's just when I get messages and

---

102. See Anderson and Balsamo, "Pedagogy for Original Synners"; Heverly, "Growing Up Digital"; Jukes et al., *Understanding the Digital Generation*; Livingstone and Brake, "On the Rapid Rise"; and Oblinger and Oblinger, *Educating the Net Generation*.

103. Charlie, Peter, and Rose did not answer the question of the duration of internet usage per day. On the other hand, in the case of Nick, he did not use the Internet much. Abigail, interview; Grace, interview; Ian, interview; Julia, interview; Kate, interview; Kris, interview; Luke, interview; Molly, interview; Nick, interview; William, interview.

start a conversation. I still do other things during KakaoTalk. With Facebook I only use it for about an hour or less per day.[104]

Ian and Grace also said that they use the Internet and especially SNSs all day with their smartphone. Ian said that "the Internet is with me all day through using Facebook and KakaoTalk during the day."[105] Grace similarly shared, "Unless I'm out or sleeping I'm using the Internet."[106] On the other hand, Nick, non-SNS user, said that he did not connect to the Internet often except when he needed it.[107]

Second, a majority of SGKA informants said that they are visual learners and prefer multimedia-based learning. Kris answered that multimedia is "a smarter alternative for education rather than reading a block of text, and it is more memorable."[108] Ian also said that "I am a multimedia/ visual learner as a boring long script of text puts my learning appetite off."[109] However, it is noted that some students who preferred visual learning also emphasized the importance of reading text. For example, Kate answered the question "Are you a multimedia learner or a text learner?" as follows: "Half half. Multimedia makes things more interesting but I can't look at a LED screen too long so a mixture is always good."[110] In addition, three students, Luke, William, and Abigail, said that they are text learners. Luke, William, and Abigail agreed that they preferred text-based learning because it is easier to memorize facts in books. They seemed to be accustomed to testing and evaluation based on a scoring system.[111] This shows that not all digital gen people are visual learners. I found that although a majority of the digital generation like multimedia-based learning, reading texts is still an important way to get information.

Third, the result of interviews with SGKA adolescents also show that not all digital gen students like the team-project learning style. Surprisingly, a considerable number of SGKA informants said that they prefer teacher-centered learning, which is not in accord with many scholars'

---

104. Julia, interview.
105. Ian, interview.
106. Grace, interview.
107. Nick said that he does not want to use SNS because communication via SNS does not seem real to him. Nick, interview.
108. Kris, interview.
109. Ian, interview.
110. Kate, interview.
111. Abigail, interview; Luke, interview; William, interview.

arguments. Julia argued, "I prefer teacher centered instruction because if you work in a team there are more chances of you being disturbed in the group and the amount of work might not be equal. I guess it would depend on who you're working with but I think I can focus more when the teacher gives instructions."[112] Similarly, Nick and Luke said that teacher-centered instruction is generally more productive and effective for them.[113] Grace also said that she likes the teacher-centered style because she is more of an independent learner.[114] On the other hand, only two students, Kris and Abigail, preferred team-project learning.[115] The rest of students prefer a more balanced mode. For example, Ian, Kate, and Molly agreed that we should decide which mode is appropriate depending on the type of task students are doing.[116] This result demonstrates that we do not need to give up teacher-centered teaching in order to educate digital gen students. Rather, educators should learn how to integrate various teaching styles depending on learning context, topic, and student.

Finally, most of SGKA informants agreed that youth groups in the KA churches need a virtual space like SNS or homepage in order to promote student participation in the activities of the group and improve the level of relationships with teachers and peers in the group. Among the four selected youth groups, three youth groups except the Central church youth group had a Facebook page for group members.[117] I found that most of SGKA students participating in their online community were satisfied with communicating with other peers via virtual space. Molly, Luke, and Kris said that their Facebook group is very helpful for youth group members to share their stories, photos, and messages. In addition, for them it seems a good channel to introduce a new activity and remind others of planned events.[118] From the same perspective, teenage students in the Central church like Kate, Ian, and Abigail demanded that their youth group make a Facebook page for group members.[119] It is also noted that there were a number of opinions about the difficulties of revitalizing

112. Julia, interview.
113. Luke, interview; Nick, interview.
114. Grace, interview.
115. Abigail, interview; Kris, interview.
116. Ian, interview; Kate, interview; Molly, interview.
117. The youth group of the Central Church did not have any online community for group members.
118. Kris, interview; Luke, interview; Molly, interview.
119. Abigail, interview; Ian, interview; Kate, interview.

such an online community. For example, Kate said that the age difference/cultural gap among students and the indifference to SNS of some group members including teachers could be an obstacle to members' active participation.[120]

So far, I have discussed four major characteristics of the lives of SGKA youth based on the interviews with fourteen SGKA teenagers, ten teachers, and four youth pastors affiliating with the four selected KA churches. This analysis has provided significant knowledge of the unique needs, issues, and situation of SGKA youth as an important consideration for creating an appropriate religious education curriculum for them.

---

120. Kate, interview.

6
The Religious Educational Performance in the Korean Australian Church

Educational Philosophy

THE EDUCATIONAL PHILOSOPHY OF the teacher/pastor participants was based on their ideas about the role of the Korean Australian (KA) church and their understanding of second-generation Korean Australian (SGKA) young people. The main purposes of religious education most mentioned by educators in the four KA churches are as follows: (1) creating a faith community and helping SGKA young people develop faith; (2) helping SGKA young people accept their Korean background by providing adequate opportunities to develop ethnic factors; and (3) building an appropriate church structure for SGKA young people so they can feel a sense of attachment to the church.

Toward a Faith Community

Above all, all Korean immigrant educators attending the interviews responded that the religious education of the Korean immigrant church should focus on building up the church as a faith community and influencing SGKA young people to have faith. Especially in relation to SGKA teenagers, many of them argued that it is very important for adolescents to find faith because adolescence is the period when a personal identity is established.

Judy, a forty-seven-year-old teacher in the East church, would like the Korean immigrant church to be a warm faith community in which people can feel a sense of attachment to other members as a family because she believes that through such warm relationships faith will develop.[1]

Sam, a twenty-one-year-old 1.5-generation teacher attending the Northeast church, also argued that it is very important to provide SGKA youth with opportunities to experience God's love, the fundamental truth of Christianity, in the church so that they may accept faith and further develop it.[2]

Robert, the fifty-five-year-old head teacher in the youth group of the Southeast church, said that nurturing faith is the most important thing in church education, so the church should be a community for faith. He argued that if SGKA young people find it difficult to have faith in the Korean church for some reason or other, parents or church leaders should help them find an appropriate church suitable for their faith development because developing faith is the core of the church.[3]

As such, all teacher/pastor participants underlined the importance of faith development in religious education because they believed that nurturing faith is the essential purpose of religious education in the church. It was remarkable that their emphasis on faith education is also closely related to their understanding of the identity crisis of SGKA young people. All of them thought that most SGKA teenagers are consciously or unconsciously undergoing identity confusion between the two cultures and many of them have experienced racial discrimination slightly or seriously.

Considering her 1.5-generation son's case, Isabella, the fifty-year-old head teacher in the youth group of the Northeast church, said that the biggest concern of SGKA teenagers is the issue of identity. As all SGKA young people live between Australian and Korean cultures, they are likely to continually ask themselves, "Who am I?" and struggle to establish their own identity between the two worlds. For her, the quality of their lives depends on the degree of identity achievement. Thus, she said that the core role of the Korean ethnic church for SGKA young people is to help them establish a healthy identity.[4]

Robert also argued that the biggest issue for SGKA adolescents is the matter of identity. He said that the issue seems hidden in many cases

---

1. Judy, interview.
2. Sam, interview.
3. Robert, interview.
4. Isabella, interview.

because SGKA teenagers hardly mention it to church teachers, but when he talks to them personally, he finds that most of them have undergone a slight or serious identity crisis and a sense of marginalization.[5]

Most teacher/pastor informants believed that faith can provide SGKA young people with an alternative identity to overcome the marginalization that ethnic minorities often experience.

Ben, the thirty-nine-year-old SGKA pastor in charge of the youth group in the Southeast church, also argued that almost every SGKA young person tends to undergo identity confusion. He said that since the two cultures are changing rapidly, the hyphenated identity of SGKA adolescents is also continually evolving according to the transformation of the two cultures, which seems to cause them to feel unstable in terms of identity. He argued that Christian identity based on faith is relatively firm and solid, while cultural identity cannot provide SGKA young people with a stable identity because culture changes rapidly.

> I have come to the point of being completely content with who I am, but I think if (this is one of the things that is really important about second gen ministry) you base your identity on culture, this means you will always be shifting. The Gospel actually says our identity is not in culture, but it is in Christ. The focus of second generation ministry is personal relationship with Christ. Once you have this relationship, your identity is with Christ and Christ alone. Everything else fits into place, based on who Christ is and how God calls us to live as his children. So, an almost forty year old second generation versus a grade seven second generation, who both have their identity firmly in Christ, they have a lot of things in common. And they may choose to act in different ways, but the common threads are all in Christ. And that is fine.[6]

Mark, the thirty-two-year-old youth pastor in the East church, also argued that Christian identity seems the only alternative identity helping SGKA teenagers resolve the problem of identity confusion. He claimed that SGKA people seem not to be able to achieve a true identity even though they decide on a cultural identity by themselves, whether Korean or Australian, because only faith can recover the true self created by God. Once they have faith in Christ, he insisted, the issue of whether Korean or Australian does not matter because in faith the two different

5. Robert, interview.
6. Ben, interview.

cultures both seem important and can be mixed into a third culture with little problem.[7]

Ralph, the thirty-eight-year-old youth pastor in charge of the youth group of the Central church, similarly considered faith as the only way for SGKA adolescents to overcome diverse problems caused by their minority status in Australia. He claimed that once they have a Christian identity as children of God, they can subdue negative feelings, and not adhere to racially disadvantaged environments because faith provides them with a bigger picture in terms of identity so that they may establish firm identities regardless of their cultural status in the mainstream society.[8]

Henry, a twenty-six-year-old SGKA teacher in the Southeast church, shared his experience of growing up as a SGKA in terms of the importance of faith as a solution to identity confusion as follows:

> I guess cultural identification is better now than back when I was in youth group. I had no idea. But however, there are many variables and factors that do play with this and I do feel that culturally the youth may know who they are, but also they have no idea who they really are. I guess they have a sense of an identity, but they don't understand the trueness of that identity. . . . A Christian identity should be developed over anything else. An identity in Christ is so much more important and valued.[9]

Toward a Matrix of Ethnic Identity

Many teacher/pastor informants, especially those attending the Korean-speaking youth group, argued that although faith is the fundamental identity that SGKA teenagers ought to establish, the religious education of the Korean immigrant church should also help SGKA teenagers develop a Korean identity in relation to their psychological well-being. They argued that if SGKA young people regard themselves only as pure Australians, they are likely to feel more confused or rejected because they are likely to be categorized as ethnic minorities based on racial appearance. On the contrary, they claimed, when they accept their Korean background and enjoy their heritage within Australian society, they become able to create a balanced identity. Similarly, Denisha Anbu argues

7. Mark, interview.
8. Ralph, interview.
9. Henry, interview.

that faith can provide ethnic minority people with a stable identity, but faith itself cannot resolve cultural identity confusion. So, ethnic minority young people should accept both cultures with a balance within faith for creating a healthy identity.[10]

For Jarvis, a twenty-one-year-old SGKA teacher in the East church, it is very important that SGKA teenagers have a Korean identity for their psychological well-being. From his own experience as a SGKA, he acknowledged that SGKA young people are likely not to feel accepted as true Australians by the mainstream because of racial difference.

> I think all second-generation Koreans need to have a Korean identity. That's what I realized when I was an adolescent. It doesn't matter how non-Koreans think you are; the fact is that you are Korean. The use of the Korean language definitely helps to use more and more Korean ways of living. Informing them about what Korean culture is about is important. It helps with their relationship with their parents and friends.[11]

Mark also argued that when SGKA people are in childhood, they tend not to be aware of their racial difference. However, in the course of growing older, he claimed, they might notice that they cannot be accepted as true Australians because they are Asian. He asserted that if they do not grasp this reality at a younger age like adolescence, they might experience more serious confusion and isolation when they do understand it at an older age. On the contrary, if they realize it at a younger age, he argued, they might be able to reduce their sense of shock and establish a healthy identity.[12]

Sam similarly claimed that in the course of growing older, SGKA young people become aware that they cannot but be Korean. He said that attending the Korean ethnic church seems helpful for SGKA teenagers to have an ethnic identity because in the church they have occasion to meet Korean people and speak the Korean language. He said that the Korean church should provide various opportunities encouraging SGKA young people to accept more positively their Korean heritage. However, at the same time, he strongly criticized the way that the Korean church unilaterally pushes SGKA people to follow Korean ways of living.[13]

10. Anbu, "Multiple Identities," 134.
11. Jarvis, interview.
12. Mark, interview.
13. Sam, interview.

The Religious Educational Performance

At this point, however, it should be noted that their emphases on Korean identity was for creating a balanced identity between the two worlds. That is, as SGKA young people seem more accustomed to Australian ways of living than Korean culture because they have lived most of their lives in Australia, many Korean educators argued that SGKA youth should open up their Korean side in order to gain balance between the two cultures.

Sam argued that in adolescence teenagers try to decide on one culture; otherwise they are likely to feel isolated or marginalized. However, he said that only when they fully experience both cultures can they establish a healthy identity. He shared his own experience as follows:

> In terms of identity, we tend to view it as a black and white issue, like we are Koreans or Australians. Especially, while adolescents are still young, they tend to think they should belong to a group; otherwise, they tend to think they don't belong anywhere. For example, they say, "As I'm not comfortable with Koreans, I should be a pure Australian." I felt that way too. Even before entering university, I felt like a Korean when I was with Korean peers, while I was an Australian with Australian people; I was very confused.... So, I decided that "I'm grey; I'm in the middle." However, I came to realize that I don't need to select one side and give up the other; I don't need to take an exclusive stand. I can embrace both cultures. This is a healthy identity.[14]

Isabella also asserted that it is important to educate SGKA young people to accept both cultures in a balanced way, because both cultures are critical parts of their lives. In order to do this, the Korean ethnic church, an important Korean community for immigrants, should be balanced in terms of cultural preference. She said that multicultural education is a suitable approach for SGKA young people.[15]

On the other hand, it is remarkable that those working for the English-speaking youth group of the Southeast church argued that the Korean-centered atmosphere of the Korean ethnic church is likely to be an obstacle to creating a balanced identity. For them, emphasizing an ethnicity-centered religious education might result in a monocultural education rather than a multicultural one.

Andrew, a twenty-one-year-old SGKA teacher in the Southeast church, argued that the Korean ethnic church has tended to be

14. Ibid.; translation into English.
15. Isabella, interview.

regarded as a Korean-only community, but it should be open to all ethnic people in Australia.

> Often more conservative voices of the choice argue that Korean church should be for Koreans only—that cultural homogeneousness should be maintained and any type of "westernization" or "Australianization" should be discouraged. An ethnic church that thinks like that will eventually have no future—so many second-generations have left the church because of this attitude. Thus, its main roles should be not of isolation from Australian society—but integration/pathways. The ideal ethnic church would be active in the local community, using its resources to edify others and the body of Christ.[16]

Ben argued that the ultimate purpose of his youth group is to spread the gospel to other English-speaking ethnic people in Australia, and furthermore build a community able to embrace them all.[17]

As such, there were two understandings of multicultural ministry in the KA church: one group argues that multicultural ministry is to embrace the two cultures in a balanced way, while the other argues that multicultural ministry is to open the church beyond Koreans to other ethnic groups. However, I found in this research project that the ministries generated by both groups are a kind of monocultural ministry in that one culture has dominated the other in some way, consciously or unconsciously.

Toward a Comfortable Place for SGKA Youth

Last but not least, some educator participants argued that the religious education of the Korean church should try to make the church environment a comfortable place for SGKA teenagers. They claimed that a considerable number of SGKA young people want to lead a faith life with people who have the same experience of growing up as theirs, so if the Korean church provides an appropriate church structure and atmosphere for them, they may settle into the Korean ethnic church more easily.

Sam claimed that educators or church leaders in the Korean church should create a haven for SGKA teenagers to encourage a sense of belonging to the church and to open themselves to other members so that

16. Andrew, interview.
17. Ben, interview.

The Religious Educational Performance

they may enjoy a Christian relationship with them and be influenced by them rather than by the secular culture.[18]

Karen, a twenty-two-year-old 1.5-generation teacher in the Southeast church, shared her experience of when she attended an English-speaking local church. She enjoyed English language sermons, but she felt a sense of isolation among the church members but did not know why. Consequently, she returned to the Korean church although there were still some problems with the church she needed to address.[19]

Ben argued that the gospel can be more easily spread through heart language which consists of the mother tongue and a comfortable culture. It is true that English is the first language of SGKA people, but simultaneously Korean culture is also an indispensable part of their lives because they have grown up in a Korean immigrant family. In a local church, they can understand sermons perfectly, but as an ethnic minority they do not feel the heart language.[20]

However, for Korean educators, the Korean ethnic church does not seem to be a comfortable place for SGKA adolescents for a number of reasons. Three factors were most mentioned by the teacher/pastor participants: relationship with Korean international students, language barriers, and a first-generation-centered church structure. It is noted that their understanding of the difficulties of SGKA teenagers' adjustment to the Korean ethnic church are quite consistent with the sharing of SGKA youth discussed in the last chapter.

First, a number of educator informants said that many SGKA teenagers have relational problems with Korean overseas students, which tend to make them feel a sense of isolation in the church.

Jarvis argued that many SGKA adolescents have difficulty in communicating with Korean overseas students because of cultural differences. For example, in the case of SGKA boys, they tend to follow Australian football or cricket, so like to talk about these sports, while Korean overseas students tend to have an interest in Korean pop culture or other sports like soccer or baseball. As a result, it is not easy to find common topics between the two parties. Consequently, many SGKA students in

---

18. Sam, interview.
19. Karen, interview.
20. Ben, interview.

his church feel isolated and fail to settle into the church because they are the minority in the youth group.[21]

Jarvis said that SGKA teenagers ought to open their minds to Korean overseas students and be on good terms with them. From his own experience, he argued that it would be beneficial for SGKA young people to acknowledge a different culture and value system through spending time with Korean students. He shared that in his childhood he was not open to Korean students in the church, and consequently became isolated and this was harmful to the process of his identity achievement.[22]

Sam expressed similar opinions about the relationship between the two groups. He said that there are many cases where the two groups cannot keep company because of cultural differences. He maintained that SGKA youth and Korean international students can communicate with each other in English or in Korean, but they cannot understand each other's culture or preferences. As Jarvis indicated, Sam argued, there are few common interests between the two parties, so they are likely to feel alienated and distant from one another. In addition, he argued that the real problem is that the two parties tend not to make an effort to understand and accept one another because they are too young. Also, he said in his youth group there is little educational effort and no appropriate systems for strengthening the connection between the two groups.[23]

On the other hand, it is remarkable that there were three teachers, Judy, Isabella, and Albert, all first-generation teachers, who said that they believed there was not much of a problem in terms of the relationship between the two parties in the Korean ethnic church. In spite of the fact that the matter of the relationship with Korean overseas students was mentioned by many SGKA students as a critical issue in terms of their church life, many first-generation teachers or leaders—like these three teachers—tended not to take it seriously, so there was little educational effort to resolve the problem.[24]

Second, all Korean educators in the interviews admitted that many SGKA adolescents in the Korean ethnic church, especially those attending the Korean-speaking youth group, have some difficulty in understanding Korean sermons or expressing their opinions in the Korean language.

21. Jarvis, interview.
22. Ibid.
23. Sam, interview.
24. Albert, interview; Isabella, interview; Judy, interview.

Many teachers/pastors argued that the language barrier could be a big obstacle to SGKA teenagers' faith development.

Thus, most of the Korean teacher/pastor participants agreed with the necessity for an English-speaking education for SGKA adolescents in the Korean church. However, it is noted that there were various opinions about English ministry for SGKA young people in the Korean church. Teachers/pastors involved with the Korean ministry for SGKA teenagers tended to stress a Korean-English integration model, while educators participating in the English ministry tended to stress an English dominated model for multiethnic ministry beyond SGKAs.

For example, Mark argued that religious educators in the Korean ethnic church should develop a Korean-English balanced model for educating SGKA teenagers. If we lean toward a one language dominated structure, he claimed, we are most likely to lose one of them. For him, although it is important to educate SGKA teenagers with their first tongue, it is also significant to help them develop Korean language by providing them with various opportunities to use the Korean language.[25]

On the contrary, Henry who is ministering with the Southeast church youth group pursued an English-speaking ministry embracing all nations and ethnicities as follows:

> Church is church—we're all a part of one cause, which is to bring people to Jesus Christ and share His story and love to all that walk the earth. The main role for anyone would be to continually allow this flow to continue. I don't believe that the church should be different because of different ethnicity. We have one God—and we're one under His name.[26]

It is also noted that there were two teachers who objected to the necessity of an English-speaking ministry for SGKA young people in the Korean ethnic church.

Sophie, a forty-two-year-old teacher in the Central church, argued that although she knows that there are some SGKA teenagers who experience difficulty in understanding Korean, teachers in the Korean church should educate them in Korean because they have been using Korean at home since their childhood.[27]

---

25. Mark, interview.
26. Henry, interview.
27. Sophie, interview.

In the case of Albert, the thirty-nine-year-old head teacher in the youth group of the East church, he agreed with the necessity for English-speaking education for SGKA teenagers in the Korean church, but argued that nevertheless the Korean church should keep a Korean-speaking ministry for youth because there would be a continual influx of Korean students into Australia. From his perspective, SGKA teenagers might be able to go to an English-speaking local church but it is too hard for Korean international students or newly immigrant students to attend a local church. He argued that the Korean church should be more concerned about students who have limited proficiency in English.[28]

Finally, the Korean culture–centered atmosphere in the church was mentioned by many Korean educators as an obstacle to moulding the church into a comfortable place for SGKA adolescents.

Jarvis claimed that in many cases traditional Korean culture and values have been the first consideration in the church rather than biblical culture and values. He took the Confucian way of thinking as a representative example; for instance, he said, the hierarchical church structure based on age or church position is an obstacle and prevents the church from being a faith community as well as a comfortable place for SGKA young people.

> One thing I hope Korean churches get rid of is rank (age). That is one thing that is really annoying. I know it is Korean culture, but if you want to have a healthy church, you have to get rid of rank. Many times I have expressed my feelings amongst adults. I have always been told "stop being rude." Being rude is one thing, but not listening is also bad. A child doesn't become rude if you listen. An adult's response will affect the child's response. That is something Korean churches struggle with a lot. Children or leaders of youth groups, or leaders of young adult groups can't voice themselves because they are intimidated with adults telling them that they are rude. It's like "you're a kid, I'm an adult, I'm wiser than you, I can make the decisions and this is what's happening, so you run off and we'll look after it." You are not going to run a healthy church if you don't listen to young kids/adult groups. This may be for all churches. Investment into youth/young adult groups is not being done. That is a tragedy. Adults think their group is the most important thing. Adults

---

28. Albert, interview.

think the money that is left over by them goes to the younger groups. This is something I struggled with in youth group.[29]

From the same perspective, Sam argued that Korean culture seems to dominate biblical or Christian culture in his church, which he believes has been a hindrance to being a faith or love community. He claimed that in such an atmosphere young people seem to be forced to respect and obey unconditionally what older people say simply because they are older than them. He insisted that such an atmosphere worsens the relationship between the first-generation and second-generation in the church. SGKA young people, he said, are accustomed to an egalitarian culture, so most of them hate the Korean chronological rank.[30]

To sum up, many Korean educators argued that religious education for SGKA adolescents growing up in the Korean Australian church should make continual efforts to create a faith community for developing faith, a matrix of Korean identity for building a balanced identity, and a comfortable place for SGKA young people to feel a sense of belonging to the church. I found that their opinions on the purpose of religious education in the Korean ethnic church are closely related to their general understanding of the lives of SGKA young people. It is noted, however, that the fact that today's SGKA adolescents are the digital generation was not fully considered in the educational philosophy of teacher/pastor informants. Although most of teacher/pastors informants recognized that today's SGKA young people are very different from them in terms of teaching-learning methodologies, ways of communication, and the level of utilizing digital technology, there were few mentions of SGKA teenagers' digital ways of learning, thinking, and communicating in relation to educational philosophy.[31] It was found that this lack of knowledge of SGKA young people as the digital generation in their educational philosophy is directly connected to their general practices of religious education and their understanding of curriculum.

29. Jarvis, interview.

30. Sam, interview.

31. It is also noted that compared to the SGKA participants' frequent mention of their school life, especially of peer relationships in school, there were few mentions of the matter in the interviews with educator participants. See Albert, interview; Andrew, interview; Ben, interview; Henry, interview; Isabella, interview; Jarvis, interview; Judy, interview; Karen, interview; Mark, interview; Paul, interviewed by author, Melbourne, Australia, October 24, 2011; Ralph, interview; Robert, interview; Sam, interview; Sophie, interview.

General Practices of Religious Education

The Image of Church Educators

On the question of the image of church educators, almost every teacher/pastor participant said that the church educator is a mentor, a spiritual guide, or a helper who assists students to develop their faith.

Isabella argued that the church teacher is a helper for student faith development. She expressed her opinion of the church educator's role as follows:

> A Christian education teacher is not a leader who leads the students in his or her direction, but a helper who listens to the students' stories and assists them to live their own lives. From the perspective of Christian education, a teacher is a person who helps students to have faith in God. . . . Christian education teachers need to listen carefully to the personal concerns or problems of students as in the course of speaking about their issues students might be able to resolve the matter for themselves.[32]

Mark explained the role of the church teacher using the term *coaching*. For him, the Christian religious education teacher is not a manager who commands or instructs, but a coach who cooperates with the students. A coach builds a relationship of friendship with students rather than the kind of relationship that exists between subordinates and superiors. He argued that "if teachers cannot feel sympathy with students, they are most likely to miss the most important thing in educating them."[33] He claimed that in leadership in church education a coach is better than the traditional, charismatic leadership as a manager.[34]

Albert argued that the teacher should have a deep concern and love for SGKA in order to be a mentor for them. He shared his own experience of how he tried to communicate with students through playing together or spending time together in spite of the language barrier, and he found that they readily opened their minds. Based on this experience, he claimed that love and concern is much more important than language.[35]

---

32. Isabella, interview; translation into English.
33. Mark, interview; translation into English.
34. Ibid.
35. Albert, interview.

The Religious Educational Performance

In addition to this emphasis on a close relationship with students as a mentor, a helper or a coach, other factors like a healthy faith, accurate biblical knowledge, a sound theological foundation, and a mind that is open to different cultures and values were often mentioned by the teacher/pastor informants as important talents for teachers.

Building a Close Relationship with Students

Almost every educator informant in the four KA churches argued that a religious education teacher in the church should be a mentor, a helper or a coach for the faith development of SGKA young people, and for this to happen he or she should establish a personal relationship with students. It is remarkable, however, that almost every teacher/pastor said that they have not spent enough time and energy to build up such a warm relationship with the students because of their hectic schedules or busyness with other things. All participants said that they have few meetings with students except on Sundays.

Andrew agreed that building a warm relationship with his students is a critical part of his education in the church, but he shared that it is very hard for him to connect with them. "It is extremely hard to do this with so many kids—extremely hard! It is taxing on resources, time, and effort. Ideally I would like to have a warm relationship with the kids but I only have it with a few."[36]

Sam also claimed that the relationship between teacher and students is one of the most important factors in religious education, but he said that normally he did not meet with his students except for the Bible study session of his youth group on Sundays. He argued that as a church teacher sharing a sense of intimacy with his students is one of the most difficult things in educating them. He himself feels that he needs to make communication with his students a priority.[37]

Judy spoke candidly of her difficulties in making her class a warm community because it is very difficult for her to spend enough time with her students because of her busyness as well as the students' hectic lives. So, she has tried to have a meeting in school holidays because she believes

---

36. Andrew, interview.
37. Sam, interview.

that spending time together with students is a starting point for forming a loving relationship with them.[38]

Likewise, although almost every teacher/pastor participant agreed with the importance of creating a warm relationship with students, most of them have not spent enough time and energy doing this mainly because of their busyness. It is interesting that most of the teacher/pastor participants did not consider using SNS as an alternative, even though they know that most of today's students are active users of SNS for peer communication.[39] Many teachers/pastors in this research were using SNS personally to converse with friends and colleagues, but did not actively use it as a way for communicating with their students. In the case of some educators, they did not like to use SNS. For example, Jarvis said that he does not communicate with his students via SNS because he does not like this method.[40] In the case of Judy, she said that she does not feel comfortable using SNS and objects to spending lots of time on chat through SNS.[41] Consequently, although three youth groups had at least one account of SNSs for promoting communication among members, many teacher/pastor participants did not use virtual spaces as a channel for connecting with their students.

Furthermore, through interview findings I found that most educators in the four KA churches tend to regard youth group ministry as Sunday School ministry, and so limit their responsibility to Sundays. This seems to be the main reason why they have not invested time and energy in creating a loving relationship with students on weekdays. Their understanding of the youth group as the Sunday School tends to cause them to focus on teaching rather than on genuine meeting or deep sharing. Normally, they seem to regard their main responsibility as teaching students in a group Bible study session according to materials suggested by the pastor in charge of the youth group. Most of the participants said they usually spend most of the group Bible study time, about thirty to forty minutes, in talking about what they are supposed to teach or cover so they cannot afford to spend time to build closer relationships with students in the small group session. The given time is normally not enough to even accomplish what they intend to teach.

38. Judy, interview.

39. As indicated in chapter 5, this research showed that all the SGKA informants except Nick were using SNSs to communicate with their peers.

40. Jarvis, interview.

41. Judy, interview.

In spite of the fact that most teacher/pastor participants in the four KA churches highly valued building up a loving relationship between teacher and students, and creating the youth group as a faith community or a comfortable place for SGKA adolescents, their practical performance of religious education in the church was limited to teaching in group Bible study sessions on Sundays. As a result, there seems little time for developing a sense of intimacy among group members either on Sundays or on weekdays, which causes a huge discrepancy between their words and actions in terms of their educational philosophy and their ideas about church teachers. Limited communication tends to result in a superficial relationship between teacher and students and is likely to have a negative impact on faith education in the church.

Preparation for Group Bible Study

Through interviews, most teacher/pastor participants reported that they regard teaching in small groups on Sundays as the main task of church teachers. It is closely related to their understanding of the ministry of a Sunday School teacher. However, it was found that most of them did not spend much time in preparation for group study. Many teachers mentioned their busy daily lives as the main reason for this, but at the same time they seemed not to consider Bible study preparation as a top priority on weekdays.

For example, Judy said that she has not spent enough time in preparing the next Bible study session although she feels the responsibility.[42] In the case of Jarvis, his multiple ministries in his church have been a huge obstacle to his commitment to youth ministry. He said that it is very hard to spend time preparing the next Bible study session because he is not only a teacher in his youth group, but also a leader in his young adult group and a member of the worship team for the main service of his church.[43]

In the case of Paul, the thirty-two-year-old pastor in charge of the youth group of the Northeast church, he was very aware of the teachers' limited preparation for the group Bible study because he has long struggled with this matter. As an alternative, he changed the Bible study

---

42. Ibid.
43. Jarvis, interview.

materials from a Korean textbook to a self-designed question sheet based on the day's sermon for group discussion. He argued as follows:

> Most of the teachers don't prepare for the group Bible study enough during the week and tend to lead the session after looking materials over. As a result, in many cases even teachers don't understand what they are supposed to teach or share in the group Bible study.... The current methodology that leading the group discussion according to the questions suggested seems easy for them if they carefully listen to the day's sermon.... At first, I provided the question sheet a week before in order to help teachers prepare beforehand. However, I found that they didn't, so nowadays I provide it on the spot before the group discussion.[44]

Ironically, such materials seem to make teachers less inclined to invest their time and energy on weekdays in preparation for their ministry. For instance, Sam shared that he spends little time preparing the next Bible study session on weekdays because the content for the Bible study is based on the Sunday's sermon. He cannot prepare for it although he wants to.[45]

In spite of the teachers' inadequate preparation for the group Bible study, among the four KA churches selected as research sites, only two youth groups, the Southeast church and the Central church, provided a preparation class for teachers to study the content before the group study on Sundays or on weekdays. The other two youth groups did not provide teachers with opportunities to look at materials together with the pastor's exposition before the group Bible study session. The youth pastor in the Northeast church, Paul, thought that it is not necessary because he is using the day's sermon as the content for group discussion,[46] while the youth pastor in the East church, Mark, said that he has not been able to do it mainly because he could not find a suitable time and place on Sundays.[47]

---

44. Paul, interview; translation into English.
45. Sam, interview.
46. Ben, interview; Paul, interview.
47. Mark, interview.

Communication with Parents

In the case of teacher participants in this research, all of them said that they usually do not connect with parents because they find it very difficult. This is inconsistent with their agreement on the importance of parents' cooperation in religious education for their children.

Some teacher/pastor participants argued that the non-Christian behavior of some parents attending the church tends to lead their children to perceive hypocrisy among the parents. They argued that this negative experience results not only in the children tending to lose trust in their parents, but it also hinders them from developing Christian faith. Many educators, especially pastors, regarded parental lack of faith as the biggest obstacle in educating SGKA young people in the church. Since many non-Christians go to the Korean ethnic church in Australia for various reasons other than religious ones, such as social, educational, or business purposes, many SGKA young people tend not to be educated in a Christian way at home or are not encouraged by parents to be involved in church activities, especially in the case of senior secondary students who face examinations in order to enter university.

Paul argued that from his vantage point, the uncooperative attitude of parents is the biggest difficulty in ministering to SGKA adolescents in his youth group. He shared his experience as follows:

> I think that the biggest concern about youth ministry in my church comes from parents, especially their unbelief and lack of cooperation. Although students want to learn more about Christianity or become more actively involved in the youth group, unless their parents cooperate, it is hard for them. The matter of transport is a good example. Since it is hard for SGKA young people to come to the church alone because of limited public transportation in Melbourne, if parents don't want to attend the church, students can't come. . . . Even if students want to join in the extra bible study group beginning after lunch, if parents don't stay at the church after lunch, they can't attend. . . . Sometimes, SGKA teenagers feel confused when their parents educate them differently from church teachers or pastors. For example, the church educators emphasize developing their faith first, while parents place more emphasis on improving their academic ability; church educators encourage them to attend the

church every Sunday, while parents tell them not to go to the church especially during examinations.[48]

Ralph also claimed that parents' lack of belief seems the most difficult obstacle in the religious education of SGKA young people in the Korean ethnic churches. He said that since many parents in the Korean church are non-Christians, this is a serious limitation in nurturing SGKA teenagers to be Christians because the cooperation of parents is critical in educating them appropriately.[49]

Robert argued that parents' relative indifference to their children's faith compared to their academic achievement is one of the biggest problems to be resolved in order to help SGKA adolescents improve their faith. For example, he said that some older SGKA students cannot come to the church because of extracurricular tutorials on Sundays organized by parents.[50]

Nevertheless, all four youth groups relied upon the teacher's individual efforts to connect to parents without developing any communication strategies. Only the youth group of the East church has a general meeting with parents once or twice a year, while the other three youth groups did nothing to improve the connection with parents. In the case of young adult teachers compared to adult teachers, communicating with parents seems very difficult because of the age gap, language barriers, or lack of familiarity with the parents. Above all, their lack of concern about connecting with parents seems the biggest reason for their not communicating with them. In this regard, all the head teachers participating in the interview project, like Isabella, Albert, and Robert, argued that one of their important tasks is to create a bridge between teachers and parents, but little effort was made except to ask teachers to connect regularly with parents.[51]

There were some suggestions for resolving the current poor level of communication with parents. For example, Paul argued that some special education for parents such as discipleship training is urgently needed.[52] Ben also agreed on the necessity for some education for parents, but he

---

48. Paul, interview; translation into English.
49. Ralph, interview.
50. Robert, interview.
51. In the Central church, there was no head teacher at the time of interview project; Albert, interview; Isabella, interview; Robert, interview.
52. Paul, interview.

felt it is not a matter that his youth group could handle, but a matter about which the whole church congregation should be concerned.[53] In addition, Ralph said that he is planning to systematically visit all his students' houses the following year in order to talk with students as well as their parents.[54]

Recruitment and Regular Training for Teachers

Most of the teacher informants in the four KA churches said that they became teachers after being approached by the pastor or other teachers. All teacher participants shared the fact that they were not educated for their role. In this respect, all pastors in the four KA churches agreed that there is currently no special training for new teachers in their youth groups mainly because of limited educational resources as well as a lack of teachers. In the case of the youth groups in the Northeast church and the East church there was just a certain period of probation before being appointed as a regular teacher in charge of a small group, whereas in the other two youth groups there was no specific process of teacher recruitment except some criteria for selecting teachers.

Among the four pastor participants, Paul, the youth pastor in the Northeast church, showed the keenest interest in more systematically and carefully recruiting new teachers although he could not organize a preparation program for teacher volunteers. He shared his ideas about selection of church teachers as follows:

> I am selecting teachers very carefully because teachers are in charge of precious children. If teachers stumble, such precious children easily get lost. So, I try to be thorough in the process. There are a few critical criteria for recruiting teachers. First of all, I select the person who really wants to do this job; I do not accept anyone who is suggested by someone. Secondly, I select the person who is able to keep attending the youth group for at least a year or more. Finally, I expect them not to be late or absent without notice.... After being selected based on these criteria, they should go through a probationary period before being appointed to be a general teacher who can teach students in a small group.... For example, even if more than a hundred students attend our youth group, if there were only four trained

---

53. Ben, interview.
54. Ralph, interview.

teachers, I would lead the youth group with them. It would be much better than selecting anyone who is not prepared to commit to being a teacher simply because they are short-handed.[55]

On the other hand, in respect to regular training for teachers, the Southeast church has a relatively good system because there are sufficient human and material resources compared to the other three churches. At the time of the interviews, there were about sixty teachers working for all educational departments in the church including the youth group. The church has provided teachers with regular opportunities, like annual seminars or special lectures, for teachers to improve their teaching-related abilities. However, in the case of the other three churches, there is little church support because the churches are relatively small, and each youth group has to prepare teacher training themselves.

In the case of the youth group of the Northeast church, teachers have a fortnightly Bible study program with the youth pastor. Paul said that strictly speaking it is not educational training for teachers, but a general Bible study for discipleship.[56] In the case of teachers in the Central church, they have gathered with the senior pastor or the youth pastor once a week to study what they are to teach on the coming Sunday. This is the only time teachers are educated for teaching in the youth group.[57] In the case of the youth group of the East church, there was no special meeting for the purpose of training or educating teachers. Instead, a few times teachers attended a combined teacher seminar provided by an association of some small churches located in Melbourne, but Albert said that it had little effect on teachers.[58] Thus, all teacher informants in the three youth groups often mentioned the necessity of appropriate training programs for them.

Understanding of Curriculum

Most of the teacher informants tended to lack confidence when talking about curriculum because of their limited knowledge of the curriculum. In general, they were inclined to consider curriculum as a guideline or

---

55. Paul, interview; translation into English.
56. Ibid.
57. Ralph, interview.
58. Albert, interview.

a framework for teaching, or a sequence of content to be taught. They tended to identify curriculum with textbooks.

For example, Jarvis understood curriculum as "sets of guidelines" that provide criteria for what to teach or how to teach.[59] Isabella argued that curriculum is a framework for adequate teaching.[60] Albert said that "curriculum is a kind of foodstuffs prepared for nurturing students."[61]

In relation to their understanding of curriculum, it was noted that most of the teacher participants said that planning or selecting curriculum was not their job, but the pastor's responsibility. The teacher's job was just to follow the guidelines suggested by the pastor in charge of the youth group.

Judy argued that "normally curriculum is provided by the pastor, so I invest my time and energy in thinking how to use it effectively, not worrying about making or selecting the curriculum myself."[62] In the same way, Albert claimed that it is the pastor's job to plan a curriculum, while it is the teacher's responsibility to apply it appropriately in the course of educating the students.[63]

Besides, it is remarkable that many teacher informants said that for various reasons they are not satisfied with the current curriculum of their youth group.

Isabella argued that the current curriculum of her youth group, a self-designed discussion formula prepared by her youth pastor, seems not to be systematic. She also worried about a lack of consideration of the suitability of the current material for group discussion because of the age differences in the group. She claimed that from an educational perspective it seems inappropriate that the same questions are given to all students regardless of their age, interests, and situations. In addition, she argued that curricular flexibility is essential because every textbook needs to be adapted in some way to suit particular students and their educational contexts.[64]

As referred to above, Jarvis considered curriculum as sets of guidelines for appropriate teaching. However, in his view, there have not been

59. Jarvis, interview.
60. Isabella, interview.
61. Albert, interview.
62. Judy, interview; translation into English.
63. Albert, interview.
64. Isabella, interview.

firm guidelines in his youth group since he became involved in youth ministry as a teacher. He argued that while the youth pastor seems to have a solid vision for the group, he has not provided teachers with firm sets of guidelines to realize that vision. Jarvis wondered about the connection between the pastor's vision and what he teaches. From his perspective, inconsistency results from the lack of solid sets of guidelines in the first place.[65]

Robert referred to the difficulty of finding adequate textbooks for his students, especially for SGKA young people, who are growing up in the context of the Korean ethnic church. In the case of his youth group, the English translation of a Korean monthly devotional magazine designed for teenagers was imported and used as a textbook for group study in the last four years. But he argued that it did not seem suitable for SGKA adolescents in spite of the English-language version because the themes and the content were often irrelevant to their lives as an ethnic minority in Australia. He claimed that it is very hard to find English or Korean textbooks suitable for the context of the Korean migrant church. In his view, to filter or amend the content of textbooks is a realistic option.[66]

Similarly, Sophie claimed that it is difficult to develop a textbook suitable for SGKA young people. Instead, it seems enough to transform Korean or English published textbooks into revised versions after filtering the content carefully.[67]

As such, all the teacher informants tended to identify curriculum as a guideline like textbooks indicating what and how to teach. Thus, for them selecting appropriate textbooks was the most important thing in terms of curriculum. In choosing suitable materials, they emphasized issues related to language, culture, and life context more than anything else. However, it is noted that no one mentioned today's students' digital life style as a curriculum consideration.

The basic curriculum understanding of the pastor informants in the research was not different from that of the teacher participants discussed above. All pastor participants saw curriculum as a guideline or a sequence of content to be taught, so in relation to curriculum they focused primarily on educational materials like textbooks for group study sessions. Like the teachers, they thought that selecting or planning curriculum is their

---

65. Jarvis, interview.
66. Robert, interview.
67. Sophie, interview.

responsibility rather than the teachers, but agreed that it is very hard to find an appropriate textbook for SGKA adolescents in the KA church because of language barriers, culture gaps, and differences in context. Remarkably, they also did not consider today's SGKA young people's digital ways of living in terms of curriculum.

Ralph said that he thinks curriculum is about the learning-teaching sequence. He also argued that "the curriculum of the youth group should be consistent with the ministerial vision of the senior pastor of the church because teaching in the youth group must be consistent with the direction of the whole church ministry."[68] However, he confessed that he has very limited knowledge of curriculum and has not considered the matter of curriculum in depth. In regard to materials for group study, a textbook—the *Westminster Shorter Catechism*—was chosen by the senior pastor, and used in the youth group before he came to the church. In terms of curriculum development for SGKA students, he indicated that the language barrier is one of the critical issues.[69]

Paul also shared that he has relatively little knowledge of curriculum, so does not think about it profoundly although he has designed material for group discussion in his youth group. He argued that when he used a Korean textbook introduced by his predecessor, he found it difficult to apply the content to the life context of his students and to invite them to participate in group discussion. This is the reason why he decided to create a three-question sheet based on the day's sermon in order to improve the level of student involvement in the Bible study session. However, he said that he does not have a whole-year plan for his self-designed discussion material. Instead, he has made it under the existing conditions. In relation to curriculum planning, he underlined the importance of the student active participation and sharing of their stories rather than the teachers' unilateral instruction.[70]

Ben has also been preparing self-designed material for group discussion based on his sermon because he could not find an appropriate textbook for his students. As indicated above by Robert, his youth group used the English-language version of a Korean devotional magazine for adolescent Christians, but he stopped using it after 2010 as he concluded that it did not work for SGKA students who are currently the majority

---

68. Ralph, interview; translation into English.
69. Ibid.
70. Paul, interview.

in his youth group, for Korean textbooks do not address the Australian context and culture. In addition, he has not been able to find English textbooks suitable for his students because they do not consider the specific context of Korean migrants and their culture. Likewise, in his view, it is hard to find a textbook that contains various cultural spectrums in it. As a result, he concluded that it is important to keep a balance between education based on a solid curriculum and education that is flexible and capable of adaptation to local circumstances.[71]

Mark understood curriculum more broadly than the other three pastors. He explained his concept of curriculum as follows:

> I consider curriculum in a broad sense.... Curriculum is a kind of manual necessary for ministering to a congregation, including the ministerial vision and direction of the pastor in charge of a group.... A textbook is a very important part of curriculum, but it should not be identified as curriculum itself.[72]

However, he also showed a tendency to focus mainly on textbooks or teaching materials when asked to present an opinion on curriculum. His youth group has been using a Korean Bible study textbook series published by a Korean Presbyterian denomination which was introduced by a former youth pastor. He decided to keep using it although he thought it was second-best. In terms of curriculum development in the context of the Korean Australian church, he argued that two matters should be considered carefully: language and cultural sympathy.[73] Pastors' understanding of curriculum and their curricular efforts in their youth groups will be investigated in more detail in the next chapter through an analysis of the current curriculum of each youth group.

Likewise, almost every teacher/pastor participant considered curriculum primarily as a guideline, framework, or manual for the teaching ministry or the sequence of the content to be presented. Most of them identified the textbook for group Bible study sessions with the curriculum itself. This phenomenon was demonstrated well through the fact that they talked mostly about textbooks when asked about curriculum. Most of the teacher/pastor informants argued that it is very hard to find textbooks suitable for teenage students including SGKA young people growing up in the context of the Korean Australian church. Korean textbooks are most

---

71. Ben, interview.
72. Mark, interview; translation into English.
73. Ibid.

The Religious Educational Performance

likely not to consider the Australian context and culture, while Australian ones do not take Korean culture and values into account. In fact, there are few textbooks designed for second-generation people living between the two worlds. Consequently, finding suitable textbooks has been the most essential curricular issue in most of the Korean ethnic churches.

This textbook-centered curriculum understanding is closely related to Tyler's curriculum model for schooling, the standardized model that is assumed to be applied to all educational environments. As in Tyler's rationale, most of the teacher/pastor participants understood curriculum as a teaching plan for transmitting knowledge systematically and effectively in order to achieve the selected purposes. However, as discussed earlier, Tyler's schooling paradigm is inappropriate for religious education for faith because faith as knowledge of God is totally different from knowledge based on the modern objectivistic epistemology which is the foundation of Tyler's curriculum model. Nevertheless, transmitting knowledge-out-there based on Tyler's schooling-instructional paradigm has long been a major curriculum model for the churches. As a result, the curriculum understanding of the teacher/pastor informants was generally limited to the issue of choosing textbooks indicating content and methodology.

In addition, their indifference to today's SGKA adolescents' digital ways of learning, thinking, and communicating shows that their understanding of curriculum is based on an analog-based curriculum. As analyzed in chapter 2, analog-based curriculum is grounded in a deep-rooted manufacturing mode, *component-based modularity*, and in a mass communication paradigm. Component-based modularity tends to result in a hierarchical collaboration model and passive service for component replacement. On the other hand, a mass communication paradigm would cause a teacher-centered and offline-dominated curriculum. These curricular characteristics are not appropriate for current student life styles.

7
An Analysis of the Current Religious Education Curriculum of the Korean Australian Church

THE CURRICULAR EFFORTS OF the teacher/pastor participants were limited to selecting textbooks or preparing teaching materials for group Bible study sessions. However, as curriculum includes all activities and events designed to have educational benefits, I will examine three major curricular factors of the Korean youth groups such as the Sunday sermon[1], textbooks for group Bible study, and various educational activities. It is also noted that the current curricula of the four selected youth groups are not only for second-generation Korean Australian (SGKA) students because there are students of diverse backgrounds in all the youth groups, like 1.5- or second-generation students, Korean international students, and newly immigrated students. Thus, in the process of curriculum planning, not only SGKA young people, but other students have also been considered.

The Youth Group of the Southeast Church

Sunday Sermon

Ben, the thirty-nine-year-old SGKA youth pastor, argued that the most important aspect of youth ministry is to help students meet Jesus Christ personally and so become his disciples. Ben said, "Haksengbu [Youth group] ministry is to raise, equip, prepare and send out this high school aged generation to be missionaries for Christ in their schools and families all for God's glory."[2] Therefore, his Sunday sermons focus on encourag-

---

1. All the four pastors in charge of the selected youth groups have not preached from the lectionary. Instead, they have made their own preaching plans depending on their contexts.

2. Ben, interview.

ing youth to be missionaries and ambassadors for God's kingdom. Based on this perspective, he has prepared the Sunday sermon according to a short-term sermon plan based on topics or books of the Bible. For example, at the time of his interview, he had just finished a nine-week sermon program on the *fruits of the spirit*, referring to Galatians 6:22–23. Before that, he preached to students on the Epistle of James for eight weeks.

Another significant purpose of his ministry is to develop the Korean ethnic church to be a multiethnic church welcoming other ethnic people as well as Koreans. For Ben, the Korean ethnic church should not be limited only to Korean people. Rather, the church should be open to all ethnic people in Australia to spread the gospel to them. In order to carry out a multiethnic ministry beyond a Korean-only church, he insisted, an English dominated structure needs to be developed rather than a Korean-English integration model in the youth group. Thus, since he came to the church, all his sermons to the group have been preached in English. Even guest speakers who were invited to preach to the students in the youth group have mostly been English speakers.[3]

Ben's multiethnic church driven ministerial vision has permeated his sermons and his philosophy of religious education. It is not surprising that his ideas of an English-speaking multiethnic ministry have a strong impact on the teachers and students in his youth group. I found in this interview project that many teacher/student participants attending the Southeast church youth group agree that the Korean ethnic church should do an English-speaking ministry for a multiethnic congregation.

In relation to his pursuit of a multiethnic church rather than a Korean-only one, however, there seem to be a few problems. First, as Ben indicated, about 40 percent of the students in his youth group are Korean-speaking people such as Korean international students or new immigrants. This means that a considerable number of students in the youth group have difficulty in understanding English sermons. Nevertheless, the education of the Southeast church youth group was monocultural with an Australian culture–centered perspective. If the group adheres to an English dominated educational structure aiming to embrace other ethnic people, not considering the situation of Korean-speaking students, those who lack English proficiency are not likely to be educated appropriately and may leave the church. This is another monocultural

---

3. Ibid.

education similar to the situation in which Korean culture dominates in church education.

Second, the pursuit of a multiethnic church is likely to cause conflict with first-generation church leaders and members in the Southeast church. Most of the first-generation Korean Australians are inclined to consider the Korean immigrant church as a haven for Korean Australians.[4] In the course of serving a Korean Australian (KA) church in Melbourne as an associate minister for six years, I discovered that very few first-generation people think that the Korean ethnic church should become a multiethnic church. It was remarkable that even those parents who strongly defend the necessity of English ministry for SGKA young people in the Korean ethnic church want a church life with their children at the same church even if they cannot worship together with them because of the language difference. Most of those parents seem indifferent to the Korean ethnic church developing as a multiethnic congregation.

Even Robert, the fifty-five-year-old head teacher, argued that the Korean ethnic church should develop a structure for two congregations to lead a church life together under the one roof enabling the two parties to worship separately in their first language, but to continually associate with one another within the same church structure. He claimed that in this context SGKA young people are able to experience and learn about the good traditions of Korean Christianity, such as attending the church every Sunday, passionate prayer, ardor for the Bible, financial commitment, and respect for elders.[5] While Ben also argued for the paradigm of the two congregations under one umbrella using the term *inter-dependent model*, the connection between first-generation and second-generation was less emphasized. Rather, he underlined the independence of an English-speaking congregation in building a multiethnic congregation within the Korean ethnic church.[6]

However, Andrew, a twenty-one-year-old SGKA teacher, claimed that the segregationist attitude which ignores the opinions of Korean-speaking church members is not helpful. Rather, he insisted that a cooperationist paradigm should be developed between the two groups as follows:

> The establishment of such close relationship requires fluency in Korean and is a huge practical requirement. If the EM [English

---

4. Albert, interview.
5. Robert, interview.
6. Ben, interview.

ministry] pastor doesn't know Korean—it is often very hard to establish any sort of amiable relationships with the first generation leaders. Often the first generation leaders are too set in their ways to learn English in any proficient way. Therefore, it's up for the EM pastor to be able communicate the NEED for the ministry—but also be congruent with the overall church vision. There needs to be unity in purpose, theology, and vision. If the EM pastor doesn't submit to these concepts—then there is destructive disunity. It requires a certain submission from the EM pastor to really think of the EM as part of the whole—an overall community. It's counter-productive to operate in isolation. Also, both parties need to really come together with the goal of church edification in mind. Senseless and counter-productive church politics and bureaucracy can often harm this objective.[7]

Textbooks for Group Bible Study

Ben has, since 2011, chosen a discussion-centered format without a textbook as the main method of the group Bible study in his youth group, and ceased using *Sena*, the English-language version of a Korean devotional magazine for teenagers. Instead of using a fixed textbook, he normally provides teachers a week in advance with information about his sermon for the following Sunday so that they can prepare. He shared two reasons as to why he decided on this format.

First, he said that he likes the current discussion-centered structure as it is very hard to find appropriate textbooks for his youth group because of the language gap and cultural differences. He underlined that good textbooks are connected to current culture, so that they are not out of context. He insisted, however, that there are few materials, whether Korean or English, which adequately contain rapidly changing cultural trends in them. Furthermore, he argued that it seems impossible for a textbook to be fully linked to the current culture and to cover various cultural spectrums. Thus, he decided to deal with culturally critical topics or individual issues in his Sunday sermons rather than to expect a textbook to cover them. In this respect, he argued that "textbooks and other curriculum date quickly, so the role of the minister is very important. They

---

7. Andrew, interview.

have the task of theological engagement and discipleship. Any textbook needs to be adapted to suit individual contexts."[8]

Second, he argued that he prefers the current textbook-free group study based on the day's sermon because it enables teachers to be flexible. For him, it is important to keep a balance between following a fixed curriculum and educating students in ways that relate to issues and contexts. He agreed that if there is no curriculum for church education, the pastor and teachers might easily lose educational direction and consistency. However, he argued that if they have clear ministerial visions and concrete educational purposes, it would not be difficult to educate students without a curriculum.[9] This statement shows that he identified textbooks with curriculum.

The main purpose of the current discussion-based group study is, he insisted, to improve the students' faith through active dialogues between the teacher and students. He argued that educators should create "a small group to encourage and urge one another on in faith to actively be missional wherever the Lord places us."[10]

The sermon-based group discussion style of the youth group has an advantage in terms of the connection between the day's sermon and the group Bible study. In the course of group discussion, students will be reminded once again of the content of the day's sermon and may be able to apply it directly to their real life-contexts. The level of discussion is liable to become deeper and develop into a sharing of their life situations. In addition, such sharing might help strengthen the relationship between the teacher and students. These are the reasons why Ben originally introduced the textbook-free group discussion style.[11]

However, the teacher participants involved in the youth group also outlined some weaknesses. First of all, the level of success of the methodology seems to depend largely on the individual teacher's ability. Since there is no fixed textbook or guideline for the teacher to follow or refer to in the course of leading a discussion, teachers need to prepare well and have good communication skills for satisfactory group sharing. In this regard, Karen, a twenty-two-year-old 1.5-generation teacher, said that it is not easy to decide on topics suitable for group discussion based on the

---

8. Ben, interview.
9. Ibid.
10. Ibid.
11. Ibid.

content of the day's sermon even if the pastor explains a week in advance what he will talk about in the next sermon. In addition, since she is not accustomed to leading this kind of group Bible study, she sometimes feels confused or inadequate especially when students do not respond to her questions.[12]

From Andrew's perspective, the current sermon-based group discussion style of the youth group seems to depend on the appropriateness of the pastor's sermon. If the sermon fits the life-context of students, the group discussion is satisfactory. Otherwise, the discussion might not be dynamic because the topic is out of context. Andrew argued that a relevant sermon is the most important thing in terms of the group discussion: "Often the sermons this year have been rather ineffective in terms of topic. For example, nine weeks on the fruits of the spirit was not a fruitful exercise. When the preaching became a bit more expository such as on the book of James we saw some actual productive discussion between the class members."[13]

Educational Activities

The youth group organizes a camp for students once a year. At the time of the interview project, the camp was the only educational activity of the group. Ben has organized it normally in the Easter season and invited one or more guests as the main speaker(s) during the camp. Thus, the camp becomes a sermon-centered conference. Students have the opportunity to listen to new sermons from new preachers and be challenged by them, but the impact seems limited or superficial because the speakers do not know the real context of the youth group. Students are impressed or challenged not by their pastor but by external guests, so it is difficult to follow up any change in the direction of spiritual development in the ordinary context of the youth group. This is most likely to result in a disconnection between the camp and normal worship.

For youth pastors, an invitation to guest speakers is easier in terms of the preparation of the annual church camp than preparing special sermons themselves in addition to their routine responsibility to preach every Sunday. However, considering that the camp is a marvellous opportunity to meet the same students in a different time and environment, it

---

12. Karen, interview.
13. Andrew, interview.

is worth spending time and energy for such special occasions. The camp might then be an educational bridge connecting their education before and after the camp. Of course, sometimes the challenge from external guest speakers might create good educational benefits for the group, but this is not necessarily the case.

In addition to the church camp, there is another camp called Youth Melbourne Jesus Conference (hereafter YMJC) presented, since 2007, under the auspices of the Melbourne Korean Minister's Association. YMJC is a good opportunity for students to listen to the stories of guest speakers and to meet students who attend other churches. Many students of the youth group of the Southeast church have attended it every year since 2007.[14] However, there are limitations in terms of educational benefits because it is an annual event focusing on worship rather than educational programs that are intentionally designed with consideration of the specific context of the group.

The Youth Group of the Northeast Church

Sunday Sermon

Paul, the thirty-two-year-old youth pastor, argued that one of the core purposes of religious education in his youth group is to help teenage students establish a Christian world view or Christian sense of values. Otherwise, in his view, most Christian adolescents are likely to be infected with secular materialism. Thus, he said that his sermon planning is closely related to this educational purpose.

For him, another important factor related to the Sunday sermon is to preach simply and plainly so students can understand it easily and it is connected to their life contexts. He claimed that if the sermon is too difficult for students, or neglectful of their context, they tend to be inattentive.

The third factor that he is concerned about in preparing a Sunday sermon is the appropriateness of the sermon topic for group discussion because his sermon is the basis for the small group discussion after worship. When he came to the current youth group as a pastor about a year ago, a Korean Bible study textbook was being used for the group Bible study session. However, he found it difficult to get the students to

14. Ben, interview.

participate in the group study with the Korean material, so he decided to stop using it. Instead, every week he makes a three-question sheet based on the day's sermon as material for group discussion to improve the level of student participation. I will investigate the three-question sheet in detail in the section on textbooks.[15]

Considering these three factors, he usually prepares a Sunday sermon according to Christian themes or the liturgical season. However, he said that he does not have a yearlong sermon plan, but depending on circumstances makes a 4–6 week sermon series. He shared his opinion on this matter as follows:

> I don't have a year-long plan for sermon themes or directions. . . . If I had a fixed plan, sermons would be more systematic. They could be easily boring because they are likely to be repetitious during a certain period. . . . Thus, I try to prepare a Sunday sermon to fit special insights or challenges given to me rather than follow a fixed plan.[16]

With respect to the Sunday sermon, he expressed a difficulty caused by the language barrier. That is, many SGKA students cannot fully understand his Korean sermon. He argued that such a language gap is most likely to hinder SGKA students from concentrating on the sermon, which makes it very hard to establish a rapport with them. In addition, he argued that it is hard for him to select appropriate topics for his students because there is a wide spectrum of students in his youth group: 1.5- and second-generation students, newly immigrated students, and long-term Korean international students. In addition, choosing adequate themes for SGKA young people is difficult because of his limited knowledge of the lives of SGKA teenagers; he frankly said that he knows little about Australian school life which hugely influences SGKA adolescents.[17]

Textbooks for Group Bible Study

The youth group of the Northeast church currently uses a group discussion format rather than a teacher-centered structure in the group Bible study session. This change is based on Paul's educational philosophy. He believes that the most important thing in a group Bible study is student

15. Paul, interview.
16. Ibid.; translation into English.
17. Ibid.

participation. He stresses the need to create an environment in which students are easily able to express their opinions.

> I've emphasized that teachers should focus on listening to students' stories or ideas rather than on inculcating students with what they deem important. I think that church based religious education shouldn't be a kind of schooling in which teachers are supposed to give correct answers, while students are supposed to accept and memorize them without fully understanding them. Rather, religious education in the church should aim for a structure in which students are able to express their opinions freely, with teachers listening to them carefully. The main role of teachers is not to teach students, but to help them express their ideas in group Bible study sessions.... Thus, our group study is a talk-show; the teacher is a M.C., students are guests who are invited to share their stories, and the theme of the talk-show is the day's sermon. The core of this structure is to create a haven to encourage students to speak and participate.[18]

In this regard, the three-question sheet given to teachers by Paul is a kind of script for a talk-show-like group discussion in the youth group and the questions are based on the content of the day's sermon.

For example, Paul preached to students based on Matthew 7:13–14 on September 4, 2011. The title of the sermon was "The Narrow Gate" and the content was about priority in life. In the sermon, he argued that only those who put God's will as the top priority of their lives are able to enter the narrow gate. He then took the story of the temptation of Jesus as an example. Since Jesus accepted God's word as his first priority, he could win a great victory over Satan's temptations and keep going through the narrow gate.[19]

Based on this title and the content of his sermon, he provided teacher and students with three opening questions for group discussion on the same Sunday as follows: (1) What are top priorities in your life? (Money, dream, honor, good occupation, parents, friends, appearance, and so on); (2) What are the big temptations or obstacles hindering you from living up to God's words? (Computer, parents, laziness, friends, and so on); and (3) How can you change the top priorities of your life to

---

18. Ibid.; translation into English

19. Paul, "Jobeun mun" [Narrow gate], sermon preached at the youth group of the Northeast church, September 4, 2011.

the Current Religious Education Curriculum 185

God's will rather than your will? (We should set correct life priorities to change our lives.)[20]

The main purpose of using this three-question sheet based on the day's sermon is to boost student participation. In addition to this aim, he presented four other purposes. First, he wants to check how much students understood his sermon by monitoring the degree of student comprehension. Second, he expects students to connect what they have heard or discussed to their lives through expressing their ideas and listening to the opinions of others. Third, the current format of group Bible study, namely, group discussion, is appropriate to teachers who tend not to invest much time and energy in preparing the session on weekdays. He argued that if teachers listen to the sermon carefully, they will be able to lead the discussion without problems. Finally, considering the limitations of time and venue in relation to group Bible study, he believes that this discussion style is appropriate to the context of his youth group. Normally teachers are allotted at best half an hour to lead the group Bible study, which is too short to invite students to freely express their ideas under the traditional teaching-centered structure.[21]

Paul mentions three points as the strengths of the current discussion style. He believes that it enables students to share their stories and thoughts, and their participation tends to make them apply what they have heard to their life context. Second, he argues that it helps students to remember the sermon in the course of discussing topics related to the preaching. Finally, it helps teachers to use the given time to listen to student opinions, and develop a closer relationship with them rather than teaching what they are supposed to cover in a one-sided way.[22]

On the other hand, he presented the poor communication skills of the teacher as one of the biggest problems:

> One of the biggest weaknesses is related to the quality of the teachers. This is really huge. . . . The success of the talk-show-like group discussion depends largely on the teacher's ability to extract students' inner stories by using the three questions. If the teacher can't play this role satisfactorily, the group discussion tends to fall down. . . . Simply speaking, if a M.C. can't

---

20. Paul, material for the group Bible study session in the youth group of the Northeast church, September 4, 2011.

21. Paul, interview.

22. Ibid.

lead a talk-show appropriately, the show is most likely to lose its direction.[23]

Paul also shared about his personal situation like physical and/or spiritual condition, language barriers, and cultural differences as other concerns in making the three-question sheet for the group discussion. In terms of SGKA students, he was mostly concerned about their understanding of his sermon and the questions.

The teacher participants attending the Northeast church, Isabella and Sam, also expressed various opinions on the talk-show-like group discussion and the three-question sheet based on the day's sermon.

Isabella, the fifty-year-old head teacher, was satisfied that these questions are usually connected to concrete life issues of the students, so seem to help them participate in the discussion more actively. In the case of SGKA teenagers, group discussion seems more appropriate than teaching directed study because of language and cultural barriers. However, she was concerned that the question sheet is given to all age groups without consideration of age differences. In her view, it is not good to ask all students the same questions since the developmental stages and life interests are different according to age. She preferred to use specialized textbooks designed by age or grade. In addition, she felt there needed to be more consistent and systematic themes for the group discussion.[24]

Sam, a twenty-one-year-old 1.5-generation teacher, argued that when he used the former textbook imported from Korea, it was very hard to dialogue with students because he had to spend most of his time of his group Bible study delivering the content. On the contrary, the current question sheet is simple to understand and good for discussion with the students. It seems good for SGKA students who are accustomed to presentation-centered education. Many of the questions are applicable to the lives of students. However, he wanted to get the questions a week before in order to be familiar with the topics and have enough time to think about various sub-questions. He also expressed difficulties related to limitations of time and place.[25]

---

23. Ibid.; translation into English.
24. Isabella, interview.
25. Sam, interview.

Educational Activities

In the youth group of the Northeast church, there are two activities designed for achieving educational outcomes: extra Bible study for those who wish to learn more about the gospel (hereafter wishers) and the annual youth camp.

Paul said that about ten students attend a Bible study that he presents after lunch for wishers. He uses an adult Bible study textbook designed for discipleship training, tuning the level of difficulty according to the participants. Since wishers come to the group voluntarily, there is an atmosphere of passion for God's Word. However, he shared that parental noncooperation has been a significant obstacle to encouraging more students to join in the extra Bible study.

Another educational activity in the youth group is the youth camp held once a year. Paul said that the main purpose of the camp is to present opportunities for the student spiritual development through preaching, deep prayer, and special events. In his view, the camp is also a good occasion for students to develop closer relationships with other friends as well as with teachers. In addition to the church camp, the students of the group have attended YMJC every year like the youth in the Southeast church.

The Youth Group of the East Church

Sunday Sermon

Mark, the thirty-two-year-old youth pastor, argued that the Korean ethnic churches should do their best in nurturing the following generation to be God's people. Therefore, more than anything else, they should focus on Christian education for the second-generation. In this regard, Mark claimed that the most important purpose of his youth ministry is to equip students to have faith in God. In order to realize this vision, he emphasized the sermon in Sunday worship and fellowship in the small group sessions. To draw student attention to his sermon, he said, he plans it carefully.

Above all, he argued that the sermon should be fun, so he tries to provide amusement for students in his preaching. However, for him, the language barrier and cultural difference are huge obstacles to connecting with the students, especially with SGKA adolescents. For example, he shared a Sunday when he made a joke using an episode of a famous

Korean comedy show during the preaching, but few SGKA students could understand and laugh even though many SGKA teenagers watch Korean drama or entertainment shows regularly. He found the lack of cultural sympathy with students to be one of the biggest problems in communicating with them through the Sunday sermon. This shortage of cultural sympathy might result from a combination of language barriers and different cultural preferences.[26]

In addition, he said that he normally prepares Sunday sermons according to a concrete sermon plan in order to make them consistent and systematic. The sermon plan consists of various short-term projects categorized by topics like love, commitment, endurance, and so on. He said that he does not prepare his Sunday sermons in relation to the group Bible study session because he wants to talk about various Bible topics and stories beyond the content of the textbook that his youth group is using for the group Bible study. He shared that if he prepares Sunday sermons according to the textbook, students would be learning the same content twice in a day, which might be good for their memory, but is liable to limit their learning. This is the reason why he decided to use a published textbook as material for group Bible study rather than to use his Sunday sermon.[27]

Textbooks for Group Bible Study

The youth group of the East church had used a Korean textbook series for teenagers, *Click Bible Series*, for about two years before Mark came to the church a year ago. The textbook series consists of twenty-six small books categorized into three major themes: Scripture, Teenage Christian Life, and Discipleship. These three themes are divided into two stages according to the degree of difficulty: basic course and advanced course. There is no further division according to grades, but the basic course is suitable for students in year seven to nine, while the advanced one is for those in year ten to twelve. Each course has thirteen books. These books are not designed to be used step by step. Rather, users can start to use any book depending on the context of their own youth group.[28]

---

26. Mark, interview.
27. Ibid.
28. Educational Research & Development, *Click Bible Series: Jesus Christ (Basic Course 2)*, 65.

the Current Religious Education Curriculum 189

In the case of the youth group of the East church, the two courses have been used in turn as all secondary school students attend the group together. The three themes of the series have also been selected in turn in order to improve the diversity in terms of the topics. Currently, the group is using a booklet in the series, *Jesus Christ*, which is part of the basic course on the theme of the Scripture.

The book *Jesus Christ* consists of fourteen chapters designed to teach about Jesus Christ in the group Bible study for fourteen weeks. The fourteen chapters are divided into two sections: His Story and Jesus Who Came to the Lost. Each section has seven chapters respectively. The content and purpose of the booklet is outlined in the preface. The book focuses on the life of Jesus: His birth, ministry, miracles and parables, death, and resurrection. However, the emphasis of the textbook is not on information about Jesus' ministry, but on helping students experience a life-changing encounter with Jesus Christ. Thus, in the preface two purposes are expressed for the course of study: (1) students will learn about Jesus' life and work, and will come to resemble him as a disciple; and (2) they will believe in Jesus as Messiah, Son of God, through the stories of his deep love and marvellous miracles.[29]

Each chapter in the book is composed of four parts: Ice Break, Toward Forest, Toward Tree, and Toward Life. The section Ice Break is preparation time in which students get ready to start; Toward Forest is the part when they are offered an overview of the chapter; the part of Toward Tree is a time to study the core content of the chapter; the final part is Toward Life in which the core principles of the study are applied to the lives of individual students. In the whole process, cooperative learning among students is strongly emphasized rather than the teacher's unilateral instruction. In order to develop cooperative learning, each part is designed to encourage students' participation and active discussion by providing food for thought, questions or group activities.[30]

In Mark's view, the series seems suitable for his students including SGKA students who have poor Korean proficiency because the content is simple and easy to teach and learn, and furthermore there are numerous illustrations and comments so that adolescents can easily understand the content. This is the main reason why he decided to keep using it although

---

29. Ibid., 1.
30. Ibid., i.

he was not involved in the process of selecting it.[31] Albert, the thirty-nine-year-old head teacher, also thought that the simplicity and plainness of the series are its best merits.[32]

In addition, it is noted that the Click Bible Series is designed to improve students' active participation through cooperative learning. The series developers argue that the church teacher should guide the class towards improving student-centered learning, criticizing traditional teacher dominated learning.[33] Considering that shallow and superficial relationships between the teacher and students were mentioned by the teacher/pastor interview participants as one of the biggest problems in the religious education of the Korean ethnic church, the merits of cooperative learning are worth studying further in order to improve the educational situation in the KA churches.

The fact that there is a guidebook for educators for each Bible study booklet in the series is another strong point. As discussed earlier, the problem of insufficient preparation during the week by the teachers for the group Bible study has been a huge concern in all the four youth groups. Nevertheless, there was limited support for enhancing the level of the teachers' preparation in all the youth groups at the time of the interviews. In this respect, providing teachers with a well-organized handbook seems beneficial for the teachers' preparation.

On the other hand, a few limitations of the book were mentioned by the pastor/teacher participants in the East church.

First, Mark argued that when using the book, it is hard to educate students according to their specific concerns because the book does not consider the age difference and the different developmental stages of the students.[34] *Click Bible Series* is divided into two stages in terms of the level of difficulty, not by the age difference. In addition, the fact that the series was designed for the life-contexts of adolescents living in Korea means that there are limitations in applying the content to SGKA students. For instance, Judy, a forty-seven-year-old teacher, said that some stories and examples in the introduction and final application seem a bit strange to

---

31. Mark, interview.

32. Albert, interview.

33. Educational Research & Development, *Click Bible Series: Jesus Christ (Basic Course 2)/ Handbook*, 5.

34. Mark, interview.

Korean Australian people. The language barrier is another obstacle to using this material with SGKA adolescents.[35]

Second, Albert said that the content of some chapters is too simple and superficial to discuss in detail. Since the purpose of the series is not to transfer knowledge of Scripture or Christian dogmas, but to strengthen a student-centered learning structure, the focus is on providing food for thought or insightful questions to encourage students' involvement rather than on presenting well-organized lessons. Consequently, the content of the booklet is likely to be narrow or superficial. Albert shared that there was an occasion when the teachers themselves developed one chapter into a four-week program because they believed the topic worth studying in detail.[36]

Educational Activities

In the youth group of the East church, an annual youth camp and an extra Bible study for wishers are provided for students as educational activities.

First, for Mark, the church camp may create an opportunity to encourage teenage students to open their hearts to the gospel. Mark said that the camp should be fun because when students have really enjoyable experiences at the camp they are most likely to open their minds and accept Scripture with their hearts.[37] In the same vein, Albert claimed that the church camp is one of the greatest occasions for youth to encounter God personally. So, in his view, the camp should be prepared as an educational activity. In his opinion, YMJC is also a good vehicle for providing students with such an opportunity.[38]

In addition, an extra Bible study has been organized for wishers on Sundays after lunch. Because Mark leads the young adult service at the same time, the extra session has been led by a Korean guest pastor who is staying in Australia temporarily. Because of a shortage of human resources, Mark has been in charge of the two groups, the youth group and the young adult group, which has some limitations in ministering to the two groups.[39]

35. Judy, interview.
36. Albert, interview.
37. Mark, interview.
38. Albert, interview.
39. Mark, interview.

In relation to the educational activity, it was remarkable to listen to Mark's plan for a discipleship class. He said that he is thinking of beginning a discipleship class for leaders and wishers commencing the following year. His idea of the discipleship class is based on the concept of *life-coaching* which focuses on helping students lead a devout daily life rather than transplanting Christian dogmas or knowledge of the Scripture. For example, he said that the pastor or the teacher in charge of the discipleship class receives a weekly plan of daily devotions from students every week and encourages them to follow the plan. He claimed that church teachers cannot create a warm relationship with their students with only the Sunday Bible study session. They should connect with students during the week. In this respect, his idea of life-coaching seems an alternative to the traditional Sunday group study–centered relationship between teacher and students.

He also argued that the life-coaching should develop into *learning-coaching* because almost every teenage student is concerned about their academic success. Learning coaching means actively helping students' learning at school by providing tutors, study groups, and educational materials. He shared some success stories of the learning-coaching from his former youth ministry in Korea. At that time, he networked with young adult or adult volunteers and connected them to those who needed academic support. The learning-coaching helped a considerable number of students to improve their academic ability, and this connected to their faith development because learning-coaching is grounded on life-coaching for a pious life.[40]

His idea of the discipleship class was remarkable in the sense that it seems a practical plan to bridge the gap between Sundays and weekdays, the gap between church life and family life and even school life. However, there needs to be further study in order to apply such concepts to immigrant adolescents growing up in the context of the Korean ethnic church.

The Youth Group of the Central Church

Sunday Sermon

Ralph, the thirty-eight-year-old youth pastor, has prepared the Sunday sermon according to the content of *Daily Bible*, a Korean monthly

---

40. Ibid.

magazine for quiet time (hereafter QT), a daily individual session of prayer or reading the Bible. The whole congregation of the East church uses the magazine not only for improving their personal devotional life, but also in daily family services at home. The youth group has also participated in the church campaign by using the teenage version of the magazine and its English version for SGKA students as supplementary educational material in addition to the *Westminster Shorter Catechism*, the fixed textbook for group Bible study sessions. Because of a lack of time, teachers cannot deal with the content of the QT magazine in the group study. Instead, Ralph refers to it continually by using its content in his Sunday sermons.

In preparing Sunday sermons based on the order of the QT book, he said that he considers three factors. First, he argues that students should learn and understand Scripture accurately and deeply. Second, from his perspective, they should apply their knowledge of Scripture to their lives. So, he has students consider how what they are learning today will affect their lives. Finally, he expects to see practical changes in students' lives. For him, the signs of change are not only the result of appropriate religious education for students, but also a basis on which to judge whether their religious education is proceeding on the right track.

Textbooks for Group Bible Study

Students of the East church youth group studied the Westminster Shorter Catechism in the group Bible study session before Ralph came to the church as a youth pastor. The senior minister of the East church chose the catechism as the group study textbook not only for youth, but also for children and young adults because he believed that it contains the core principles of Christianity. In his view, the Westminster Shorter Catechism may provide young Christians with the basic truth and groundwork necessary for leading a Christian life. Ralph also agreed with him in relation to the importance of doctrinal education. He argued that through the Westminster Shorter Catechism the God encountered in Scripture can be clearly presented to students as it summarizes all the truths of the Bible's sixty-six books. He claimed that if we Christians do not have certain knowledge of God based on the Scripture, our faith is likely to change depending on the situation. In this regard, he asserted that the purpose of studying the Catechism is to acknowledge the unchangeable character of God based on the Bible and proclaim it with one's heart regardless of one's situations.[41]

The Westminster Shorter Catechism was written by the Westminster Assembly between 1643 and 1649, during the English Civil War. At that time, the assembly produced three doctrinal statements: the Westminster Confession of Faith, the Westminster Larger Catechism, and the Westminster Shorter Catechism. David Anderson argues that "they form the doctrinal foundation of much of modern Presbyterianism."[42] Among them, the Westminster Shorter Catechism is very simple because "it was aimed primarily for children, an 'easy and short' document, as one of its supporters wrote, 'for new beginners.'"[43]

It consists of 107 simple questions; Keum San Baek categorizes them into eight parts as follows: (1) the truth of the Scriptures, Q1–3; (2) the truth of God, Q4–11; (3) the truth of man, Q12–19; (4) the truth of Jesus Christ, Q20–28; (5) the truth of Holy Spirit, Q29–38; (6) the truth of Ten Commandments, Q39–84; (7) the truth of the means of grace, Q85–98; and (8) the truth of Lord's Prayer, Q99–107.[44] Referring to Baek's classification, Ralph has led the group study on the Shorter Catechism in his youth group.

He said that students normally studied a question a Sunday, or sometimes two questions depending on the content since those questions are condensed core doctrines. The questions are provided to students in both languages to help their understanding. Currently, he uses a Korean guidebook for the catechism, *Cartoon Westminster Shorter Catechism*, as a workbook for teachers. Since its core doctrines are cartoonized, he said, the book is very helpful for teachers in understanding the catechism and preparing for the group study with students. Teachers gather once a week with the youth pastor or the senior minister to study the section for the following Sunday, using the Korean guidebook. He said, however, that there is currently no specific material provided to students. Instead, as an educational method, he has students write down the day's question and answer in their notebook and then their own opinion of it.[45] In the case of Sophie, a forty-two-year-old teacher, she said that she prepares

---

41. Ralph, interview.
42. Anderson, "Nature of Faith," 5.
43. Lee, *Understanding and Application*, xii.
44. See Baek and Kim, *Manhwa westminstersogyorimundap2*, 257–331.
45. Ralph, interview.

an introductory document related to the day's content and gives it to her students to help their understanding.[46]

Ralph argued that the greatest strength of studying the Catechism is that students can learn all the truths of Christianity written in the Scriptures and think carefully about the Christian faith. He also believed that students are likely to have objective and biblical standards of the Christian truths about God, Jesus Christ, and the Scriptures by repeatedly studying the historically confirmed confessions of the Christian faith. In addition, since children in his church also learn the Catechism, collaborative education between the children's group and the youth group becomes possible. However, for him, it is hard to find good methodologies or materials for helping students, especially SGKA teenagers, easily understand the Catechism because there are a limited number of guidebooks for young people. Besides, students often think doctrine education is boring, and this needs to be overcome for effective doctrine education.[47]

Sophie also said that it seems beneficial for students to learn all the basic truths of Christianity through the Westminster Shorter Catechism because it contains the essentials of the Christian faith. However, as she explained the meaning of Christian dogmas in Korean, she was concerned about a two-way linguistic difficulty; one, the difficulty of dogmatic terms like Justification or Sanctification, and two, the lack of Korean proficiency of SGKA students. For her, there seem few methods to overcome these difficulties except for repeated learning.[48]

Educational Activities

Ralph said that currently the church camp is a representative educational activity for youth in his church. For him, the annual church camp is a good occasion not only for intensively educating students for faith, but also for strengthening relationships between teachers and students as well as relationships among students. It is remarkable that this youth group, unlike the other three youth groups, does not attend YMJC because of church policy. However, he said that he wants to have his youth attend such joint Christian camps because there are educational benefits. He insisted that students can meet and associate with friends who attend other

46. Sophie, interview.
47. Ralph, interview.
48. Sophie, interview.

Korean churches, which tends to challenge them directly or indirectly. For example, in such camps students might gain confidence in praying or praising God in public through seeing others praying and praising.[49]

A campaign that inspires students to have a daily devotional time is another educational activity in the youth group of the Central church. The campaign has been using the English language-version of a Korean monthly magazine designed for helping teenagers lead QT. It is related to the church's policy to encourage family services at home by using the same magazine. Ralph has supported the campaign by preparing Sunday sermons according to the order of the QT magazine and asking teachers to regularly check whether their students are doing QT. In addition, he said that next year he plans to strengthen this by sending parents a weekly newsletter on the week's QT and asking parents to encourage their children to undertake QT.

Analysis and Implication: Fragmentation of Curriculum

So far, I have discussed the curricula of the four KA church youth groups selected as research sites, investigating three curriculum-related dimensions, namely, the Sunday sermon, textbooks for group Bible study, and educational activities. Among these three curricular events, almost every teacher/pastor participant in the interview project tended to identify curriculum with textbooks for group Bible study sessions. Thus, most of the interviewees' mentions of curriculum were about textbooks for the small group activity of their youth groups. However, since sermons and other educational activities are important curricular facets of the Korean ethnic churches and furthermore they are related to group Bible studies and other group programs in some way, the two aspects should be discussed together with Bible study textbooks.

First, I investigated the Sunday sermons of the four pastors from a curricular perspective. In terms of Sunday sermon, all the pastors in the four youth groups did not preach from the lectionary because lectionary preaching is not popular in the KA churches. Paul, Ben, and Mark prepared Sunday sermons according to their own sermon plans organized by topics or the Bible's books, while Ralph followed the content of a Korean devotional magazine used in his church as a guidebook for QT life.

49. Ralph, interview.

Except Ralph who has a fixed plan for preaching, the other three pastor's sermon plans seem relatively flexible or non-systematic because none of them had a long-term plan for the Sunday sermon. Instead, they all said that they usually have a short-term project like a four- to eight-week plan and prepare the following sermon plan halfway through the current one depending on the situation. This style seems good in terms of flexibility, but it is likely to result in sermons being directionless if the short-term plans are not organized systematically taking into account former sermon projects. In the case of Paul and Ben who use Sunday sermons as a basis for their youth group discussion, their group Bible studies might also lack consistency if their sermons lose coherence.

This phenomenon seems to be closely related to the fact that the Sunday sermon was not considered as a curricular component by any of the four pastors in the interview project. All the four youth pastors did not plan their sermons with a curricular perspective although they thought of the Sunday sermon as a significant educational channel for their youth ministry. In the case of the Southeast church and the Northeast church, although the youth pastor's sermons were used as curricular materials for group Bible studies, Paul and Ben did not consider various curricular dimensions except for educational objectives, such as learning experiences, organization of learning experiences, and evaluation, in preparing Sunday sermon. In this respect, the quality and effectiveness of their sermons and Bible study sessions seemed limited and inconsistent. As a result, many SGKA participants felt that many of their critical issues and interests at home and in school were not attended to consistently and systematically in the Sunday sermons and small group discussions of their youth group.

On the other hand, in the case of the East church and the Central church where Sunday sermons were not used for group Bible studies, the connection between Sunday sermon and other educational events was remarkably weak. Ralph connected his sermons to the QT campaign of his youth group, but the level of relationship between the two factors were relatively superficial, while Mark did not relate his sermons to any other youth activities. I found that many of the sermons of Mark and Ralph were also irrelevant to the lives of SGKA students.

Second, in terms of group study textbooks, there were two kinds of formats: self-designed material for group discussion based on the pastor's sermon and use of a published textbook for group study. At the two youth groups of the Southeast church and the Northeast church, the pastors provided a number of topics for group discussion based on their Sunday sermons, while the youth groups of the East church and the Central church used a published textbook as a fixed curriculum for group Bible study sessions.

In the case of the self-designed material for group discussion, Paul, the youth pastor of the Northeast church, provided teachers with a sermon-related three-question sheet as a guideline for group discussion, whereas Ben, the youth pastor of the Southeast church, did not give such material to teachers, but held a regular teacher's meeting to explain the content and points of his next sermon to help them prepare the group discussion. Both of them decided to design a sermon-centered course of learning for group discussion because they discovered that the previous textbooks used for their group study sessions were not appropriate to the context of their youth groups in terms of topics, cultural preference, and language. They also could not find an alternative. In addition, they believed that group discussion is helpful in encouraging students' active participation (Paul) and improving the degree of flexibility between curriculum and cultural contexts (Ben). However, the absence of curricular concepts and the short-term preparation for their sermons seem to be a significant problem in creating a systematic guideline for group discussion.

On the other hand, youth in the East church use the *Click Bible Series* as a textbook for group Bible study, while those of the Central church study the Westminster Shorter Catechism in small group sessions. Compared to the teachers who lead group discussion based on the pastor's sermon in the other two churches, those in the East church and the Central church seem to have a more solid curriculum in terms of content, reliability and coherence. In addition, there is a well-organized handbook for teachers, which was very different from the youth groups that use self-designed materials. However, in the case of those using a published textbook, transmitting the content is likely to be the main focus rather than encouraging student participation because of the limited group study time. It was noted, however, that this chronic tendency of transmitting knowledge out of context in the religious education of the Korean Australian churches still seems strong even in the discussion-centered group activity because of the teachers' lack of communication skills, insufficient preparation and the superficial relationship between the teacher and students.

In relation to Bible study textbooks, it is also noted that all the curricula of the four KA youth groups were monocultural and did not embrace the different kinds of students in the group. For example, in the case of the Southeast church the ministerial focus was on English-speaking 1.5- or SGKA teenagers, while the other three youth groups were dominated by the Korean-centered orientation. Furthermore, in the course of group Bible study characteristics of today's digital gen students were not actively considered; their digital ways of learning, thinking, and communicating were not part of the methodology of the small group sessions. This monocultural and analog-centered orientation was found in the Sunday sermons of all four youth pastors as well as in almost all group activities.

Finally, I have discussed the educational activities of the four youth groups. The annual youth camp was the common educational event of all the selected youth groups. In the case of the Southeast church, Ben usually invited a guest speaker and organized a conference-centered youth camp, while the other three pastors have themselves prepared special sermons for the camp and emphasized community activities for improving relationships in their youth groups. On the whole, however, those youth camps seemed to be disconnected from ordinary Sunday sermons or group Bible study sessions because they tended to be organized as an annual event rather than as an integrated curricular activity. It was remarkable that all participating youth groups, except for the Central church, have attended YMJC every year believing it helpful for the faith development of their youth.

In addition, the youth groups of the Northeast church and the East church have run an extra Bible study for wishers and both held it on Sundays after lunch. Paul and Mark said that compared to the ordinary group Bible study, most wishers tend to more actively participate in the course of learning in the extra session. It was impressive to listen to Mark's plan for starting life-coaching and learning-coaching as a means of discipleship training for students. In the case of the youth group of the Central church, a campaign for the development of a daily devotional life has proceeded using a Korean monthly magazine designed for helping QT. In the youth group of the Southeast church, there was no educational activity other than the annual church camp.

In relation to the curricula of the four youth groups, it is also noted that while all youth pastors explained the purposes of their educational activities, other curricular factors like learning experiences, organizing principles of their curricular events, and ways of evaluation were little mentioned. Especially in terms of evaluation, there was no reference to the way their educational practices could be evaluated. Consequently, since there are few ways to assess whether their educational efforts are appropriate or to what extent their educational methods are effective, they tend to repeat untested practices without adequate evaluation, which might cause superficial or stagnant education.

To conclude, through analysis of the current curricula of the four KA church youth groups, I found that the curriculum of each of the four youth groups was fragmented in the sense: (1) that the three curricular facets were separated from one another because of the textbook-centered curriculum understanding; (2) that each curriculum tended to be separated from students' daily lives at home and in school not only in its topics and content, but also in ways of learning and communicating; (3) that there was little interest in methods of assessment compared to educators' concern about the purposes of their curricular activities; and (4) that each curriculum was designed for monocultural education in spite of the multicultural environment of the youth groups. As a result, there seemed to be little educational synergy, consistency and improvement in the curriculum planning and practices of the four youth groups.

These four factors indicating the curriculum fragmentation of the four KA church youth groups are by-products of the model of transmitting knowledge-out-of-context. As analyzed in chapter 2, the paradigm of transmitting knowledge-out-of-context is based on Tyler's schooling-instructional approach and analog-based curriculum development, which shows that it is not in accord with the ways of learning, thinking, and communicating of today's SGKA young people. Besides, through examining faith in chapter 3, it was proved that the modern objectivist epistemology on which the model of transmitting knowledge-out-of-context is built is not appropriate for nurturing faith as knowledge of God. Likewise, the current curriculum paradigm of the KA churches is not suitable for religious education for faith and for education for the digital generation. Thus, a new curriculum model for SGKA teenagers should be established on a digital-based curriculum model that overcomes the schooling approach and attends to the curricular issues of the KA church.

8
A Model of Religious Education Curriculum for the Digital Generation

IN THIS CHAPTER, a new religious education curriculum model for second-generation Korean Australian (SGKA) adolescents growing up as a digital generation will be presented in order to overcome educational and curricular problems resulting from the model of transmitting knowledge-out-of-context. The new curriculum model of religious education seeks curriculum innovation for a *digital-oriented curriculum* in order to resolve the limitations of Tyler's standardized curriculum for schooling and the analog-based curriculum approach on which the model of transmitting knowledge-out-of-context is based.

Curriculum Innovation: Digital Oriented Curriculum

As proven in the analysis of interview findings and current curricula of the four KA church youth groups, the model of transmitting knowledge-out-of-context has long dominated the curricula of most Korean Australian (KA) churches. The model is greatly affected by the Tylerian schooling-instructional paradigm. To overcome the curricular limitations caused by the current model, the new paradigm constructed in this chapter will focus on *the contextualization of curriculum* rather than its standardization. The contextualization of curriculum emphasizes the context of students and involves dwelling with others and their individuality.[1]

A standardized curriculum tends to confine students to abstract conceptualization, and does not consider appropriate individual differences such as age and cultural preference. Consequently, it cannot solve various contextual problems generated in a wide range of educational environments. In creating an alternative contextualized framework, Elliot Eisner and Maria Harris's aesthetical curriculum theories and insights

1. Huebner, "Curriculum as Concern," 324–31.

will be considered as the theoretical bases for successfully addressing the limitations of Tyler's standardized curriculum for schooling.

The new model will move a step further to include *the digitalization of curriculum*. In this thesis, digital-based curriculum means a conceptual framework that help teachers understand today's digital generation and educate them in digital ways of learning, thinking, and communicating. It does not mean developing new technology-embedded digital textbooks or resources, but developing a curricular framework to guide educators in using various digital or analog materials more appropriately for religious education. Without appropriate curricular approaches, digital technologies and resources will have limited educational benefits.[2]

The digitalization of curriculum seems critical in terms of curriculum innovation. As the rapid shift from offline-centered analog material culture to the online-offline hybrid digital media culture accelerates, many changes have occurred in society, the economy, culture, education, and politics in terms of forms of communication, social interaction, work processes, and the concepts of time and space. This transformation has had a huge impact on people's lives, especially young people, causing "a generational divide between those born before the Internet Age (1969) and those who grew up being digital."[3] Thus, the traditional paper-based curriculum seems inappropriate for SGKA students who are living in a digital culture unless it is digitized in terms of concepts, resources, forms of communication, and the principles of learning and teaching. To advance the digitization of curriculum, the digital generation should, in the first place, be understood.

The Digital Generation

Young people growing up in a digital culture are dominated by digital ways of learning, thinking, and communicating which are totally different from the traditional offline analog-based modes. Those born in the digital generation are no longer a younger version of the older generation born and raised in the analog age. Steve Anderson and Anne Balsamo describe the younger generation born in the digital age as follows:

> For these students, the process of "thinking" now routinely (and in some cases, exclusively) relies on social network navigation.

2. See Scanlon and Buckingham, "Debating the Digital Curriculum," 191–205.
3. Castells, *Rise of the Network Society*, i.

A Model of Religious Education Curriculum

Data = information = knowledge is their taken-for-granted epistemology, and for many of them, every world is a game, and all the people merely players. Their imaginations are structured and shaped through encounters in different kinds of mediated worlds: RL [real life] and online games, institutional and familial, peer-based and anonymous. They move easily through different kinds of networks: social, technological, material, and virtual. Consequently, their identities are a hybrid of multiple personae performed and shaped through their participation in dispersed (mixed reality) social networks as well as within simulated virtual (gaming) worlds. In this they are the quintessential decentered postmodern subjects marked by differing intensity flows and shifting affinities. Remix is their cultural vernacular.[4]

1. Learning of the Digital Generation: Constructionism

Malcolm Brown argues that for this digital generation, learning means finding information from the various Internet-based sources and from their network members, critically evaluating the credibility of collected data, and integrating verified information to create knowledge. Thus, Brown claims that constructionism is an appropriate learning theory for today's students as follows:

> This theory holds that learners construct knowledge by understanding new information building on their current understanding and expertise. Constructivism contradicts the idea that learning is the transmission of content to a passive receiver. Instead, it views learning as an active process, always based on the learner's current understanding or intellectual paradigm. Knowledge is constructed by assimilating new information into the learner's knowledge paradigm. A learner does not come to a classroom or a course Web site with a mind that is a tabula rasa, a blank slate. Each learner arrives at a learning "site" with some pre-existing level of understanding.[5]

James Gee also argues that in a digital world, learning means not only memorizing fragmented information, but connecting and

---

4. Anderson and Balsamo, "Pedagogy for Original Synners," 244.
5. Brown, "Learning Spaces," 12.4.

manipulating it with a critical perspective.⁶ For Anderson and Balsamo, *creative and critical synthesis* is the most important skill for *digital learning*.⁷ André Mottart, Ronald Soetaert, and Bart Bonamie similarly insist that students living in the digital age are no longer mere audiences for information presented by the teacher. They are producers of new content as well as consumers of existing information through collaborative information sharing with the teacher and peers, and even with strangers in online communities.⁸

In this respect, for members born in the digital generation, school is no longer the primary space for learning as knowledge production. The learning process can occur anytime and anywhere if they have a mobile device like a smartphone or tablet linked by wireless networks.⁹ In the same vein, for today's students, teachers are not considered as the sole experts, but one of a number of reliable sources. Sometimes, a teacher's knowledge might be less current than that of the students or even inaccurate or limited. The accuracy of a teacher's instruction can be checked instantly by students and they can easily access extra information to which the teacher did not refer in the class. In some cases, teachers could ask students to explain some concepts or methods especially in relation to contemporary digital culture and new technologies. In this situation, the traditional boundary between the teacher and students can blur. Teachers should be open to learn from students, while students should be able to contribute their knowledge to the learning process.¹⁰

2. New Meaning of Teacher: Teacher as a Designer

With the new concept of learning and the multiplication of learning spaces in the digital society, a new image of the teacher is being formed: *teacher as a designer*. For example, Mottart, Soetaert, and Bonamie argue that teachers should design appropriate learning environments to enable students to actively and critically participate in the learning process, by using various learning tools and encouraging peer-to-peer information

---

6. See. Gee, *What Video Games Have*, 22–39.

7. Anderson and Balsamo use the term *digital learning*. Anderson and Balsamo, "Pedagogy for Original Synners," 245.

8. Mottart et al., "Digitization and Culture," 31.

9. Anderson and Balsamo, "Pedagogy for Original Synners," 245–46.

10. Mottart et al., "Digitization and Culture," 30–31.

A Model of Religious Education Curriculum

sharing. They propose that a good education depends on the teacher's ability to synthesize and design various resources, connect them to learning topics, and create an appropriate learning environment in which various online-offline learning channels are facilitated. In designing learning processes and environments, teachers should become service persons for students rather than authoritarian administrators.[11]

Anderson and Balsamo argue that for teachers to be educational designers, they should be accustomed to digital ways of learning, thinking, and living so that they may map out a contemporary digital landscape and fully understand the students' disposition. In addition, they should critically accommodate the advantages of new technologies in a dialectic with traditional analog-based learning.[12] Likewise, a new curriculum for the digital generation such as SGKA adolescents should be designed as an educational platform that crosses multiple channels into which the features of digital ways of learning, thinking, and living must be embedded. As Sartia Yardi argues, the framework pursues a model of active, collaborative, and engaged knowledge production.[13]

3. Educational Space: Online-Offline Hybrid Structure

Contemporary people, especially young people growing up with digital technology, lead their lives within a rapidly evolving matrix of online-offline hybrid social networks, instant interactive communication, and mobile information space. The revolution in information and communication technologies has caused huge changes in home, business, education, and social life. The traditional ways of living are rapidly being transformed.

There seems to be no exception in church life. For all church members are living in a digital society. Conventional modes of worship, meeting, and communication have changed markedly by virtue of digital technologies. For example, church has become an online community as well as a local congregation. A considerable number of churches have a church homepage on the World Wide Web on which Sunday sermons, event photos, notices, advertisement for coming events, members' stories, church information, and various useful resources can be accessed

---

11. Ibid., 30–34.
12. Anderson and Balsamo, "Pedagogy for Original Synners," 254–56.
13. Yardi, "Whispers in the Classroom," 144.

not only by church members, but also by anyone who goes to the site. The church homepage tends to be connected to sub-web pages designed for diverse church online-offline hybrid communities, encouraging members to participate in various church online or offline activities. The bigger the church is, the wider the services it can provide. The quality of such online services has already become a major factor in church growth.[14]

Various SNSs and instant messaging services are being actively used as a channel of formal or informal communication and social networking among church members. People can share their personal Facebook, Google+, or Twitter account with other group members and make them friends in order to share with each other their personal or public information such as photos, music, and videos. If a small group has a closed account under the group name within a SNS and invites only group members, it can be a virtual social space in which group members can share their interests more privately. With the spread of smartphones and tablets, real-time communication becomes possible through such an online space. Consequently, communication among church members can be expanded into life beyond the Sunday gathering. This phenomenon is applicable not only to the younger generation, but also to many middle aged people in their forties or fifties who have a certain level of SNS-related knowledge.

Such online social spaces have been actively used by youth groups as well to expand contact points with students and improve their participation. For example, in the case of the four youth groups participating in this research project, three youth groups except for the Central church operate a closed community in Facebook with similar purposes.

Necessity of a Digital-Based Curriculum

From the interview findings and an analysis of the current curricula of the four youth groups, I found that most teacher/pastor informants have not tried to actively introduce features of contemporary digital learning-teaching mode—(1) *learning as knowledge construction* rather than as memorization, (2) *teaching as designing a space for student knowledge construction* rather than as instruction, and (3) *online-offline blended space* rather than offline centered—into their sermons, teachings, and

---

14. All four KA churches participating in this interview project also have their own website.

A Model of Religious Education Curriculum

small group activities in order to adapt to the codes of their teenage students although they agreed that their students are digital generation. A few teachers and pastors introduced multimedia in educational space, used SNSs to communicate with their students, and made a group account of SNS to promote group activities, but the educational success of their efforts was limited due to the language gap, cultural difference, and especially their standardized and analog-based curricular concepts.[15]

At this point, the insight of Anderson and Balsamo in terms of using digital technologies is worth considering. They argue that if new methodologies and technologies are introduced indiscreetly without a set of philosophical, pedagogical, and curricular commitments, such application-centered strategies tend to end in failure. Thus, they claim, "We must therefore proceed from a set of flexible commitments that find resonances in the technologies we elect to use and develop."[16] In this regard, to educate adequately those born in the digital generation, the religious education curriculum should be suitably innovative. Contextualization of curriculum is still critical, but it is not enough; the role of the teacher's imagination and cognitive pluralism still seem to be essential in the learning space, however there should be more within the digital learning-teaching process. What we religious educators need today is the digitization of curriculum beyond its contextualization. It is a must rather than a choice. The statement of Doune Macdonald illustrates the reason for this:

> While the literature in the curriculum field recognizes the difficulty in creating meaningful curriculum change within current school structures, the majority of innovations and analyses are blind to the bigger and more significant questions surrounding change: Who are the young people in schools? And what, where and how do they learn? If curriculum reform continues to focus upon subjects, teachers, school-based lessons, and other modernist structures of schools that obfuscate difference, meaningful learning and the impact of technology, the reform movement will become more irrelevant to the lives of young people. "Blind," "floundering," and "failure" will be apt.[17]

---

15. Some SGKA informants also shared that it is a bit difficult to promote such a group online community with a few reasons such as the age gap and cultural difference among students and the indifference of some students and teachers to SNS.

16. Anderson and Balsamo, "Pedagogy for Original Synners," 254.

17. Macdonald, "Curriculum Change," 147.

Since the digital-oriented curriculum should be accord with today's students growing up in the digital age, it needs to promote the digital learning-teaching process—learning as knowledge construction, teaching as designing a space for student knowledge construction, and online-offline hybrid structure. For this to happen, the development of a digital-based curriculum should be undertaken on the basis of the characteristics of digital culture discussed in chapter 2. That is, a digital-based curriculum is grounded on the service-oriented paradigm instead of component-based modularity and suitable for digital mass self-communication rather than analog mass communication. A service-oriented paradigm generates: (1) open-flat collaboration networks; and (2) prompt, polyarchic, and nonlinear services. In addition, mass self-communication focuses on: (3) interactive and horizontal modes of communication; and (4) online-offline hybrid space. These four characteristics of the digital era should be embedded in the digital-based religious education curriculum for today's SGKA students, in which the features of digital learning-teaching mode can be appropriately encouraged.[18]

A New Model: Curriculum as Software

Curriculum as software is a conceptual framework for understanding digital ways of learning, thinking, and communicating and for helping teachers educate the digital generation suitably for their ways of living. The concept of software seems appropriate for describing what the digital-based curriculum should be.

The concept of software provides an alternative image to the longstanding hardware image of curriculum in Tyler's standardized approach. Many scholars have criticized Tyler's concept of curriculum as hardware. For example, Mary Boys has criticized Tyler's curriculum approach as a production-oriented curriculum.[19] In the same vein, Pamela Mitchell argued that Tyler's curricular rationale is a blueprint for curriculum

---

18. Since digital-oriented curriculum is based on a service-centered and mass self-communication paradigm, it seems an economic-based model of curriculum. However, digital-oriented curriculum is based not only on economic, but also on a social, cultural, cognitive, and epistemological paradigm in which digital ways of thinking, learning, and communicating are addressed and integrated. In a digital-based curriculum, students are not only consumers, but also creators, distributers, and re-creators.

19. Boys, *Biblical Interpretation*, 207.

production.[20] Elliott Eisner insisted that under Tyler's standardized curriculum model curriculum development is like assembling components in the assembly line in a factory.[21] Eisner argued that curriculum as hardware cannot be applied to all educational environments because educational spaces are not like factories.[22] Arthur Applebee also claimed that curriculum as hardware is "perfectly appropriate to a curriculum that construes knowledge as fixed and transmittable—as something 'out there' to be memorized by students.... Such a curriculum of knowledge-out-of-context may enable students to do well on multiple-choice items."[23]

Curriculum as software, on the contrary, underlines being optimized suitably for educational environments and users rather than production itself. The core of curriculum as software is focusing on a process to fit the particular educational environment and the particular users—teachers and students—for whom a curriculum is designed. Thus, the construction of curriculum as software is not a one-time production, but a continual process to be updated and upgraded according to the specific educational space and users. Curriculum as software is also appropriate for individualization and customization of curriculum which is against the standardization of curriculum. Considering that Diana Oblinger and James Oblinger argue that individualization and customization are critical in teaching the digital generation,[24] curriculum as software is a suitable framework for educating today's SGKA young people growing up in the digital age.

In addition, the concept of software provides scaffolding suitable for embracing the characteristics of the digital culture. Analog culture is closely connected to component-based modularity and mass communication, while digital culture is based on service-oriented modularity and mass self-communication. Analog ways of working are intertwined with the modern manufacturing paradigm focusing on a hierarchical network of collaboration in which users are regarded as passive receivers. It is also based on a mode of mass communication in which information transmission is most likely to be unilateral and in most cases happens in offline spaces. On the other hand, digital ways of working are done within

20. Mitchell, "What Is 'Curriculum'?," 363.
21. Eisner, *Educational Imagination*, 361.
22. Ibid., 7.
23. Applebee, *Curriculum as Conversation*, 32–33.
24. Oblinger and Oblinger, "Is It Age or IT," 2.16.

a service-oriented paradigm emphasizing continual updates, open-flat collaboration networks, interactive and horizontal communication, and online-offline hybrid spaces. These four digital features will be embedded in the development process of curriculum as software in which the three features of digital learning-teaching mode—learning as knowledge construction, teaching as designing a space for student knowledge construction, and online-offline blended space—are emphasized.

First, curriculum as software is designed on the basis of an open-flat collaboration network mode in which curriculum is no longer the exclusive property of a small number of professionals. Instead, the curriculum planning process should be open not only to a small number of scholars, professional educators, and church leaders, but also to teachers, parents, and even students. The process of decision making would then be flat rather than hierarchical. The opportunity would be also open to the whole congregation in the church so that all church members may take responsibility for faith education for the following generation rather than such responsibility being limited to the Sunday School ministry.

Second, curriculum as software is service oriented. Like software, the service that curriculum pursues requires maintenance, repair, and ultimately upgrade. The reliability and durability of a curriculum depends largely on the quality of service. The service should be prompt, accurate, and service oriented. To do this, curriculum developers should continually connect to users and listen to their problems and suggestions. Then, such user experiences must be embedded in service packs for fixing problems and/or improving functions in the next upgraded version. This integrating service model of maintenance, repair, and upgrade is a key characteristic of curriculum as software. Under this concept, curriculum planning would be a continually upgraded process being connected with the former and the next version rather than a one-time product.

Third, curriculum as software is developed within an interactive and horizontal communication mode. Traditionally, teachers have tended to be regarded as users of curriculum; they use it in order to educate their students. Students seem to have been considered as a mass audience for teacher-centered instruction according to the curriculum. In this situation, the main form of communication in class is most likely to be one-way, so there seems little room for students to participate in and contribute to the learning process. On the other hand, within the new religious education curriculum model, students as well as teachers are users of curriculum. Students should be able to use curriculum as

A Model of Religious Education Curriculum

software freely so that they may create knowledge themselves analyzing all information obtained through given educational resources or activities within their educational contexts. The teacher's major role is to help them do it appropriately by designing learning space through integrating the educational environment, educational materials, and the curriculum.

Finally, for promoting a digital learning-teaching process based on active two-way communication between the teacher and students, educational spaces should be mobile. Traditionally, communication between the two parties has been class-bound, resulting in many limitations such as time restraints and class atmosphere. However, if educational environments are expanded to an online-offline hybrid from the offline-only mode, opportunities for student-centered communication would be increased.[25] Within the online-offline hybrid structure, educational practices and communication can occur outside educational institutions. Especially in the case of church based religious education, educational practices can continue even on weekdays.

As such, curriculum as software is a good framework for embracing the four characteristics of digital culture, that the digital ways of learning-teaching interaction may be appropriately fostered.

Designing a Curriculum as Software: Four Stages

Under the new concept of curriculum as software, curriculum is considered all educational activities designed for obtaining educational benefits beyond the textbook-centered curriculum understanding. Thus, in the process of curriculum development, various curricular factors including textbooks, sermons, camps, or excursions, should be developed together and integrated with each other within a certain curricular perspective for getting educational synergy. For instance, when developing a Bible

---

25. Glen Smith and Hermann Kurthen divide the online-offline hybrid learning structure into three forms depending on the level of utilization of online activities: web-enhanced, blended, and hybrid. A *Web-enhanced* course is the first stage e-learning; in it only a few online documents such as a syllabus are available. On the contrary, in a *blended* course, more diverse online activities are introduced like online quizzes and online discussions. They argue that in a blended course such online activities make up less than 45 percent. If the rate of such online activities is more than 45 percent and less than 80 percent, the course is *hybrid*. On the other hand, they describe a class with 80 percent or more e-learning as *fully online*. In this book, an online-offline hybrid learning space means the blended and hybrid courses. See Smith and Kurthen, "Front-Stage and Back-Stage," 457.

study course, not only content and unit structure of the new course, but also appropriate Sunday sermons and extra activities should be designed as educational channels for maximizing the educational effects of the new Bible session. An example of developing a Bible Study program for SGKA teenagers within the model of curriculum as software will be presented as follows.

The design process of curriculum as software is based on the basic procedure of software programming: *analysis, design, simulation,* and *service.*[26] These four stages are not based on a linear process, but a spiral movement. Service, the last stage, is oriented to updates and upgrades, so is directly related to the analysis stage of the next version of curriculum.[27]

1. Analysis

The first step is analysis. Analysis is advance preparation for designing a course. There are a number of critical assessments to be undertaken in this phase before fashioning a curriculum.

First, the former curriculum is analyzed. This is a stage for a critical evaluation of the former curriculum, which is a significant starting point for curriculum development. At this stage, curriculum planners should critically investigate the pros and cons of the previous curriculum in light of any new information, and then decide what to keep, what to improve, and what to give up in the construction of new curriculum. In this process, educational critique is critical to illuminate the qualities of the former educational programs.[28] For Eisner, educational criticism means *the art of disclosure.*[29] He argues that to disclose hidden values

---

26. Jiang et al., "Exploration of the Relationship," 279–81.

27. In the new curriculum model, the primary role of the teacher is to help students realize God's revelation for them. To help each learner achieve God's will, the teacher should assist students to comprehend God's revelation as a partner of God, and should also understand their needs as a service person. It is noted that the starting point for Christian education should not be the needs of students, but God's revelation for each student. However, identification of God's revelation for each student is a challenge. For this, as I presented in the section on Implications for the Religious Education Curriculum in chapter 3, religious education for faith should be pedagogia Dei, faith community centered, prayer centered and participation focused education. These four implications can be a framework and process for the teacher to help students realize God's will for them. This new model has integrated the four points.

28. Eisner, "Preparing Teachers," 105.

29. Eisner, *Educational Imagination*, 215.

A Model of Religious Education Curriculum

and meanings of educational practices, educational connoisseurship is essential. "Connoisseurship, generally defined, is the art of appreciation. It is essential to criticism because without the ability to perceive what is subtle and important, criticism is likely to be superficial or even empty."[30]

Educational criticism based on educational connoisseurship is also necessary in the second phase of analysis which is user experience evaluation. User experience in relation to the former curriculum should be examined by listening to the teachers and students who have used the curriculum. Their dispositions, opinions, and understanding in terms of curriculum need to be investigated along with their curricular preferences, experience of difficulties and suggestions for a richer curriculum. The evaluation of user experience should reveal curricular characteristics in given educational environments and their advantages and/or limitations. This curricular data should be addressed in the development of a new curriculum.

Third, based on the results of curriculum evaluation and analysis of user experience, curricularists determine the direction, goals, and content of the new course. Under the new curriculum model, the new course should be a framework for integration of the educational environment, resources, and users so that students can achieve new educational outcomes by creating their own knowledge through a creative and critical synthesis of diverse learning opportunities in the course. The new educational program ought not to be undertaken solely within a teacher-centered instructional paradigm. Instead, the new pedagogical ideas should be achieved through students' active involvement in knowledge construction within their educational situations.

2. Design: Interactive Communication-Based Design

Curriculum as software should be designed on the basis of a teacher-student interactive communication paradigm. The whole design process should be open to all youth group members and church members so that they may participate and interact freely in the process. The role of curriculum planners is to network people, create a space for them to participate in the design process, and integrate people's ideas so as to be appropriate to the educational context. There are three design processes:

---

30. Ibid.

course structure design, unit structure design, and the design of educational materials.

First, curriculum designers set out the whole framework based on the direction, goals, and content of the new course determined at the analysis stage. At this stage, topics and questions for the organization of units are necessary for the overall design.

For example, suppose that after analyzing the former curriculum and listening to the feedback from users curriculum planners decide to launch a new Bible study course with the title "Prayers in the Old Testament." The main purpose of the new program is to have students learn about the power of prayer from characters in the Bible and to lead a life of prayer themselves. The chosen topic for unit organization is "Contexts of Prayer." According to the theme, after discussing and listening to diverse members, six units are composed as follows: Repent (e.g., Hezekiah's prayer), Despair (e.g., Hannah's prayer), Intercession (e.g., Abraham's prayer), Commitment (e.g., Jeremiah's prayer), Praise (e.g., David's prayer), and Ministry (e.g., Joshua's prayer). Each unit also has a few subunits related to the subtopic.

Curriculum designers should then integrate each unit so that students may learn the overall content repeatedly, for instance, by continually revisiting previous topics with a new perspective. For such an intertwined unit structure, the relationships among the units should be emphasized and reorganized. Applebee describes it as an *integrated curriculum*. He stresses the importance of integration of each part as follows:

> Though such a course must begin somewhere, books and ideas introduced early will be continually reconstrued as new ideas are encountered. As the course continues, participants will construct a shared representation of the curricular domain, and may very well redefine the topic with which they began. The knowledge they develop will be richly contextualized knowledge-in-action, developed through sustained conversation about related ideas.[31]

This integration of each unit is very important so as to enable students to synthesize the information and knowledge obtained in the learning process of the course. Otherwise, they may have fragmented knowledge-out-of-context. The primary concern of course design is to build educational scaffolding for students to create knowledge

---

31. Applebee, *Curriculum as Conversation*, 77–78.

A Model of Religious Education Curriculum

themselves rather than passively receive it from teachers. To do this, the course should be considered as the domain in which the skills of creative and critical integration of diverse information are emphasized and developed. For the teacher and students to fully understand the course as a framework for digital learning, if necessary, *a preparation unit* can be provided before beginning the course in order to explain why curriculum as software should be implemented for educating the digital generation and how they do it under the new curriculum model.

Second, in this stage various educational activities are also organized in reference to the whole framework of the new Bible study program in order to have educational synergy and lead holistic education. For instance, a Sunday sermon series can be prepared in relation to the determined theme of the new course. In addition to its content, Sunday sermons can be a domain for basic or advanced learning for the new Bible course by introducing various formats like drama, talk-show, or testimony. Furthermore, extra educational activities can be planned, such as excursions or mini-camp. For example, considering the new Bible program theme is "Context of Prayer," curriculum designers might be able to plan a Sunday excursion to a memorable place related to prayer. Such extra activities can be a good vehicle for students to realize the purpose of planned educational programs. At this point, curriculum developers' creative imagination and cognitive pluralism are essential.

Likewise, the course structure design attends not only to the whole plan of a program in terms of content, but also to other educational events for maximizing the educational effects of new courses.

The 4R Movement

Once the course structure is designed, the unit structure should be constructed. Since the purpose of curriculum as software is to encourage students to integrate all the results of the learning practices and create their own knowledge, the skills of critical synthesis should be fostered in a teaching-learning process in each unit. Here, the teaching-learning process encouraging student knowledge construction for digital learning is called the 4R movement: *reflection, reinterpretation, re-formation,* and *re-creation*. The teacher should lead a class based on the 4R scheme so that students can create knowledge themselves through synthesizing diverse concepts and ideas. Considering that the group Bible study class in KA church youth groups is normally thirty to forty minutes in length, each stage should be less than ten minutes. The teacher might be able to organize the four movements flexibly depending on topics and situations.

The first movement is reflection. Reflection provides a domain for students to think about and express their ideas on the day's topic. The teacher should encourage students to reflect upon what they are learning rather than instruct them to memorize it. Reflection may start with a few questions related to the day's topic. For instance, suppose that today's topic is about Hannah's prayer (1 Sam 1:10–18), the second subunit in the topic of *despair*. A teacher may ask the teenage students to research a few questions in some resources given to them or on the Internet with their own smartphone, like: Who is Hannah? Why did she pray to God? What happened to her? Why did she commit Samuel to God? The students could then summarize the results of their search, and prepare a one-minute presentation rather than the teacher explaining it.[32]

In the process of searching, summarizing, and preparing a briefing, students can reflect upon the questions themselves. This is just an example of reflection. The bottom line is that, at this stage, the teacher should encourage students to reflect upon the day's topic themselves. To do this effectively, the teacher needs educational imagination. When there is a lack of time or other difficulties in designing reflection time in a class, the teacher could give students homework to prepare for the next Sunday's topic by using various reference books or the Internet at home and summarizing the results in a short report in their own language for presentation the following Sunday.[33] In this way, weekdays become reflection time, and the teacher can begin the class on Sunday from the second stage after listening to each student's presentation prepared at home.

The second movement is reinterpretation. Here, students are provided with opportunities to rethink, broaden, and deepen their ideas about the day's topic which have been generated in the process of earlier reflection. Listening to other people's ideas, watching an insightful movie clip, or learning Bible stories and reading theological comments in relation to the topics are good methods for students to reinterpret their opinions. To continue the above example, after searching the given

---

32. In the case of SGKA student participants in this research project, most of them had a smartphone.

33. Lee Vukich and Steve Vandegriff underline the importance of assignment in religious education for youth referring to the principle of readiness. Vukich and Vandegriff, *Timeless Youth Ministry*, 306–8.

A Model of Religious Education Curriculum

questions, summarizing, and preparing a presentation of Hannah's prayer in the class or as homework, students are given a chance to present their ideas about the topic. After listening to all the students' ideas, the teacher should epitomize them in order for students to keep them in mind. The teacher can then show an insightful video clip or picture, play music, or tell a story related to the topic in order to help students participate in the process of reinterpretation. Various ideas, comments, insights, questions, or challenges might stir students into reinterpretation of their experiences and opinions, and ultimately into contemplating God's ideas. Reinterpretation is preparation for the next movement, re-formation.

Third, re-formation is a movement where students are encouraged to re-form their ideas on the topic by critically synthesizing diverse information obtained through the reflection and reinterpretation stages. Compared to the process of reinterpretation in which students are encouraged to view the topics from new angles and so enlarge the range of their knowledge, in the stage of re-formation they are invited to further create new knowledge by critically evaluating given information in a process of creative dialogue with peers and the teacher. Re-formation is the stage in which learning as knowledge construction takes place in the 4R movement.

Conversation with other students, especially with those who have different values and ideas, seems to be helpful for students in synthesizing diverse information to create their own knowledge. For, as Robert Slavin argues, "in their discussions of the content, cognitive conflicts will arise, inadequate reasoning will be exposed, and higher-quality understandings will emerge."[34] For this, the teacher invites students to participate in discussion of the topic. At this point, the teacher's ability to create insightful, biblical, and discussable questions that can intrigue students is essential. The conversational skills of teachers in creatively leading group discussion are also important to help students participate actively. In designing and leading group discussion, the teacher has students revisit previous units with the day's topic so that students may understand the day's learning in a more integrated perspective. Depending on topics or situations, the teacher can choose various discussion formats, for example, free talking, panel discussion, team debate, the forum or colloquy.[35]

---

34. Slavin, *Cooperative Learning*, 16.

35. For more information of various methods in group discussion, see Vukich and Vandegriff, *Timeless Youth Ministry*, 331–54.

The final movement is re-creation. Re-creation is the time when students create their new life based on new knowledge or insights constructed through former three stages. Re-creation is the ultimate purpose of a unit designed according to the 4R movement and further becomes a starting point for reflection on the following units. At this time, it is particularly important to provide students with various opportunities to put their thoughts in order and then express them in their own language in order to bear in mind what they have newly realized. The teacher should focus on encouraging students to respond holistically rather than simply intellectually to what they have learnt that day. This should be the call to obedience rather than memorization. Re-creation is the stage in which students decide to re-create their knowledge and life style in relation to the day's topic into obedience. Without the determination to obey, the knowledge obtained in the class is likely to be at best intellectual belief rather than faith as holistic knowledge of God.[36]

It is noted that various creative methods are needed depending on topics or situations in order to design and lead the process of re-creation appropriately. As an example, writing a journal seems a good way for students to re-create their knowledge and life style into obedience. Here, as guidance, the teacher can suggest a few questions, like: "What did you feel was most impressive or challenging today?" and, "What will you do in your life in relation to such insights?" In the course of writing a short statement, students might be able to summarize what they learnt and felt through reflection, reinterpretation, and re-formation, and then determine to re-create their lives. In addition, if students upload their journals to their online community as blogs or Facebook at the end of the class or as an assignment, they might be able to revisit it later with new experiences and check how they re-created their lives after the determination. Revisiting such journals might be a good opportunity to be connected with another reflection, reinterpretation, re-formation, and re-creation. Furthermore, parents can follow their children's learning progress and encourage them by writing a comment, which might provide another educational possibility. Although many teenagers would be reluctant to open their social media to their parents, it could be a good educational

---

36. As indicated in chapter 3, Calvin and Barth commonly emphasized the importance of obedience in knowing God. For them, obedience is not only an essential fruit of faith, but also a starting point for faith through building a close relationship with God. Thus, from their perspectives, without obedience it seems impossible to have faith.

A Model of Religious Education Curriculum

channel for encouraging parents to participate in the process of religious education and engage in an educational dialogue with their children. However, when using the online community as a learning space, education on issues of privacy is necessary to protect student privacy.[37]

The parable of the Good Samaritan in Luke 10:25–37 is a good example of education based on the 4R movement. One day, a scholar of religion stood up to test Jesus, asking, "Teacher, what must I do to inherit eternal life?"[38] Jesus did not answer the question directly. Instead, he asked the lawyer to reflect and express his idea, replying, "What is written in the Law? How do you read it?"[39] The scholar presented his opinion: "Love the Lord your God with all your heart and with all your soul and with all your strength and with all your mind; and love your neighbor as yourself."[40] This is reflection. After listening to his ideas, Jesus commented on it and challenged him to live so. Then, the person responded promptly, asking "Who is my neighbor?"[41] Jesus answered by telling a story, the parable of the Good Samaritan. In it, Jesus drew a strong contrast between those who know the law and those who practice the law in their lives. Furthermore, he argued that the spirit of the law is beyond people's racial, religious, and cultural prejudice. The story was possibly a shock to the religious scholar. This is reinterpretation where new ideas or unexpected directions are encountered.

Reinterpretation is closely intertwined with re-formation. After finishing the parable, Jesus asked him, "Which of these three do you think was a neighbor to the man who fell into the hands of robbers?"[42] The lawyer replied that the one who had mercy on him was a neighbor to the needy. In Scripture, there is no information about how the scholar responded, how long it took until he answered, or to what extent his reaction was sincere, but at least his answer shows that his idea of neighbor

---

37. It is also noted that education for using technology responsibly should be offered to students regularly in order to cope with various ethical issues related to using technology such as sexting, cyber-stalking, and cyber-bullying. Preparing students to be responsible digital citizens is critical for achieving education benefits through the new paradigm. In this model, it is essential for students to actively participate and contribute in the process of learning as knowledge construction through using technology in our digital age.

38. Luke 10:25 NIV.

39. Ibid.

40. Luke 10:27 NIV.

41. Luke 10:29 NIV.

42. Luke 10:36 NIV.

was undergoing re-formation. Seeing that the scholar's opinion was being re-formed, Jesus encouraged him to create a true life through re-creating his beliefs: "Go and do likewise."[43] This is an invitation or a challenge to a re-creation of his life.

The 4R movement seems suitable for curriculum as software. In each stage, students seem to be able to actively participate in the learning process and create knowledge themselves by searching, summarizing, evaluating, discussing, integrating, and collaborating with the teacher and other peers. It is noted that the teacher's educational and religious imagination, cognitive pluralism, and their spirituality being open to the work of the Holy Spirit are definitely needed for them to guide 4R based education.[44]

In addition, the teacher should consider (1) all dimensions of faith, (2) the life context of students, and (3) the educational issues of the KA church as filters in designing a unit suitable for SGKA young people to develop faith, lest the unit should be another type of transmitting knowledge-out-of-context. For this, it is helpful to constantly refer to the chart (table 5) indicating all the factors to be considered in establishing a curriculum as software for SGKA adolescents growing up in the KA church. Since it seems impossible to embrace all aspects in a unit, it is necessary to decide what characteristics are to be addressed or avoided in the particular unit. However, it does not mean that analog ways of learning and communicating, such as linear/logical access, processing one thing at a time, text based teaching, teaching as talking, and memorization emphasized structure, should be renounced in curriculum as software. On the contrary, the teacher should utilize both approaches in a balanced way depending on topic and context. I found that a considerable number of SGKA informants prefer a blended approach between analog and digital ways in their educational context.

---

43. Luke 10:37 NIV.

44. As all terms have pros and cons, the terms—reflection, reinterpretation, re-formation, and re-creation—have strong and weak points simultaneously. The terminology of 4R movement, however, appropriately contains the educational philosophy and epistemology for which the new curriculum model pursues. For example, the name "reflection" can emphasize the importance of student's thinking and reasoning. The name "reinterpretation" can stress that student should be provided various opportunities to rethink, broaden, and deepen their ideas about the day's topic. The title "re-formation" can highlight the importance of student's learning as knowledge construction rather than transmitting-knowledge-out-of-context. The final stage of "re-creation" aims for life changing through continual obedience.

Table 5. Three Filters for Designing a 4R Movement Embedded Unit

Faith	Life Context of SGKA Teenagers	Educational Issues of The KA Churches
1. Personal	1. Multicultural Society	1. Textbook-Centered Education
2. Spiritual	– Twofold Identity Development	2. Disconnection From Student' Lives at School and Home
3. Participatory	2. Digital Culture	
4. Communal	– Open-Flat Collaboration Network	3. Absence of Educational Evaluation
	– Service Oriented	
	– Interactive Communication	4. Monocultural Education
	– Offline-Online Hybrid Space	

Once the whole course and the structure of each unit are established, materials and activities suitable for each unit should be provided, considering educational contexts and user status. At this time, curriculum developers need to interconnect with the various extra events planned at the stage of the course structure design. There are two ways of designing educational materials available at the level of church based religious education: *self-design with selective approach* and *joint design in a project team*. There are pros and cons for both approaches, so curriculum planners should select one of them depending on the course topics or situations. The whole course structure and the 4R movement should be foundational frameworks for designing educational materials for each unit.

First, it is necessary to select appropriate sections from a wide range of resources and reorganize them suitably for the specific unit, because it seems extremely hard to find a single resource suited to the new program. It is particularly important that curriculum designers should utilize various resources chosen intentionally on the basis of the 4R movement considering the whole course structure so that all unit materials may be designed to be systematically interconnected. If such a selective approach is taken, curriculum planners with rich educational imagination might be able to see there are a variety of educational resources from various disciplines available to them. In order to supply students with diverse materials and programs, online-offline blended resources should be utilized.

Curriculum designers need to be content curators. Content curation is the process of searching for appropriate content in the vast amounts of source material and adding value to it.[45] In this sense, a content curator is a person who filters various sources of information online as well as offline with professional and creative perspectives, selects content that is appropriate for the topic and the context, and organizes and shares it in a way that is relevant for the unit of work.[46] As a content curator, curriculum planners should look at a range of resources, assess the educational implications, and decide which resource seems appropriate for their students, teachers, and situations. Otherwise, their collected educational materials might be fragmented, incoherent, and inappropriate for use in particular educational environments.

To curate content, curriculum designers should realize that this is the era of mass self-communication in which people not only consume content, but also recreate, reorganize, and distribute them creatively through various channels using micro media such as SNSs and blogs. It is noted that recently lots of curation platforms based on social media have emerged, such as *Flipboard*, *Pinterest*, or *Scoop.it*. These services provide platforms to collect information from various sources of mass and micro media. Users of such services can share their curated content with friends using SNSs directly in the platform. As such, SNSs are not only micro media for personal communication, but also a curation platform themselves in which a flow of information and recent trends are discovered. Thus, curriculum designers as content curators should have SNS channels not only to communicate with their students and teachers, but also as a way of being open to new developments. Relevant content curation might decide on the quality of the collected resources and their relevance for educational practice.

At this stage, there are two issues to be considered. The first issue is about copyright permission. Curriculum designers and teachers should

---

45. Abrams et al., "Emergent Micro-Services," 173.
46. Wuebben, *Content Is Currency*, 247.

be very careful not to infringe copyright in using online or offline resources in religious educational activities. Many church members seem to assume that they can use online or offline materials for educational purposes in a church setting without the copyright owner's permission. However, churches in Australia do not have a general exemption from copyright law. Australian Copyright Council states, "There are no general provisions in the Copyright Act allowing churches to use copyright material without the copyright owner's permission. Under copyright law, churches and other religious organizations are in the same position as non-profit organizations, companies, local councils and individuals."[47]

Sharing content with other people via SNSs or SNS-connected curation platforms or linking to it in websites or blogs is relatively secure from copyright issues because both of them just provide a link to original content. However, when posting content on websites or blogs, emailing it, or using it offline by printing or photocopying, curriculum developers and teachers should check for copyright information related to the material before using it.[48] If copyright has expired or there is a special copyright statement such as *Creative Commons License* (CCL) that allows the use and distribution of copyrighted work under certain conditions, they can use it in accordance with the conditions.[49] Otherwise, they should get the copyright owner's consent or a license from the authorized agency in order to reproduce, communicate or adapt it.

However, there are some special situations in which church members do not need permission or a license to use copyright material. For example, when their use of content is fair dealing for research, review, parody, or criticism, when they perform live music during church services including weddings and funerals, when they play recorded music for the benefit of the church in church activities, when they make a copy by hand in Sunday School classes, or when they screen small sections of a film for educational instruction in Sunday School classes, they do not need the copyright owner's permission if they clearly indicate the source.[50] The matter of copyright is very complex, so to avoid infringing copyright, church groups need to be educated in regard to copyright law.

47. Australian Copyright Council, "Churches and Copyright."

48. Australian Copyright Council, "Websites & Copyright."

49. For more information of *Creative Commons License*, see van Eechoud and van der Wal, "Creative Commons Licensing."

50. See. Australian Copyright Council, "Churches and Copyright"; Australian Copyright Council, "Films, DVDs, Videos and TV." For accounts of the fair dealing

The second issue is about the time needed to find and organize diverse resources. One method for resource management is to make a database for educational materials. If curriculum planners systematically collect good resources in their database and index them, it will save time and energy massively. In addition, as discussed above, for effective data collection through content curation and time-saving, it is recommended to utilize SNSs or SNS-connected curation platforms appropriately and creatively.

Curriculum planners can also design educational materials for each unit by forming a project team out of youth group teachers, church members, and even external guests. After the project team has been composed, all the team members gather regularly to be educated about the purpose and design of the new course, the whole course structure, and the unit structure based on the 4R movement. A unit is then allotted to one or two members respectively with basic information supplied like the unit title and related Bible passages; each member should design materials based on the 4R system. After all unit materials are submitted, the whole team gathers together again to be informed of other unit materials and to discuss them in order to improve the level of quality and to coordinate the units into a program.

The whole process of joint design would normally take two to three months. This project team–styled design also meets the two issues discussed above: copyright and time. For the satisfactory process of joint design, the role of curriculum planners is essential. For efficient collaborative work, it is recommended that curriculum planners use cloud computing based services such as *Dropbox*, *Evernote*, or *Google Drive*. Utilizing such services allows all members of the team to share content in real time anywhere as soon as the material is uploaded into a shared directory. It also allows prompt discussion of the appropriateness of the collected data, which might save time and energy.

3. Simulation

The third stage of developing a course is simulation that is inevitable as in the process of software development. Software is created through repetitive simulations. At this stage, software developers check whether the software operates according to their design. If problems are found, they need to discover the source of the problems, fix them and simulate again.

---

exceptions, see Australian Copyright Council, "Fair Dealing."

A Model of Religious Education Curriculum

Only after they confirm that the software operates without a problem, will it be released to customers.

The process of simulation is also very significant in planning a course in curriculum as software. Since curriculum as software pursues a contextualized curriculum suitable for the educational environment and the users, the level of suitability must be checked through simulation. In addition, as the primary purpose of curriculum as software is to encourage students to create knowledge by synthesizing diverse information, curriculum designers should investigate how appropriate each unit of the new course is in providing students with a framework for knowledge construction by simulating the course. Thus, simulation seems indispensable in designing curriculum as software.

To simulate the new course, curriculum designers first choose a teacher and a small number of students to be a pilot group. They explain curriculum as software to the teacher and students in the pilot group who will implement a month-long sample unit of the new course to be a framework for knowledge construction, leading the class based on the 4R system. After simulating sample units within a specified period, curriculum planners will analyze the results of simulation in light of the analysis and design of the new course. In the course of such simulation analysis, some aspects would become more central and other factors less central, which would be helpful in addressing weak points and improving the new course. The improved course needs to be simulated again to confirm that the changes are appropriate.

4. Service

The final stage of planning curriculum as software is service. Traditionally, the construction process of a curriculum tends to finish as soon as the curriculum is released to the public. However, under the new curriculum model, the level of success of the new course depends on the quality of curricular service after release. The service for curriculum users focuses on maintenance, repair, and upgrade of the structure and content of units, considering any change to the educational environment and the users' status. For example, to provide teachers with various opportunities to prepare effectively for the next sessions or to equip them with a wide range of creative resources on a regular basis, services for maintenance are required. If there are reports of difficulties in relation to structure, methodology, or content, curriculum planners should check whether those problems are limited to certain units or groups or found in all units or groups, and then should take appropriate follow-up measures depending on what is necessary to fix them. This is service for repair. Difficulties and their solutions should be recorded and reflected upon thoroughly in the process of designing the next curriculum for upgrade.

To carry out these services, curriculum designers should always be connected with users—teachers and students, being sensitive to their experiences and suggestions. With the new curriculum model, curriculum as software, the role of church curriculum planners cannot be limited to selecting or making materials. Rather, their primary role should be serving users as they lead their classes to be a domain for knowledge construction, by continually designing and redesigning learning environments and educational practices through the continuing curricular process of analysis, design, simulation, and service. To create a group or a page in Facebook is a good way to connect users online as well as offline and facilitate their interaction by receiving their feedback and providing solutions or general information related to curriculum in the space.

Curriculum Education: Recruiting Curriculum Coordinators

For this alternative model to be realized in the educational environments of the KA church, I argue that education about curriculum is critical. One of the important reasons that various new curriculum models could not be adequately applied to church educational practices until now seems to be the lack of curriculum education at the church level. Although a wide range of religious education curriculum models are created in order to overcome the defects of the schooling-instructional model, if educators stick to the teacher-centered schooling paradigm there would be little change in the field. Thus, curriculum education for teachers is significant because the success of curriculum innovation suitable for new generations and new environments depends totally on the quality of the paradigm shift in their curriculum understanding.

Curriculum education for frontline educators should be a continuing process rather than a one-time seminar. To do this, above all, church leaders who plan curriculum such as the senior pastor or the pastor in charge of the youth group should be equipped with basic curriculum

A Model of Religious Education Curriculum

knowledge and should become *curriculum coordinators who organize various people and things in the process of curriculum planning*. Their primary role as curriculum coordinators is to *design* educational environments, creatively *network* various people to generate educational synergies, and *curate* content to provide appropriate educational materials. The church should then train some teachers, such as the head teacher to be lay curriculum coordinators cooperating with the youth pastor in the group in order to retain consistency of curriculum policy and planning regardless of the regular change of pastors.

The process of recruiting lay curriculum coordinators at the church level needs a long-term plan. Church leaders should build a structure of educational ministry in which the new curriculum model—curriculum as software—is emphasized and encouraged enough to transform teachers' traditional curriculum understanding through various educational channels such as internal and external seminars, and curriculum workshops. There should also be opportunities for the recruited lay curriculum coordinators to cooperate with youth pastors by jointly designing educational space, networking people, and curating content for educational materials.

Furthermore, lay curriculum coordinator(s) and the youth pastor in each group can gather together as a curriculum research team. Through this team collaboration, they can design the whole church as educational space and network the whole congregation so they can be involved in the process of curriculum development. The curriculum research team can also establish an educational database for education resources, activities, and information suitable for their contexts and students by researching and filtering various materials. In addition, the curriculum of each group can be connected with other groups through team work so that all students from preschoolers to young adults can be educated consistently and coherently.

Through such continual designing, networking, and content curation by church leaders and lay curriculum coordinators, an educational course can be a framework not only for the teacher to integrate educational environments and available materials, but for students to learn holistically, by critically synthesizing information from various sources to create knowledge.

Relevance of Curriculum as Software

Relevance to Religious Education for Faith

So far, I have discussed the necessity of a digital-oriented curriculum for educating digital generations such as SGKA teenagers. Curriculum as software has been presented as a new religious education model suitable for those born in the digital era. The new paradigm designs a course for students to create knowledge themselves by synthesizing diverse information in digital ways of learning, thinking, and communicating. To design a learning space according to the new model of curriculum as software, the software programming procedures are critically applied in the planning process: analysis, design, simulation, and service. At this point, we religious educators should ask a significant question: "Is curriculum as software relevant to religious education for faith?"

Based on the faith understanding of Calvin and Barth I have argued that faith is knowledge of God. In chapter 3, I investigated what faith is, how faith is achieved, and how faith is communicated through analyzing Calvin and Barth's understanding of faith. Even though they were separated by a period of nearly four hundred years and there is the continuity and discontinuity between their perceptions of faith, it was found that both of them agree that faith is personal, spiritual, participatory, and communal knowledge of God. To nurture all these dimensions appropriately, I proposed four directions for a new religious education curriculum suitable for faith as follows: (1) pedagogia Dei (God's education); (2) faith community based education; (3) prayer-centered spiritual education; and (4) participation promoting education. Curriculum as software can be a good framework for incorporating these curricular insights for designing a religious education curriculum for faith.

First, curriculum as software seems to be solid ground for the first principle for establishing an alternative curriculum paradigm: *pedagogia Dei*. Pedagogia Dei means that the only subject of religious education is God because people can know God only through God's revelation to them. The essence of God's revelation is the incarnation of Jesus Christ, so all educational programs must be connected to Jesus Christ. In understanding divine revelation through Jesus Christ, the help of the Holy Spirit is indispensable. Thus, pedagogia Dei is inherently Trinitarian education. In pedagogia Dei, teachers are partners participating in God's education, whose primary role is to help people recognize and realize

A Model of Religious Education Curriculum

God's revelation through Jesus Christ in their daily lives. Thus, religious educators need a paradigm shift in understanding the teacher's role, for example, from human centered to God centered, from instruction centered to hospitality centered. Palmer explains the importance of hospitality in a learning space as follows:

> Precisely because a learning space can be a painful place, it must have one other characteristic—hospitality. Hospitality means receiving each other, our struggles, our new born ideas with openness and care. It means creating an ethos in which the community of troth can form, the pain of truth's transformation be borne.... Hospitality is not only an ethical virtue, but an epistemological one as well. So the classroom where truth is central will be a place where every stranger and every strange utterance is met with welcome.[51]

In this regard, curriculum as software can be a desirable framework for pedagogia Dei in that the model is service oriented rather than teaching centered, in which the teacher's primary role is stated to serve students in cooperation with God rather than control them. Furthermore, the new model leaves an open-ended learning space which can be open to the unexpected rather than being dominated by prescribed directions and goals.

Second, curriculum as software seems helpful for developing faith community education. Calvin and Barth both argued that faith is a communal rather than individual knowledge of God, so it can be developed only in the church as a faith community. From the same viewpoint, C. Ellis Nelson claims that a person learns the meaning of faith and how to believe in God through his or her relationship with their faith community, family, and church congregation. If faith is distorted or absent in relationships in the faith community, faith cannot be nurtured appropriately because it is communicated by a believing community.[52] For Nelson, "the congregation is not the sum of individual believers. It is a dynamic, living reality that adjusts, adapts, modifies, and makes exception to general faith propositions which come from the past."[53]

Curriculum as software can provide a learning space suitable for faith community based education as it emphasizes an open/flat collaborative

---

51. Palmer, *To Know as We Are Known*, 73–74.
52. Nelson, *Where Faith Begins*, 106–7.
53. Ibid., 110.

network rather than a closed/hierarchical paradigm. Under the open and flat cooperation model, opportunities for participating in the process of curriculum design are open not only to a few church leaders, but also to all interested church members. The process of decision-making is also flat rather than hierarchical, so a wide range of curricular ideas might be broadly accepted and integrated. The process of religious education will then be community centered.

Third, curriculum as software seems to provide a domain for prayer-centered education. In religious education for faith, the role of prayer is very significant because prayer is an essential channel for building a personal relationship with God and for understanding God's revelation. In this respect, Calvin and Barth viewed prayer as an important vehicle in helping us to know God personally, imaginatively, and spiritually. Thus, religious educational courses for faith should be prayerful spaces for students to establish a loving relationship with God. In designing a course to be a prayerful space, close and spiritual relationships among the teacher and students are critical. Otherwise, prayer education is likely to be confined to the level of intellectual learning. Curriculum as software might be helpful for the teacher in developing closer spiritual relationships with students because it is based on interactive communication between the teacher and students. Besides, the online-offline hybrid learning space emphasized in curriculum as software might be a good platform to connect students even on weekdays, which may strengthen the quality of relationships between the two parties.

Finally, curriculum as software might encourage participation-centered education for obedience. Obedience promoting education focuses on faith as participatory knowledge of God. For Calvin and Barth, without participating in God's commandments, faith might be identified with intellectual beliefs, not being developed holistically. Obedience as participation is believed to strengthen, deepen, and broaden the life of faith. Thus, in religious education for faith, it is very important to provide people with diverse opportunities for obedient participation. The new curriculum model might be able to provide a framework for students to have faith and develop it through continually participating in God's Word and struggling to live it out in their daily lives. The 4R movement is a process designed to achieve this purpose.

Likewise, curriculum as software is an appropriate religious education curriculum model for faith. Religious educators equipped with the new curricular concepts might be able to provide educational scaffolding

A Model of Religious Education Curriculum

on which faith as personal, spiritual, participatory, and communal knowledge of God can be nurtured and developed.

Relevance to the Educational Context of the KA Church

Curriculum as software is also relevant to the educational context of the KA churches. In chapter 7, I mentioned the fragmentation of curriculum in the four selected youth groups and examined its four main causes based on the results of interviews and curriculum analysis: (1) the teacher/pastor's textbook-centered curriculum understanding; (2) the disconnection between church life on Sundays and daily life on weekdays; (3) the relative indifference to educational evaluation; and (4) the tendency toward monocultural education despite the complicated composition of groups. I found that these curriculum-related issues are closely intertwined with curriculum concepts and beliefs based on the model of transmitting knowledge-out-of-context. The new model of curriculum as software seems to provide insights and implications for resolving these curricular problems.

First, curriculum as software might overcome the teacher/pastor's textbook-centered curriculum understanding. The textbook-centered curriculum approach is a key feature of the curriculum model of transmitting knowledge-out-of-context used in most KA churches, in which teaching the content of textbooks effectively is considered most important. Under this approach, various educational efforts other than textbooks such as sermons and extra activities tend to be underestimated, so that each educational and curricular event is likely to be separated and fragmented. Religious education also tends to be identified with the Sunday School ministry, so that diverse church experiences such as liturgy, fellowship, and mission are liable not to be treated as significant educational channels.

Under the new curriculum model, however, curriculum is all educational activities planned for achieving educational benefits, so various educational events including textbooks are designed and implemented as curricular factors. Within this understanding, all educational programs can be integrated with a curricular perspective so that they can be holistic rather than fragmented education. In addition, curriculum as software is based on a belief that curriculum development should be undertaken not only by some professionals and church leaders, but also by the whole congregation within an open-flat cooperation network. The emphasis on the whole church members' participation in curriculum development means that religious education is no longer limited to the ministry of the Sunday School teachers. Rather, religious education should embrace all church members and all aspects of church life, for which curriculum as software is developed.

Second, curriculum as software seems appropriate for resolving the disconnection between church life on Sundays, and home and school life on weekdays. Many SGKA teenagers tend to feel confused in many respects between church education and school education. Since they are influenced by secular world views and values at school for five days a week, it is very difficult that church educators have only Sundays to educate their students and equip them with Christian perspectives. Considering that young people are living in a relativistic postmodern society and in the digital revolution, there needs to be a change from the traditional schooling based religious education in the Sunday School as it is disconnected from the students' daily lives and their digital ways of learning and communicating. Under the concept of curriculum as software, there seem diverse possibilities to overcome such gaps. An example is online-offline hybrid learning. If church educators introduce an online-offline hybrid learning structure into their courses, they can have a point of connection between Sunday education and students' daily lives. Through online communication they can coach students to read Scripture and pray to God on a regular basis, and listen to students' issues and advise them in a Christian way considering current students' digital ways of learning, thinking, and communicating.

In addition, such a hybrid religious education might encourage students to more actively participate in the process of faith formation than traditional class-bound education. Zhichang Xu proved this by conducting a qualitative research on hybrid learning with his college students. He reports that in the online-offline blended courses there was more active participation and meaningful collaboration among students. He further argues that "all these data indicate that the 'blended' mode of learning and teaching facilitates the shift from knowledge transmission to knowledge construction."[54] Likewise, online-offline hybrid religious education seems helpful in integrating Sunday education with students' daily lives, and encouraging their participation and cooperation in the process of faith formation.

54. Xu, "When Hybrid Learning," 164.

Third, curriculum as software might be good at resolving the issue of assessment in the KA churches. In the course of interviews with the fourteen teacher/pastor informants, there was little mention of curriculum evaluation. Through critical analysis of the current curriculum of the four youth groups, I found that there are few ways to assess the extent to which their curricular activities are appropriate for their students. As a result, most educational practices and curricular programs in the KA church youth groups tend to be routinely repeated without critical evaluation, so that their religious education activities are most likely to be out-of-context. In this respect, curriculum as software can be good alternative because curriculum assessment is critical in designing a course under the new model. Above all, the stage of analysis is for critically evaluating the former curriculum and for assessing experiences of teachers and students. Findings from such evaluation can be a starting point for designing a new educational course. The stage of simulation is also a process of evaluating curriculum. Through the process of simulation, new course and related materials and activities can be assessed before being released. In addition, the movement of service indicates that curriculum as software should be a continual process to evaluate current curricular activities as being adequate to the specific educational environments and users. The results of service-oriented practices are closely connected to the movement of analysis for a new course.

Finally, curriculum as software might provide religious teachers with a holistic view on how to educate students in a youth group where the participants have a wide range of backgrounds. In most youth groups of the KA churches, there are students of various backgrounds like 1.5- or second-generations, Korean overseas students, and newly immigrated youth. Since there are differences among them in terms of language, culture, values, and developmental experiences, it has been very hard to educate them appropriately within a group. In the traditional schooling paradigm, such differences, especially the language gap, seem too huge to overcome. Consequently, many KA churches have tended to divide their youth group into Korean-speaking and English-speaking groups or subgroups so that youth may worship or study Scripture in their own tongue. However, such *separate education* is not good for the long-term development of youth because they are deprived of many opportunities to learn from differences and expand their perspectives through relationships with peers from different backgrounds.

Religious educators equipped with curriculum as software might be able to provide a way in which students with a wide range of backgrounds can learn together by collaborating with each other. Within a course designed as a framework for knowledge construction, where the skills of creative and critical synthesis, critical evaluation, creative integration, collaboration, and multicultural perspectives are emphasized, differences can serve as rich resources for learning. Through acknowledging differences and critically integrating them, students can create new knowledge. To facilitate this *integrated education* in youth groups of the KA church, the course should be a domain for students' self-directed education through participation and collaboration rather than as a teacher-centered class.

As such, curriculum as software is relevant for resolving the four curricular problems of the KA churches found in the results of interviews and curriculum analyses. It is also remarkable that the new curriculum model provides a framework for resolving another deep-rooted educational issue in most KA churches—superficial relationships between the teacher and students. The matter of superficial relationships between the teacher and students has been a critical issue in religious education in most KA churches. Poor rapport between the two parties tends to weaken communication, and might undermine the process of religious education for faith. Curriculum as software seems helpful for the teacher in establishing a closer relationship with students because it emphasizes interactive communication between the two groups and focuses on designing an interaction-encouraged user interface. The emphasis on online-offline hybrid learning space also provides the teacher with scaffolding to reach students. Considering that most teenage students seem enthusiastic about communicating with others online through SNSs, blogs, instant messages, and email, teachers might find a way of improving the quality of their relationships with students through such digital channels.

Epilogue

THE MAIN PURPOSE OF this book is to present a religious education curriculum model for SGKA teenagers, which is an alternative to the current paradigm of transmitting knowledge-out-of-context. Based on interview findings, curriculum and document analyses, and my field experiences, I have built up a new curriculum model suitable for helping SGKA adolescents who are growing up in a digital culture to develop faith in the educational context of the KA church. However, because of the limited scope of this work, I have not been able to discuss several issues that are related to this study. These topics might be potential subjects for further study.

First, since this study has focused on the youth group, I have not discussed the religious education curriculum for SGKA preschoolers, SGKA primary school children, and SGKA young adults. Since these groups also carry out educational practices in the context of the KA church just like the youth group, results of this research project might provide insights and implications for them as well. However, as each group is different and unique, research should focus on each group's religious education practice including the curriculum. Considering that there have been few studies in the religious education of the educational departments of the KA church, more academic research on this subject is needed.

Second, the complicated student composition of most youth groups of the KA church has been a challenge for religious educators in nurturing their students appropriately because it is very hard for them to decide on topics, methods, materials, and even a language that is suitable for all group members. Consequently, there has been a tendency to divide the youth group into Korean-speaking and English-speaking youth groups especially within large churches that can afford to call English-speaking youth pastors as well as Korean ministers. On the other hand, in most medium and small sized KA churches, the tendency has been to compose small groups for Bible study based on language preference. However, there has been little research on the English-speaking ministry for SGKA young people in the context of the KA church. For example, short-term and long-term educational consequences of language-centered education separating English and Korean-speaking people have not yet been adequately studied. In this situation, unconditionally following the trend toward language based separate education seems in many respects to be a problematic practice.

Finally, research on teacher training in the Korean immigrant churches is necessary. The poor quality of educational practice by teachers in the KA churches is considered a big obstacle in implementing appropriate religious education. The effectiveness of teachers in most KA churches is limited because most are volunteers, but also because most training programs for teachers have been designed focusing on providing teaching materials and skills within the schooling-instructional paradigm. As a result, most teachers in the Korean ethnic churches in Australia tend to understand transmitting what they are supposed to teach in group Bible study sessions as their primary role. Teacher training programs should be developed with consideration of the curricular and educational situations of the KA churches. In this respect, there is an urgent need to study how curriculum for teacher training might be designed suitably for the volunteer teachers and the context of the KA churches. In a curriculum for teacher education, fostering the teacher's curricular ability should be emphasized so that teachers can be adequately equipped to contribute actively and creatively to the process of curriculum planning for their educational departments as well as for their small groups.

Further studies referred to above along with the insights and implications provided by this book will be helpful in designing more appropriate and holistic religious education in the KA churches. Further research might also sharpen and deepen this study so that more developed research might follow.

Bibliography

Abbey, Evan. "The Digital Curriculum." Paper presented at 2009 ITEC Conference, Coralville, Iowa, October 12–13, 2009.
Abrams, Stephen, et al. "An Emergent Micro-Services Approach to Digital Curation Infrastructure." *International Journal of Digital Curation* 5, no. 1 (2010) 172–86.
Anbu, Denisha. "Multiple Identities: Building and Implementing Strategies." In *Crossing Borders: Shaping Faith, Ministry and Identity in Multicultural Australia*, edited by Helen Richmond and Yang Myong Duk, 133–37. Sydney: UCA Assembly & NSW Board of Mission, 2006.
Anderson, David R. "The Nature of Faith." *Chafer Theological Seminary Journal* 5, no. 4 (1999) 1–25.
Anderson, Steve, and Anne Balsamo. "A Pedagogy for Original Synners." In *Digital Youth, Innovation, and the Unexpected*, edited by Tara McPherson, 241–59. Cambridge, MA: MIT Press, 2008.
Applebee, Arthur N. "A Sense of Story." *Theory Into Practice* 16, no. 5 (1977) 342–47.
———. *Curriculum as Conversation*. Chicago: University of Chicago Press, 1996.
Armbrust, Michael, et al. "A View of Cloud Computing." *Communications of the ACM* 53, no. 4 (2010) 50–58.
Arnota, Madeleine, and Geoff Whittyb. "School Texts, the Hidden Curriculum and the Curriculum-in-Use: A British View of Recent American Contributions to the Sociology of the Curriculum." *Discourse: Studies in the Cultural Politics of Education* 3, no. 1 (1982) 1–21.
Ashkanasy, Neal M., et al. "Leadership Attributes and Cultural Values in Australia and New Zealand Compared: An Initial Report Based on 'GLOBE Data.'" *International Journal of Organisational Behaviour* 2, no. 3 (2000) 37–44.
Australian Bureau of Statistics. "2006 Census of Population and Housing: Ancestry (Full Classification List) By Sex, Australia." http://www.censusdata.abs.gov.au/ABSNavigation/prenav/ViewData?breadcrumb=POLTD&method=Place%20of%20Usual%20Residence&subaction=-1&issue=2006&producttype=Census%20Tables&documentproductno=0&textversion=false&documenttype=Details&collection=Census&javascript=true&topic=Ancestry&action=404&productlabel=Ancestry%20(full%20classification%20list)%20by%20Sex&order=1&period=2006&tabname=Details&areacode=0&navmapdisplayed=true&.

Bibliography

———. "2006 Census of Population and Housing: Country of Birth of Person (Full Classification List) by Sex, Sydney." http://www.censusdata.abs.gov.au/ABSNavigation/prenav/ViewData?action=404&documentproductno=105&documenttype=Details&order=1&tabname=Details&areacode=105&issue=2006&producttype=Census%20Tables&javascript=true&textversion=false&navmapdisplayed=true&breadcrumb=TLPD&&collection=Census&period=2006&productlabel=Country%20of%20Birth%20of%20Person%20(full%20classification%20list)%20by%20Sex&producttype=Census%20Tables&method=Place%20of%20Usual%20Residence&topic=Birthplace&.

———. "2006 Census of Population and Housing: Country of Birth of Person by Sex for Time Series, Australia." http://www.censusdata.abs.gov.au/ABSNavigation/prenav/ViewData?action=404&documentproductno=0&documenttype=Details&order=1&tabname=Details&areacode=0&issue=2006&producttype=Census%20Tables&javascript=true&textversion=false&navmapdisplayed=true&breadcrumb=TLPD&&collection=Census&period=2006&productlabel=Country%20of%20Birth%20of%20Person%20by%20Sex%20-%20Time%20Series%20Statistics%20(1996,%202001,%202006%20Census%20Years)&producttype=Census%20Tables&method=Place%20of%20Usual%20Residence&topic=Birthplace&.

———. "2006 Census of Population and Housing: Ethnic Media Package, Persons Born in Korea, Republic of (South)." http://www.abs.gov.au/ausstats/abs@.nsf/mediareleasesbytitle/CCE35AB0F0909037CA257307001E4B2B?OpenDocument.

———. "2011 Census of Population and Housing: Age in Single Years (AGEP) by Ancestry 1st Response (ANC1P)." http://www.censusdata.abs.gov.au/webapi/jsf/tableView/customiseTable.xhtml.

———. "2011 Census of Population and Housing: Ancestry 1st Response (ANC1P) by Greater Capital City Statistical Areas (UR)." http://www.censusdata.abs.gov.au/webapi/jsf/tableView/customiseTable.xhtml.

———. "2011 Census of Population and Housing: Country of Birth of Person (BPLP) by Greater Capital City Statistical Areas (UR)." http://www.censusdata.abs.gov.au/webapi/jsf/tableView/customiseTable.xhtml.

———. "2011 Census of Population and Housing: Highest Year of School Completed (HSCP) by Country of Birth of Person (BPLP) - 4 Digit Level." http://www.censusdata.abs.gov.au/webapi/jsf/tableView/customiseTable.xhtml.

———. "2011 Census of Population and Housing: Proficiency in Spoken English (ENGP) by Country of Birth of Person (BPLP) - 4 Digit Level." http://www.censusdata.abs.gov.au/webapi/jsf/tableView/customiseTable.xhtml.

———. "2011 Census of Population and Housing: Religious Affiliation (RELP) - 1 Digit Level by Ancestry 1st Response (ANC1P) - 4 Digit Level." http://www.censusdata.abs.gov.au/webapi/jsf/tableView/customiseTable.xhtml.

———. "2011 Census of Population and Housing: Religious Affiliation (RELP) - 3 Digit Level by Ancestry 1st Response (ANC1P) - 4 Digit Level." http://www.censusdata.abs.gov.au/webapi/jsf/tableView/customiseTable.xhtml.

———. "2011 Census of Population and Housing: Total Personal Income, weekly (INCP) by Country of Birth of Person (BPLP) - 4 Digit Level." http://www.censusdata.abs.gov.au/webapi/jsf/tableView/customiseTable.xhtml.

———. "2011 Census of Population and Housing: Type of Educational Institution Attending (TYPP) by Country of Birth of Person (BPLP) - 4 Digit Level." http://www.censusdata.abs.gov.au/webapi/jsf/tableView/customiseTable.xhtml.

———. "2011 Census of Population and Housing: Unpaid Demestic Work: Number of Hours (DOMP) by Country of Birth of Person (BPLP) - 4 Digit Level." http://www.censusdata.abs.gov.au/webapi/jsf/tableView/customiseTable.xhtml.

———. "2011 Census of Population and Housing: Year of Arrival in Australia (ranges) (YARRP) by Country of Birth of Person (BPLP)." http://www.censusdata.abs.gov.au/webapi/jsf/tableView/customiseTable.xhtml.

———. "2011 Consus of Population and Housing: Language Spoken at Home (LANP) by Greater Capital City Statistical Areas (UR)." http://www.censusdata.abs.gov.au/webapi/jsf/tableView/customiseTable.xhtml.

Australian Copyright Council. "Churches and Copyright, Information Sheet G018v12, August 2012." http://www.copyright.org.au/admin/cms-acc1/_images/20113036265040468834 9ec.pdf.

———. "Fair Dealing, Information Sheet G079v06, February 2012." http://www.copyright.org.au/admin/cms-acc1/_images/9596827704f39afefd0112.pdf.

———. "Films, DVDs, Videos and TV: Screening in Public, Information Sheet G031v18, February 2012." http://www.copyright.org.au/admin/cms-acc1/_images/14726359694f388ad49e94c.pdf.

———. "Internet: Copying & Downloading, Information Sheet G056v07." http://www.copyright.org.au/admin/cms-acc1/_images/13968746614f389f7994505.pdf.

———. "Websites & Copyright, Information Sheet G057v10, August 2012." http://www.copyright.org.au/admin/cms-acc1/_images/13709001950404699c2c52.pdf.

Baek, Keum San, and Jong Doo Kim. *Manhwa westminstersogyorimundap1* [Cartoon Westminster Shorter Catechism1]. Seoul: RnR, 2010.

———. *Manhwa westminstersogyorimundap2* [Cartoon Westminster Shorter Catechism2]. Seoul: RnR, 2010.

Baillie, John. *The Idea of Revelation in Recent Thought*. New York: Columbia University Press, 1956.

Banks, James A. *An Introduction to Multiculutral Education*. Boston: Allyan & Bacon, 2008.

Barnett, Ronald, et al. "Conceptualising Curriculum Change." *Teaching in Higher Education* 6, no. 4 (2001) 435–49.

Barron, Anne. *Acquisition in Interlanguage Pragmatics: Learning How to Do Things with Words in a Study Abroad Context*. Amsterdam: Benjamins, 2003.

Barth, Karl. Anselm: *Fides Quaerens Intellectum*. Translated by Ian W. Robertson. London: SCM, 1958.

———. *Church Dogmatics*. Edited by Geoffrey W. Bromiley and Thomas F. Torrance. Translated by T. H. L. Parker. Edinburgh: T. & T. Clark, 1956. Reprint, Hendrickson, 2010.

———. *Church Dogmatics*. Edited by Geoffrey W. Bromiley and Thomas F. Torrance. Translated by T. H. L. Parker. Edinburgh: T. & T. Clark, 1961.

———. *The Epistle to the Romans*. Translated by Edwyn C. Hoskyns. London: Oxford University Press, 1933.

———. "No!" In *Natural Theology*, edited by Emil Brunner and Karl Barth, translated by Peter Fraenkel. London: Bles, 1946.

———. *The Theology of the Reformed Confessions, 1923*. Translated by Darrell L. Guder and Judith J. Guder. Edited by Eberhard Busch. Louisville: Westminster John Knox, 2002.

Bibliography

Beaumont, Tim. "Australian Values." Teaching and Learning Unit of the University of Melbourne. http://tlu.fbe.unimelb.edu.au/pdfs/GEP/GEPS210/GEP%20Sessions%2017%20&%2018%20Australian%20Values%20and%20the%20Media.pdf.

Bell, Les. "Curriculum Review and Curriculum Balance." *School Leadership & Management* 4, no. 2 (1984) 179–82.

Berry, John W. "Immigration, Acculturation, and Adaptation." *Applied Psychology: An International Review* 46, no. 1 (1997) 5–34.

———. "Social Psychological Costs and Benefits of Multiculturalism: A View from Canada." *Trames: A Journal of Humanities and Social Science* 2, no. 52/47 (1998) 209–33.

Berry, John W., et al. "Immigrant Youth: Acculturation, Identity, and Adaptation." *Applied Psychology: An International Review* 55, no. 3 (2006) 303–32.

Boyd, Danah M., and Nicole B. Ellison. "Social Network Sites: Definition, History, and Scholarship." *Journal of Computer-Mediated Communication* 13 (2008) 210–30.

Boys, Mary C. *Biblical Interpretation in Religious Education: A Study of the Kerygmatic Era*. Birmingham: Religious Education, 1980.

———. "Conversion as a Foundation of Religious Education." *Religious Education* 77, no. 2 (1982) 211–24.

———. "Language and the Bible: A Response." *Religious Education* 80, no. 4 (1985) 539–49.

———. "Learning in the Presence of the Other." *Religious Education* 103, no. 5 (2008) 502–6.

———. "Questions 'Which Touch on the Heart of Our Faith.'" *Religious Education* 76, no. 6 (1981) 636–56.

———. "The Standpoint of Religious Education." *Religious Education* 76, no. 2 (1981) 128–41.

———. "Teaching: The Heart of Religious Education." *Religious Education* 79, no. 2 (1984) 252–72.

———. "The Tradition as Teacher: Repairing the World." *Religious Education* 85, no. 3 (1990) 346–55.

Boys, Mary C., and Thomas H. Groome. "Principles and Pedagogy in Biblical Study." *Religious Education* 77, no. 5 (1982) 486–507.

Boys, Mary C., Sara S. Lee, and Dorothy C. Bass. "Forum Protestant, Catholic, Jew: The Transformative Possibilities of Educating across Religious Boundaries." *Religious Education* 90, no. 2 (1995) 254–76.

Brady, Laurie. *Curriculum Development*. 3rd ed. Englewood Cliffs, NJ: Prentice Hall, 1990.

———. "Curriculum Models and Curriculum Commonplaces." *Journal of Curriculum Studies* 14, no. 2 (1982) 197–200.

Branch, Curtis W. "Race and Human Development." In *Racial and Ethnic Identity in School Practices: Aspects of Human Development*, edited by Rosa Sheets and Etta Hollins, 7–28. Mahwah, NJ: Erlbaum, 1999.

Brandt, Ronald S., and Ralph W. Tyler. "Goals and Objectives." In *Contemporary Issues in Curriculum*, edited by Allan C. Ornstein et al., 10–19. Boston: Allyn & Bacon, 2003.

Brelsford, Theodore. "Lessons for Religious Education from Cognitive Science of Religion." *Religious Education* 100, no. 2 (2005) 174–91.

———. "A Mythical Realist Orientation for Religious Education: Theological and Pedagogical Implications of the Mythical Nature of Religious Story." *Religious Education* 102, no. 3 (2007) 264–78.

———. "Politicized Knowledge and Imaginative Faith in Religious Education." *Religious Education* 94, no. 1 (1999) 58–73.

———. "Religious Education beyond the Schooling Model." *Religious Education* 100, no. 4 (2005) 357–61.

Brimfield, Renée M. B. "Curriculum! What's Curriculum?" *Educational Forum* 56, no. 4 (1992) 381–89.

Bromiley, Geoffrey W. "Karl Barth's Doctrine of Inspiration." *Journal of the Transactions of the Victoria Institute* 87 (1955) 66–80.

Bronfenbrenner, Urie. "Developmental Ecology through Space and Time: A Future Perspective." In *Examining Lives in Context: Perspectives on the Ecology of Human Development*, edited by Phyllis Moen et al., 619–47. Washington, DC: American Psychological Association, 1995.

———. "Ecological Models of Human Development." In *Readings on the Development of Children*, edited by Michael Gauvain and Mary Cole, 37–43. New York: Freeman, 1993.

———. *The Ecology of Human Development: Experiments by Nature and Design*. Cambridge: Harvard University Press, 1979.

———. "Environments in Developmental Perspective: Theoretical and Operational Models." In *Measuring Environment across the Life Span: Emerging Methods and Concepts*, edited by Sarah L. Friedman and Theodore D. Wachs, 3–28. Washington, DC: American Psychological Association, 1999.

———. "Toward an Experimental Ecology of Human Development." *American Psychologist* 32, no. 7 (1977) 513–31.

Brown, John. "Birth of Early Korean Churches in Australia." In *30 Years Korean Ministry in Australia*, edited by Myung Duk Yang and Clive Pearson, 265–78. North Parramatta, NSW: UTC Publications, 2004.

Brown, Malcolm. "Learning Spaces." In *Educating the Net Generation*, edited by Diana G. Oblinger and James L. Oblinger, 12.1–12.22. Washington, DC: Educause, 2005.

Bruner, Jerome. *Acts of Meaning*. Cambridge: Harvard University Press, 1990.

Brunner, Emil. *Dogmatics I: The Christian Doctrine of God*. Translated by Olive Wyon. London: Lutterworth, 1949.

———. *Dogmatics II: The Christian Doctrine of Creation and Redemption*. Translated by Olive Wyon. London: Lutterworth, 1952.

———. "Nature and Grace." In *Natural Theology*, edited by Emil Brunner and Karl Barth, translated by Peter Fraenkel. London: Bles, 1946.

———. *Revelation and Reason*. Philadelphia: Westminster, 1946.

Buchanana, Michael T., and Kath Engebretsona. "The Significance of Theory in the Implementation of Curriculum Change in Religious Education." *British Journal of Religious Education* 31, no. 2 (2009) 141–52.

Burns, Robert. *Introduction to Research Methods*. Frenchs Forest, Australia: Pearson Education, 2000.

Bybee, Carl, and Ashley Overbeck. "Homer Simpson Explains our Postmodern Identity Crisis, Whether We Like It or Not: Media Literacy after 'The Simpsons.'" *Studies in Media and Information Literacy Education* 1, no. 1 (2001) 1–12.

Byrne, Gareth. "Embracing Life at Its Fullest: The Spirituality of Religious Educators and School Chaplains." In *At the Heart of Education: School Chaplaincy and Pastoral Care*, edited by James Norman, 184–96. Dublin: Veritas, 2004.

Calvin, John. *Commentary on the Acts of the Apostles*. Translated by Henry Beveridge. Edinburgh: Calvin Translation Society, 1843.

———. *Commentaries on the Epistles to Timothy, Titus, and Philemon*. Translated by William Pringle. Edinburgh: Calvin Translation Society, 1855.

———. *Institutes of the Christian Religion*. Edited by John T. McNeill. Translated by Ford Lewis Battles. Philadelphia: The Westminster, 1960.

———. *The Institutes of the Christian Religion*. Translated by Henry Beveridge. Grand Rapids: Christians Classics Ethereal Library. http://www.ccel.org.

Castells, Manuel. *The Rise of the Network Society*. Chichester, UK: Wiley, 2010.

Chaffee, Steven H., and Miriam J. Metzger. "The End of Mass Communication?" *Mass Communication & Society* 4, no. 4 (2001) 365–79.

Chatman, Celina M., et al. "Identity Negotiation in Everyday Settings." In *Navigating the Future: Social Identity, Coping, and Life Tasks*, edited by Geraldine Downey et al., 116–40. New York: Russel Sage Foundation, 2005.

Chavez, Alicia, and Florence Guido-DiBrito. "Racial and Ethnic Identity and Development." *New Directions for Adult and Continuing Education* 1999, no. 84 (1999) 39–47.

Choi, Sheena, et al. "Coming to America and Becoming American: Narration of Korean Immigrant Young Men." *International Education Journal* 2, no. 5 (2001) 47–60.

Chong, Kelly H. "What It Means to Be Christian: The Role of Religion in the Construction of Ethnic Edentity and Boundary among Second-Generation Korean Americans." *Sociology of Religion* 59, no. 3 (1998) 259–86.

Chung, Byung-Joon. "Beyond Dichotomy: The Wholistic Mission Understanding of the Australian Presbyterian Missionaries and Its Contribution to the Korean Mission, 1889–1942." ThD diss., Melbourne College of Divinity, 2004.

Chung, Mei. *Chinese Young People and Spirituality: An Australian Study*. Saarbrücken, Germany: VDM Verlag Dr. Müller, 2006.

———. "Chinese Young People in the Multicultural Society: A Generation in Between." *REJA* 22, no. 1 (2006) 23–27.

Cobb, John B., and David Ray Griffin. *Process Theology: An Introductory Exposition*. Louisville: Westminster John Knox, 1976.

Coe, George A. *What Is Christian Education?* New York: Scribner, 1929.

Côté, James E., and Charles G. Levine. *Identity Formation, Agency, and Culture: A Social Psychological Synthesis*. Mahwah, NJ: Erlbaum, 2002.

Coughlan, James E., and Deborah J. McNamara, eds. *Asians in Australia: Patterns of Migration and Settlement*. South Melbourne: Macmillan Education Australia, 1997.

Cross, William E., Jr., Lakesha Smith, and Yasser Payne. "Black Identity: A Repertoire of Daily Enactments." In *Counseling across Cultures*, edited by P. Pedersen et al., 93–107. Thousand Oaks, CA: Sage, 2002.

Cross, William E., Jr., Linda Strauss, and Peony Fhagen-Smith. "African American Identity Development Across the Life Span: Educational Implications." In *Racial and Ethnic Identity in School Practices: Aspects of Human Development*, edited by Rosa Hernandez Sheets and Etta R. Hollins, 29–48. Mahwah, NJ: Erlbaum, 1999.

Bibliography

Cully, Iris V. "Christian Education: Instruction or Nurture." *Religious Education* 62, no. 3 (1967) 255–61.
———. "Continuity within Change: Religious Education as a Calling." *Religious Education* 79, no. 1 (1984) 29–36.
———. "New Approaches to Teaching." *Religious Education* 67, no. 5 (1972) 379–83.
———. "New Models and Old Forms." *Religious Education* 72, no. 1 (1977) 33–36.
———. "Teaching History in Church Curriculum." *Religious Education* 64, no. 2 (1969) 133–37.
Darling-Hammond, Linda. "Teacher Learning That Supports Student Learning." In *Contemporary Issues in Curriculum*, edited by Allan C. Ornstein et al., 277–82. Boston: Allyn & Bacon, 2003.
Department of Immigration and Citizenship. "Community Information Summary: South-Korea-Born." http://www.immi.gov.au/media/publications/statistics/comm-summ/_pdf/korea.pdf.
Deverell, Garry J. *The Bonds of Freedom: Vows, Sacraments and the Formation of the Christian Self*. Milton Keynes, UK: Paternoster, 2008.
De Vos, George. "Ethnic Pluralism: Conflict and Accommodation." In *Ethnic Identity: Problems and Perspectives for the Twenty-First Century*, edited by Lola Romanucci-Ross et al., 1–36. Lanham, MD: AltaMira, 2006.
Dillon, James T. "The Questions of Curriculum." *Journal of Curriculum Studies* 41, no. 3 (2009) 343–59.
Doll, William E., Jr. "Foundations for a Post-modern Curriculum." *Journal of Curriculum Studies* 21, no. 3 (1989) 243–53.
———. "Prigogine: A New Sense of Order, a New Curriculum." *Theory Into Practice* 25, no. 1 (1986) 10–16.
———. "Reflections on Teaching: Developing the Nonlinear." *Teaching Education* 10, no. 2 (1999) 39–54.
———. "A Re-visioning of Progressive Education." *Theory Into Practice* 22, no. 3 (1983) 166–73.
———. "A Structural View of Curriculum." *Theory Into Practice* 18, no. 5 (1979) 336–48.
Dykstra, Craig. "The Formative Power of the Congregation." *Religious Education* 82, no. 4 (1987) 530–46.
———. "Moral Virtue or Social Reasoning." *Religious Education* 75, no. 2 (1980) 115–28.
———. "Mystery and Manners: The Task of Religious Education." *Religious Education* 79, no. 1 (1984) 61–66.
———. "Understanding the Place of 'Understanding.'" *Religious Education* 76, no. 2 (1981) 187–94.
Edgar, Barbara. "Ethnic Residential Mixing and Occupational Structure across Three Generations in Sydney and Melbourne, Australia." Paper presented at RGS-IBG Annual Conference, Manchester, UK, August 26–28, 2009.
Educational Department of the Presbyterian Church of Korea. *Gyoyukgwajung ironjichimseo (*Ⅰ*)/ iron* [Guidebook of curriculum (Ⅰ)/ theory]. Seoul: PCKBook, 2001.
———. *Gyoyukgwajung ironjichimseo (*Ⅱ*)/ yeongyeok* [Guidebook of curriculum (Ⅱ)/ domain]. Seoul: PCKBook, 2001.

Educational Research & Development. *Click Bible Series: Jesus Christ (Basic Course 2)*. Seoul: Publishing House of the Presbyterian Church of Korea, 2003.

———. *Click Bible Series: Jesus Christ (Basic Course 2) Handbook*. Seoul: Publishing House of the Presbyterian Church of Korea, 2003.

Eechoud, Mireille van, and Brenda van der Wal. "Creative Commons Licensing for Public Sector Information Opportunities and and Pitfalls." Institute for Information Law, University of Amsterdam. http://wiki.creativecommons.org/images/2/2c/Creativecommons-licensing-for-public-sector-information_eng.pdf.

Eisner, Elliot W. "Artistry in Education." *Scandinavian Journal of Educational Research* 47, no. 3 (2003) 373–84.

———. *Cognition and Curriculum Reconsidered*. 2nd ed. London: Chapman, 1996.

———. "Does Experience in the Arts Boost Academic Achievement?" *Arts Education Policy Review* 100, no. 1 (1998) 32–40.

———. *The Educational Imagination: On the Design and Evaluation of School Programs*. 3rd ed. Upper Saddle River, NJ: Prentice Hall, 1994.

———. "Humanistic Trends and the Curriculum Field." *Journal of Curriculum Studies* 10, no. 3 (1978) 197–204.

———. "Preparing Teachers for Schools of the 21st Century." *Peabody Journal of Educational Researcher* 70, no. 3 (1995) 99–111.

———. "The Promise and Perils of Alternative Forms of Data Representation." *Educational Researcher* 26, no. 6 (1997) 4–10.

———. "Reshaping Assessment in Education: Some Criteria in Search of Practice." *Journal of Curriculum Studies* 25, no. 3 (1993) 219–33.

———. "Toward a More Adequate Conception of Evaluation in the Arts." *Peabody Journal of Education* 52, no. 3 (1975) 173–79.

———. "What Does It Mean to Say That a School Is Doing Well?" In *Contemporary Issues in Curriculum*, edited by Allan C. Ornstein et al., 239–47. Boston: Allyn & Bacon, 2003.

Englund, Tomas. "Curriculum History Reconsidered." *Scandinavian Journal of Educational Research* 34, no. 2 (1990) 91–102.

Epstein, Joyce L. "Creating School, Family, and Community Partnerships." In *Contemporary Issues in Curriculum*, edited by Allan C. Ornstein et al., 354–73. Boston: Allyn & Bacon, 2003.

Erikson, Erik H. *Child and Society*. St. Albans: Triad/Paladin Frogmore, 1977.

———. Identity: Youth and Crisis. New York: Norton, 1968.

Ethier, Kathleen A., and Kay Deaux. "Negotiating Social Identity When Contexts Change: Maintaining Identification and Responding to Threat." *Journal of Personality and Social Psychology* 67, no. 2 (1994) 243–51.

Everding, Edward H., Jr. "A Hermeneutical Approach to Educational Theory." In *Foundations for Christian Education in an Era of Change*, edited by Marvin J. Taylor, 41–53. Nashville: Abingdon, 1976.

Ferdman, Bernardo, and Gabriel Horenczyk. "Cultural Identity and Immigration: Reconstructing the Group During Cultural Transition." In *Language, Identity and Immigration*, edited by Elite Olshtain and Gabriel Horenczyk, 81–100. Jerusalem: Hebrew University Magnes Press, 2000.

Fowler, James W. *Faith Development through the Family Life Circle*. New York: Bosco, 1989.

———. *Stages of Faith: The Psychology of Human Development and the Quest for Meaning*. San Francisco: Harper & Row, 1981.

Fox, Robert S. "Curriculum Development with a Purpose." *Theory Into Practice* 1, no. 4 (1962) 202–7.

Frasera, Sharon P., and Agnes M. Bosanquet. "The Curriculum? That's Just a Unit Outline, Isn't It?" *Studies in Higher Education* 31, no. 3 (2006) 269–84.

Freire, Paulo. *Pedagogy of the Oppressed*. Translated by Myra Bergman Ramos. New York: Penguin, 1972.

———. *Pedagogy of the Oppressed*. 30th anniv. ed. Translated by Myra Bergman Ramos. New York: Continuum, 2000.

French, Sabine Elizabeth, et al. "The Development of Ethnic Identity During Adolescence." *Developmental Psychology* 42, no. 1 (2006) 1–10.

Friedman, Sarah L, and Theodore D Wachs, eds. *Measuring Environment across the Life Span: Emerging Methods and Concepts*. Washington, DC: American Psychological Association, 1999.

Gallagher, Daniel. "The Obedience of Faith: Barth, Bultmann, and Dei Verbum." *Journal for Christian Theological Research* 10 (2006) 39–63.

Gallatin, Judith. *Adolescence and Individuality: A Conceptual Approach to Adolescent Psychology*. New York: Harper & Row, 1975.

Gee, James Paul. *What Video Games Have to Teach Us about Learning and Literacy*. New York: Palgrave Macmillan, 2003.

Gehrke, Nathalie J. "A Look at Curriculum Integration from the Bridge." *Curriculum Journal* 9, no. 2 (1998) 247–60.

Gergen, Kenneth J. "Psychological Science in a Postmodern Context." *American Psychologist* 56 (2001) 803–13.

Gibson, David. *Reading the Decree: Exegesis, Election and Christology in Calvin and Barth*. London: T. & T. Clark, 2009.

Glaser, Barney G., and Anselm L. Strauss. *The Discovery of Grounded Theory: Strategies for Qualitative Research*. Chicago: Aldine, 1967. Reprint, AldineTransaction, 2009.

Gökmenoglu, Tuba, et al. "Crises, Reforms, and Scientific Improvements: Behaviorism in the Last Two Centuries." *Elementary Education Online* 9, no. 1 (2010) 292–300.

Goldman, Ronald. *Readiness for Religion: A Basis for Developmental Religious Education*. London: Routledge and Kegan Paul, 1965.

Goodson, Ivor. "Curriculum Reform and Curriculum Theory: A Case of Historical Amnesia." *Cambridge Journal of Education* 19, no. 2 (1989) 131–41.

Gore, Ralph J., Jr. "Calvin's Doctrine of Inspiration." *Reformation Review* 27, no. 2 (1982) 100–114.

Government of South Australia. "Does Spiritual Wellbeing Belong in Education?" *Department of Education and Children's Services*. http://www.decd.sa.gov.au/learnerwellbeing/files/links/Does_Spirtual_Wellbeing_be.pdf.

Green, Garrett. *Imagining God: Theology and the Religious Imagination*. Grand Rapids: Eerdmans, 1989.

Greene, Maxine. "Art and Imagination." In *Contemporary Issues in Curriculum*, edited by Allan C. Ornstein et al., 36–42. Boston: Allyn & Bacon, 2003.

Groome, Thomas H. *Christian Religious Education: Sharing Our Story and Vision*. Melbourne: Dove, 1980.

———. "Conversion, Nurture and Educators." *Religious Education* 76, no. 5 (1981) 482–96.

———. *Educating for Life: A Spiritual Vision for Every Teacher and Parent*. New York: Crossroad, 1998.

———. "Religious Knowing: Still Looking for That Tree." *Religious Education* 92, no. 2 (1997) 204–26.

———. "Remembering and Imagining." *Religious Education* 98, no. 4 (2003) 511–20.

———. *Sharing Faith: A Comprehensive Approach to Religious Education and Pastoral Ministry*. San Francisco: HarperCollins, 1991.

———. "The Spirituality of the Religious Educator." *Religious Education* 83, no. 1 (1988) 9–20.

Gupta, Ankur. "Practitioner-Oriented Collaborative and Cooperative Software Maintenance." *International Journal of Intelligent Computing Research* 2, no. 1/2/3/4 (2011) 228–36.

Habets, Myk. *Theosis in the Theology of Thomas Torrance: Not Yet in the Now*. Farnham, UK: Ashgate, 2009.

Hall, Stuart. "The Local and the Global: Globalization and Ethnicity." In *Dangerous Liaisons: Gender, Nation, and Postcolonial Perspectives*, edited by Anne McClintock et al., 173–87. Minneapolis: University of Minnesota Press, 1997.

Hall, William S., et al. "Stages in the Development of a Black Identity." *ACT Research Report* 60 (1972) 1–21.

Hamelink, Cees J. "New Information and Communication Technologies, Social Development and Cultural Change." *UNRISD Discussion Paper* 86 (1997) 1–37.

Han, Gil Soo. "Expansion and Schism of Korean Churches in Australia." In *30 Years Korean Ministry in Australia*, edited by Myung Duk Yang and Clive Pearson, 279–301. North Parramatta, NSW: UTC Publications, 2004.

———. "From Overt to Covert Racial Discrimination in Australia: The Experiences of Korean Migrants." *Korean Social Science Journal* 29, no. 2 (2002) 1–13.

———. "Immigrant Life and Work Involvement: Korean Men in Australia." *Journal of Intercultural Studies* 20, no. 1 (1999) 5–29.

———. "An Overview of the Life of Koreans in Sydney and their Religious Activities." *Korea Journal* 34 (1994) 67–76.

Han, Joy J., and Gil Soo Han. "The Koreans in Sydney." *Sydney Journal* 2, no. 2 (2010) 25–35.

Hannerz, Ulf. "Studying Down, Up, Sideways, Through, Backwards, Forwards, Away and at Home: Reflections on the Field Worries of an Expansive Discipline." In *Locating the Field: Space, Place, and Context in Anthropology*, edited by Simon Coleman and Peter Collins, 23–41. Oxford: Berg, 2006.

Harris, Maria. "Art and Religious Education: A Conversation." *Religious Education* 83, no. 3 (1988) 453–73.

———. *Fashion Me a People: Curriculum in the Church*. Louisville: Westminster John Knox, 1989.

———. "I from Myth to Parable: Language and Religious Education." *Religious Education* 73, no. 4 (1978) 387–98.

———. "The Imagery of Religious Education." *Religious Education* 78, no. 3 (1983) 363–75.

———. "Religious Educators and the Comic Vision." *Religious Education* 75, no. 4 (1980) 422–32.

———. *Teaching and Religious Imagination: An Essay in the Theology of Teaching*. San Francisco: Harper & Row, 1987.

---. "Teaching the Null Curriculum: The Holocaust." *British Journal of Religious Education* 11, no. 3 (1989) 136–38.
---. "Weaving the Fabric: How My Mind Has Changed." *Religious Education* 79, no. 1 (1984) 18–23.
---. "Women Teaching Girls: The Power and the Danger." *Religious Education* 88, no. 1 (1993) 52–66.
Harris, Maria, and Gabriel Moran. *Reshaping Religious Education: Conversations on Contemporary Practice*. Louisville: Westminster John Knox, 1998.
Hertzog, Nancy B. "The Creation of a School and Curriculum Reform." *Journal of Curriculum Studies* 29, no. 2 (1997) 209–32.
Heverly, Robert A. "Growing Up Digital: Control and the Pieces of a Digital Life." In *Digital Youth, Innovation, and the Unexpected*, edited by Tara McPherson, 199–218. Cambridge: MIT Press, 2008.
Hofstede, Geert H. *Culture's Consequences: International Differences in Work-Related Values*. Beverly Hills: Sage, 1980.
Hoju hanin osipnyeonsa Pyeonchan wiwonhoe. *Hoju hanin osipnyeonsa* [50-year history of Koreans in Australia]. Seoul: Doseo-chulpan jinheung, 2008.
Holcomb-McCoy, Cheryl. "Ethnic Identity Development in Early Adolescence: Implications and Recommendations for Middle School Counselors." *Professional School Counseling* 9, no. 2 (2005) 120–27.
Holder, Rodney. "Karl Barth and the Legitimacy of Natural Theology." *Themelios* 26, no. 3 (2001) 22–37.
Hubner, Jamin. "Biblical Inerrancy: What Calvin Really Believed." *RealApologetics.org*. http://www.realapologetics.org/blog/2010/02/09/biblical-inerrancy-what-calvin-really-believed.
Huebner, Dwayne E. "Christian Growth in Faith." *Religious Education* 81, no. 4 (1986) 511–21.
---. "Curriculum as Concern for Man's Temporality." *Theory Into Practice* 26, no. S1 (1987) 324–31.
---. "Educational Foundations for Dialogue." *Religious Education* 91, no. 4 (1996) 582–88.
---. "Religious Education: Practicing the Presence of God." *Religious Education* 82, no. 4 (1987) 569–77.
---. "Religious Metaphors in the Language of Education." *Religious Education* 80, no. 3 (1985) 460–72.
Huebner, Dwayne E., et al. "From Theory to Practice: Curriculum." *Religious Education* 77, no. 4 (1982) 363–436.
Hunsinger, Deborah van Deusen. *Pray without Ceasing: Revitalizing Pastoral Care*. Grand Rapids: Eerdmans, 2006.
Im, Janice H. "An Ecological Examination of Ego and Ethnic Identity Formation within Second Generation Korean-Americans." MS diss., Virginia Polytechnic Institute and State University, 1999.
Jüngel, Eberhard. *God as the Mystery of the World: On the Foundation of the Theology of the Crucified One in the Dispute Between Theism and Atheism*. Translated by Darrell L. Guder. Grand Rapids: Eerdmans, 1983.
Jiang, James J., et al. "An Exploration of the Relationship between Software Development Process Maturity and Project Performance." *Information & Management* 41 (2004) 279–88.

Jukes, Ian, et al. *Understanding the Digital Generation: Teaching and Learning in the New Digital Landscape*. Kelowna, Canada: 21st Century Fluency Project, 2010.

Jun, Sung Pyo, and Gordon M. Armstrong. "Status Inconsistency and Striving for Power in a Church: Is Church a Refuge or a Stepping-Stone?" *Korea Journal of Population and Development* 26, no. 1 (1997) 103–29.

Jupp, James, ed. The *Australian People: An Encyclopedia of the Nation, Its People and Their Origins*. North Ryde: Angus & Robertson, 1988.

Kagan, Spencer. *Classbuilding: Cooperative Learning Activities*. San Clemente, CA: Kagan Cooperative Learning, 1995.

———. *Cooperative Learning*. San Clemente, CA: Kagan Cooperative Learning, 1994.

Kameniar, Barbara. "Shaking Religious Education: A New Look at the Literature." *Religious Education* 102, no. 4 (2007) 403–18.

Kang, Joseph J. "Karl Barth as a Scholar and Interpreter of John Calvin." *Calvin Nondan* 24 (2004) 193–226.

Kang, S. Steve. "Reflections upon Methodology: Research on Themes of Self Construction and Self Integration in the Narrative of Second Generation Korean American Young Adults." *Religious Education* 96, no. 3 (2001) 408–15.

———. "The Socioculturally Constructed Multivoiced Self as a Framework for Christian Education of Second-Generation Korean American Young Adults." *Religious Education* 97, no. 1 (2002) 81–96.

———. *Unveiling the Socioculturally Constructed Multivoiced Self: Themes of Self Construction and Self Integration in the Narratives of Second-Generation Korean American Young Adults*. Lanham, MD: University Press of America, 2002.

Kelman, Herbert C. "The Place of Ethnic Identity in the Development of Personal Identity: A Challenge for the Jewish Family." In *Coping with Life and Death: Jewish Families in the Twentieth Century*, edited by Peter Medding, 3–26. Oxford: Oxford University Press, 1998.

Kennedy, William Bean, et al. "Interpreting the History of Religious Education in the Twentieth Century: Responses to Brian Tippen." *Religious Education* 88, no. 4 (1993) 606–38.

Kibria, Nazli. *Becoming Asian American: Second-Generation Chinese and Korean American Identities*. Baltimore: Johns Hopkins University Press, 2002.

Kihlstrorm, John F., et al. "Self and Identity as Memory." In *Handbook of Self and Identity*, edited by Mark R. Leary and June Price Tangney, 68–90. New York: Guilford, 2003.

Kim, Henry H., and Ralph E. Pyle. "An Exception to the Exception: Second-Generation Korean American Church Participation." *Social Compass* 51, no. 3 (2004) 321–33.

Kim, Ji Hwan. "Hanin dongpo sahoeui seongjanggwa geu jiljeok byeonhwa 2000 nyeon ihu" [The development and qualitative transformation of Korean community in Australia since 2000]. In *Hoju hanin osipnyeonsa* [50-year history of Koreans in Australia], edited by Hoju hanin osipnyeonsa Pyeonchan wiwonhoe, 96–125. Seoul: Doseo-chulpan jinheung, 2008.

Kim, John Mann-Souk. "Koreans." In *The Australian People: An Encyclopedia of the Nation, Its People and Their Origins*, edited by James Jupp, 659–60. North Ryde: Angus & Robertson, 1988.

Kim, Jung Ha. *Bridge-Makers and Cross-Bearers: Korean-American Women and the Church*. Atlanta: Scholars, 1997.

Kim, Myung Yong. "Kalbareutui seongryeongron" [The Holy Spirit in the theology of Karl Barth]. *Jangsin Nondan* 38 (2010) 91–117.

Kim, Pyeong-Gook, and J. Dan Marshall. "Synoptic Curriculum Texts: Representation of Contemporary Curriculum Scholarship." *Journal of Curriculum Studies* 37, no. 3 (2005) 291–311.

Kim, Rebecca. "Second-Generation Korean American Evangelicals: Ethnic, Multiethnic, or White Campus Ministries." *Sociology of Religion* 65, no. 1 (2004) 19–34.

Kim, Young-Seok, et al. "A Cross Cultural Issues of Korean Immigrants in America." *Journal of Welfare for the Aged* 14 (2006) 1–16.

Klein, Peter D. "Epistemology." In *Routledge Encyclopedia of Philosophy*, edited by Edward Craig. London: Routledge, 1998.

Kliebard, Herbert M. "Curricular Objectives and Evaluation: A Reassessment." *High School Journal* 51, no. 6 (1968) 241–47.

Knight, George P., et al. "A Social Cognitive Model of the Development of Ethnic Identity and Ethnically Based Behaviours." In *Ethnic Identity: Formation and Transmission among Hispanics and Other Minorities*, edited by Martha Bernal and George Knight, 213–34. Albany: State University of New York Press, 1993.

Knight, Peter T. "Complexity and Curriculum: A Process Approach to Curriculum-Making." *Teaching in Higher Education* 6, no. 3 (2001) 369–81.

Ko, Yong Soo. *Mannamui gidokgyo gyoyuksasang* [Christian education ideology in "meeting"]. Seoul: PCTS, 1994.

Koo, Haesook. "Negotiating Ethnic Identities: A Study of Korean Americans and Adoptees in Minnesota." PhD diss., University of Minnesota, 2008.

Kooi, Cornelis van der. *As in a Mirror: John Calvin and Karl Barth on Knowing God: A Diptych*. Translated by Donald Mader. Leiden: Brill Academic, 2005.

Korean Ministers Association in Melbourne. "2011 Teacher Survey of Joint Teacher Seminar." November 5, 2011.

Kreider, Alison, "1949: Ralph W. Tyler Publishes Basic Principles of Curriculum and Instruction." Ontario Institute for Studies in Education of the University of Toronto. http://fcis.oise.utoronto.ca/~daniel_schugurensky/assignment1/1949tyler.html.

Kysilka, Marcella L. "Understanding Integrated Curriculum." *Curriculum Journal* 9, no. 2 (1998) 197–209.

Lakeland, Paul. *Postmodernity: Christian Identity in a Fragmented Age*. Minneapolis: Augsburg Fortress, 1997.

Lawton, Denis. "Common Curriculum or Core Curriculum." *International Journal of Research & Method in Education* 3, no. 1 (1980) 5–10.

Lee, Dong Hee. *Understanding and Application of Westminster Shorter Catechism*. Fairfax, VA: Xulon, 2002.

Lee, Gyung Sook. "A Narrative Analysis of the Labour Market Experiences of Korean Migrant Women in Australia." PhD diss., University of Sydney, 2005.

———. "Hanindeului jikeopgwa gajeong saenghwal" [Koreans' occupation and family life in Australia]. In *Hoju hanin osipnyeonsa* [50-year history of Koreans in Australia], edited by Hoju hanin osipnyeonsa Pyeonchan wiwonhoe, 208–32. Seoul: Doseo-chulpan jinheung, 2008.

Lee, Hyeok Kyu. "Damunhwa gyoyukgwa goyyukgwajeong" [Multicultural education and curriculum]. In *Damunhwa gyoyukui ihaereul wihan goyyang goyjae jeosul*, edited by Young Dal Cho, 31–84. Seoul: Ministry of Education & Human Resources Development, 2008.

Lee, James Michael. "Hope in Instructional Practice." *Religious Education* 67, no. 5 (1972) 368–74.

———. *The Content of Religious Education: A Social Science Approach*. Birmingham, AL: Religious Education, 1985.

Lee, Jung Young. *Marginality: The Key to Multicultural Theology*. Minneapolis: Fortress, 1995.

Lee, Kyoo-Min. "Gidokgyo gyoyukgwa sinanggongdongcheui sangkwansung yeongu: L. Sherrill eui sinsangongdongche gaenyeome daehan bipanjeok sungchaleul jungsimeuro" [An inquiry of the correlation between Christian education and faith community: With an emphasis on the critical reflection of L. Sherrill's concept of faith community]. *Gidokgyo gyoyukjeongbo* 14 (2006) 7–41.

Lee, Sang-Taek. *New Church, New Land: The Korean Experience*. Melbourne: Uniting Church, 1989.

Lee, Won Il. *Haeseokhakjeok sangsangryeokgwa gidokgyo gyoyukgwajeong* [Hermeneutical imagination and Christian education curriculum]. Seoul: PCK, 2004.

Leith, John H. "Presbyterian Church, Reformed." In *Encyclopedia of Religion*, edited by Lindsay Jones. 2nd ed. Farmington Hills, MI: Thomson Gale, 2005.

Le Pere, Garth, and Kato Lambrechts. "Globalisation and National Identity Construction: Nation Building in South Africa." In *Identity? Theory, Politics, History*, edited by Simon Bekker and Rachel Prinsloo, 11–38. Pretoria: Human Sciences Research Council, 1999.

Lipman, Matthew. "Critical Thinking: What Can It Be?" In *Contemporary Issues in Curriculum*, edited by Allan C. Ornstein et al., 149–56. Boston: Allyn & Bacon, 2003.

Little, Sara. "Expressions of Gratitude for Randolph Crump Miller." *Religious Education* 97, no. 4 (2002) 292–95.

———. "Religious Instruction." In *Contemporary Approaches to Christian Education*, edited by Jack L. Seymour and Donald E. Miller, 35–52. Nashville: Abingdon, 1982.

———. "Theology in Religious Education." In *Foundations for Christian Education in an Era of Change*, edited by Marvin J. Taylor, 30–40. Nashville: Abingdon, 1976.

Livingstone, Sonia, and David R. Brake. "On the Rapid Rise of Social Networking Sites: New Findings and Policy Implications." *Children and Society* 24 (2010) 75–83.

Lovat, Terence J. "Curriculum Theory: The Oft-Missing Link." *Journal of Education for Teaching* 14, no. 3 (1988) 205–13.

———. *What Is This Thing Called Religious Education? Summary, Critique and a New Proposal*. Wentworth Falls, Australia: Social Science, 1989.

Lyotard, Jean F. "Defining the Postmodern." In *The Cultural Studies Reader*, edited by Simon During, 142–45. London: Routledge, 2000.

Macdonald, Doune. "Curriculum Change and the Post-modern World: Is the School Curriculum-Reform Movement an Anachronism?" *Journal of Curriculum Studies* 35, no. 2 (2003) 139–49.

Mack, Natasha, et al. *Qualitative Research Methods: A Data Collector's Field Guide*. Research Triangle Park, NC: Family Health International, 2005.

Marcia, James E. "Development and Validation of Ego Identity Status." This Week's Citation Classic. *Current Contents* 48, November 26, 1984. Originally published *Journal of Personality and Social Psychology* 3 (1966) 551–88.

McNamee, Sheila. "Therapy and Identity Construction in a Postmodern World." In *Constructing the Self in a Mediated World*, edited by D. Grodin and T. R. Lindlof, 141–55. London: Sage, 1996.

McNamee, Sheila, and Kenneth J. Gergen. *Relational Responsibility: Resources for Sustainable Dialogue*. London: Sage, 1999.

McRobbie, Angela. *Postmodernism and Popular Culture*. London: Routledge, 1994.

Melbon-haningyohoe Yeoksa-pyeonchan wiwonhoe. *Melbon-haningyohoe samsipnyeonsa 1973–2003* [30-year history of the Korean Church of Melbourne 1973–2003]. Melbourne: Korean Church of Melbourne, 2003.

Miller, Donald E. "The Developmental Approach to Christian Education." In *Contemporary Approaches to Christian Education*, edited by Jack L. Seymour and Donald E. Miller, 73–102. Nashville: Abingdon, 1982.

Miller, Randolph Crump. *The Clue to Christian Education: A Constructive Contribution to the Theory and Practice of Christian Education*. New York: Scribner, 1950.

———. *Education for Christian Living*. 2nd ed. New York: Prentice Hall, 1963.

Min, Pyong Gap. "Severe Underrepresentation of Women in Church Leadership in the Korean Immigrant Community in the United States." *Journal for the Scientific Study of Religion* 47, no. 2 (2008) 225–41.

Min, Pyong Gap, and Dae Young Kim. "Intergenerational Transmission of Religion and Culture: Korean Protestants in the US." *Sociology of Religion* 66, no. 3 (2005) 263–82.

Mineva, Silvia. "Identity, Otherness and Their Postmodern Ethical Discourse." *European Journal of Science and Theology* 3, no. 2 (2007) 31–39.

Ministry of Foreign Affairs and Trades. "The Statistics of Korean Migrants to Overseas, 1962–2009." http://www.index.go.kr/egams/stts/jsp/potal/stts/PO_STTS_IdxSearch.jsp?idx_cd=1684&stts_cd=168401&clas_div=&idx_sys_cd=&idx_clas_cd=1.

Mitchell, Pamela. "What Is 'Curriculum'? Alternative in Western Historical Perspectives." *Religious Education* 83, no. 3 (1988) 349–66.

———. "Why Care about Stories? A Theory of Narrative Art." *Religious Education* 86, no. 1 (1990) 30–43.

Moore, Basil. *Religion Education: Issues and Methods in Curriculum Design*. Underdale, Australia: University of South Australia, 1991.

Moore, Mary Elizabeth. "Inclusive Language and Power: A Response." *Religious Education* 80, no. 4 (1985) 603–14.

———. "Stories of Vocation: Education for Vocational Discernment." *Religious Education* 103, no. 2 (2008) 218–39.

———. "Teaching Christian Particularity in a Pluralistic World." *British Journal of Religious Education* 17, no. 2 (1995) 70–83.

Moore, Mary Elizabeth, et al. "Realities, Visions, and Promises of a Multicultural Future." *Religious Education* 99, no. 3 (2004) 287–315.

Moore, Russell D. "Natural Revelation." In *A Theology for the Church*, edited by Daniel L. Akin, 71–117. Nashville: B & H Academic, 2007.

Moran, Gabriel. "The American Experience." *Religious Education* 76, no. 3 (1981) 243–57.

———. "Interest in Philosophy: Three Themes for Religious Education." *Religious Education* 81, no. 3 (1986) 424–45.

———. "The Intersection of Religion and Education." *Religious Education* 69, no. 5 (1974) 531–41.

———. *Religious Education as a Second Language*. Birmingham, AL: Religious Education, 1989.

———. *Religious Education Development: Images for the Future*. Minneapolis: Winston, 1983.

———. "Religious Education: Past, Present and Future." *Religious Education* 66, no. 5 (1971) 335–40.

———. "Revelation as Teaching-Learning." *Religious Education* 95, no. 3 (2000) 269–83.

———. "Still to Come." *Religious Education* 98, no. 4 (2003) 495–502.

Mottart, André, et al. "Digitization and Culture." *Interactive Educational Multimedia* 8 (2004) 24–38.

Muller, Johan. "Forms of Knowledge and Curriculum Coherence." *Journal of Education and Work* 22, no. 3 (2009) 205–26.

Muller, Richard. *Dictionary of Latin and Greek Theological Terms*. Grand Rapids: Baker, 1985.

Nagel, Joane. "Constructing Ethnicity: Creating and Recreating Ethnic Identity and Culture." *Social Problems* 41 (1994) 152–76.

Nahm, Gi Young. *Melbon-haningyohoeui yeoksa 1973–1996* [A history of the Korean Church of Melbourne 1973–1996]. Melbourne: Hatch, 2003.

———. "Biktoria haninhoe (VIC)" [The history of Korean society in Victoria]. In *Hoju hanin osipnyeonsa* [50-year history of Koreans in Australia], edited by Hoju hanin osipnyeonsa Pyeonchan wiwonhoe, 326–69. Seoul: Doseo-chulpan jinheung, 2008.

Neff, Kristin D., and Roos Vonk. "Self-Compassion versus Global Self-Esteem: Two Different Ways of Relating to Oneself." *Journal of Personality* 77, no. 1 (2009) 23–50.

Neiman, Bennett, and Julio Bermudez. "Between Digital and Analog Civilization: The Spatial Manipulation Media Workshop." In *ACADIA '97: Representation & Design*, edited by J. Peter Jordan et al., 131–37. Conference of the Association for Computer Aided Design in Architecture, Cincinnati, October 3–5, 1997.

Nelson, C. Ellis. "Can Protestantism Make It with the 'Now' Generation?" *Religious Education* 64, no. 5 (1969) 376–83.

———. "Formation of a God Representation." *Religious Education* 91, no. 1 (1996) 22–39.

———. "Is Church Education Something Particular?" *Religious Education* 67, no. 1 (1972) 5–16.

———. "Pause for Station Identification." *Religious Education* 67, no. 1 (1972) 37–41.

———. "The Relation of Seminary Training to Congregational Education." *Religious Education* 63, no. 4 (1968) 301–8.

———. "Toward the Year 2003." *Religious Education* 79, no. 1 (1984) 101–8.

———. *Where Faith Begins*. Atlanta: John Knox, 1967.

Nelsona, Marc, et al. "Concepts of Curriculum." *Teaching and Learning in Medicine* 4, no. 4 (1992) 202–5.

Nemoianu, Virgil. *Postmodernism and Cultural Identities: Conflicts and Coexistence*. Washington, DC: Catholic University of America Press, 2010.

Nicole, Roger. "John Calvin and Inerrancy." *Journal of the Evangelical Theological Society* 25, no. 4 (1982) 425–42.

Niebuhr, Richard H. *Faith on Earth: An Inquiry into the Structure of Human Faith*. New Haven: Yale University Press, 1989.

Njus, David, and Dan R. Johnson. "Need for Cognition as a Predictor of Psychosocial Identity Development." *Journal of Psychology: Interdisciplinary and Applied* 142, no. 6 (2008) 645–55.

Norman, Stanton R. "Human Sinfulness." In *A Theology for the Church*, edited by Daniel L. Akin, 409–78. Nashville: B & H Academic, 2007.

Oblinger, Diana G., and James L. Oblinger, eds. *Educating the Net Generation*. Washington, DC: Educause, 2005.

———. "Is It Age or IT: First Steps toward Understanding the Net Generation." In *Educating the Net Generation*, 2.1–2.20. Washington, DC: Educause, 2005.

Oh, In Tak, et al. *Gidokgyo gyoyukron* [Christian education theory]. Seoul: KCCE, 1984.

O'Leary, Daniel J., and Teresa Sallnow. *Love and Meaning in Religious Education: An Incarnational Approach to Teaching Christianity*. Oxford: Oxford University Press, 1982.

Ornstein, Allan C. "Philosophy as a Basis for Curriculum Decisions." In *Contemporary Issues in Curriculum*, edited by Allan C. Ornstein et al., 3–9. Boston: Allyn & Bacon, 2003.

Ornstein, Allan C., et al. *Contemporary Issues in Curriculum*. 3rd ed. Boston: Allyn & Bacon, 2003.

Osmer, Richard R. "Faith Development in the Adult Life Cycle: A Review." *Religious Education* 84, no. 4 (1989) 483–93.

———. "James W. Fowler and the Reformed Tradition: An Exercise in Theological Reflection in Religious Education." *Religious Education* 85, no. 1 (1990) 51–68.

———. *Teaching for Faith: A Guide for Teachers of Adult Classes*. Louisville: Westminster John Knox, 1992.

Padilla, Armado M., and William Perez. "Acculturation, Social Identity, and Social Cognition: A New Perspective." *Hispanic Journal of Behavioral Sciences* 25, no. 1 (2003) 35–55.

Pal, Jiban K. "Social Networks Enabling Matrimonial Information Services in India." *International Journal of Library and Information Science* 2, no. 4 (2010) 54–64.

Palmer, Parker J. "The Conversion of Knowledge." *Religious Education* 74, no. 6 (1979) 629–40.

———. *The Courage to Teach: Exploring the Inner Landscape of a Teacher's Life*. San Francisco: Jossey-Bass, 1998.

———. "Divided No More." *Change: The Magazine of Higher Learning* 24, no. 2 (1992) 10–17.

———. "Good Talk about Good Teaching." *Change: The Magazine of Higher Learning* 25, no. 6 (1993) 8–13.

———. "Good Teaching: A Matter of Living the Mystery." *Change: The Magazine of Higher Learning* 22, no. 1 (1990) 11–16.

———. "The Heart of a Teacher Identity and Integrity in Teaching." *Change: The Magazine of Higher Learning* 29, no. 6 (1997) 14–21.

———. "A New Professional: The Aims of Education Revisited." *Change: The Magazine of Higher Learning* 39, no. 6 (2007) 6–13.

———. *To Know as We Are Known: Education as a Spiritual Journey.* San Francisco: Harper & Row, 1983.

———. "Ways to Deepen Our Educational Agenda." *Change: The Magazine of Higher Learning* 26, no. 3 (1994) 40–41.

Park, Andrew Sung. *From Hurt to Healing: A Theology of the Wounded.* Nashville: Abingdon, 2004.

———. *The Wounded Heart of God: The Asian Concept of Han and the Christian Doctrine of Sin.* Nashville: Abingdon, 1993.

Park, Byung Tae. "Hanin dongpo sahoeui jeongchak 1968–1979" [The settlement of Korean community in Australia 1968–1979]. In *Hoju hanin osipnyeonsa* [50-year history of Koreans in Australia], edited by Hoju hanin osipnyeonsa Pyeonchan wiwonhoe, 38–72. Seoul: Doseo-chulpan jinheung, 2008.

Park, Byung Tae, and Yang Hoon Cho. "Hanin dongpo sahoeui yeokdongjeok baljeon 1980–1999" [The dynamic development of Korean community in Australia 1980–1999]. In *Hoju hanin osipnyeonsa* [50-year history of Koreans in Australia], edited by Hoju hanin osipnyeonsa Pyeonchan wiwonhoe, 74–95. Seoul: Doseo-chulpan jinheung, 2008.

Park, Jong Soo. "A Study of Religious Education Pedagogy for Second-Generation Korean-Australian Adolescents: Threefold Structure for an Alternative Model to the Schooling Paradigm." MTheol thesis, Melbourne College of Divinity, 2010.

Park, Sang-Jin. "A Curriculum Model of Christian Education for Faith as Knowing God: A Critique of the Tylerian Model and a Search for an Alternative on the Basis of New Epistemology." PhD diss., Union Theological Seminary and Presbyterian School of Christian Education, 2001.

———. "Gidokgyo gyoyukgwajeong ironui chegyejeok bunryue gwanhan yeongu" [A study of a systematic classification of Christian education curriculum theories]. In *21segi gidokgyo gyoyukui gwajewa jeonmang* [The task and prospect of Christian education for the 21st century], edited by Ko yong-soo chongjang hwagapginyeom nonmungip Pyeonchan wiwonhoe, 157–82. Seoul: Jeyoung, 2002.

———. *Gidokgyo gyoyukgwajeong Tamgu* [A search for Christian education curriculum]. Seoul: Presbyterian College and Theological Seminary Press, 2004.

Park, Seounggyu. "Kalbareut sinhakeseo ihaereul chuguhaneun sinangui wichiwa uiui" [The position and meaning of faith seeking understanding in Karl Barth's theology]. *Jangsin Nondan* 39 (2010) 175–97.

Parramatta Diocesan Schools Board. "Minimum Professional Requirements for Religious Education Teachers." Catholic Education Diocese of Parramatta. www.parra.catholic.edu.au/_resources/re-accred-parra-policy.pdf.

Pautler, Albert J. "Curriculum Leadership, Innovation, and Change." *Community College Journal of Research and Practice* 16, no. 2 (1992) 133–40.

Perrott, Elizabeth, et al. "An Investigation into Teachers' Reactions to a Self-instructional Microteaching Course." *Innovations in Education and Teaching International* 13, no. 2 (1976) 25–35.

Phinney, Jean S. "Ethnic Identity: Developmental and Contextual Perspectives." Paper presented at the Notre Dame Conference on Culture and Diversity (ND-CCD), South Bend, Oct. 31–Nov. 1, 2004.

———. "Ethnic Identity in Adolescents and Adults: Review of Research." *Psychological Bulletin* 108, no. 3 (1990) 499–514.

Phinney, Jean S., Cindy Lou Cantu, and Dawn A. Kurtz. "Ethnic and American Identity as Predictors of Self-Esteem among African American, Latino, and White Adolescents." *Journal of Youth and Adolescence* 26, no. 2 (1997) 165–85.

Phinney, Jean S., Gabriel Horenczyk, et al. "Ethnic Identity, Immigration, and Well-being: An Interactional Perspective." *Journal of Social Issues* 57, no. 3 (2001) 493–510.

Phinney, Jean S., and Anthony D. Ong. "Conceptualization and Measurement of Ethnic Identity: Current Status and Future Directions." *Journal of Counseling Psychology* 54, no. 3 (2007) 271–81.

Piaget, Jean. "Development and Learning." In *Piaget Rediscovered*, edited by Richard E. Ripple and Verne N. Rockcastle, 7–20. Ithaca, NY: Cornell University, 1964. Reprinted in *Readings on the Development of Children*, edited by Mary Gauvain and Michael Cole, 19–28. New York: Freeman, 1997.

Pinar, William F. "Crisis, Reconceptualization, Internationalization: U.S. Curriculum Theory Since 1950." Paper presented at East China Normal University, Shanghai, May 2007.

———. "Currere: Toward Reconceptualization." In *Curriculum Theorizing: The Reconceptualists*, edited by William F. Pinar, 396–414. Berkeley: McCutcheon, 1975.

———. "'Dreamt into Existence by Others': Curriculum Theory and School Reform." *Theory Into Practice* 31, no. 3 (1992) 228–35.

———. *International Handbook of Curriculum Research*. Mahwah, NJ: Erlbaum, 2003.

———. "Internationalism in Curriculum Studies." *Pedagogies: An International Journal* 1, no. 1 (2006) 35–42.

———. "The Method of 'Currere.'" Paper presented at the Annual Meeting of the American Research Association, Washinton, DC, April 1975.

———. "The Reconceptualisation of Curriculum Studies." *Journal of Curriculum Studies* 10, no. 3 (1978) 205–14.

———. "Whole, Bright, Deep with Understanding: Issues in Qualitative Research and Autobiographical Method." *Journal of Curriculum Studies* 13, no. 3 (1981) 173–88.

Pisano, Gary P., and Roberto Verganti. "Which Kind of Collaboration Is Right for You?" *Harvard Business Review*, December 2008, 3–9.

Portes, Pedro. "Ethnicity and Culture in Educational Psychology." In *Handbook of Educational Psychology*, edited by D. Berliner and R. Calfee, 331–57. New York: Macmillan Library Reference, 1996.

Power, William L. "Imago Dei—Imitatio Dei." *International Journal for Philosophy of Religion* 42 (1997) 131–41.

Prensky, Marc. "Digital Natives, Digital Immigrants, Part 1." *On the Horizon* 9, no. 5 (2001) 1–6.

———. "Digital Natives, Digital Immigrants, Part 2: Do They Really Think Differently?" *On the Horizon* 9, no. 6 (2001) 1–6.

Priestley, Jack G. "Towards Finding the Hidden Curriculum: A Consideration of the Spiritual Dimension of Experience in Curriculum Planning." *British Journal of Religious Education* 7, no. 3 (1984) 112–19.

Randall, P. E., and C. Gibb. "Concepts of the Curriculum: The Curriculum—Why Has INSET Failed?" *Educational Psychology in Practice* 4, no. 1 (1988) 29–35.

Reeves, Thomas C. "Established and Emerging Evaluation Paradigms for Instructional Design." In *Instructional Development Paradigms*, edited by Charles R. Dills and Alexander J. Romiszowski, 163–78. Englewood Cliffs, NJ: Educational Technology, 1997.

Richmond, Helen. "Becoming a Multicultural Nation and Multicultural Church." In *30 Years Korean Ministry in Australia*, edited by Myung Duk Yang and Clive Pearson, 439–61. North Parramatta: UTC Publications, 2004.

Richter, Alexander, and Michael Koch. "Functions of Social Networking Services." In *COOP '08: The 8th International Conference on the Design of Cooperative Systems*, 1–12. Carry-le-Rouet, France, May 20–23, 2008.

Rivas-Drake, Deborah et al. "A Closer Look at Peer Discrimination, Ethnic Identity, and Psychological Well-Being among Urban Chinese American Sixth Graders." *Journal of Youth and Adolescence* 37, no. 1 (2008) 12–21.

Rosenberg, Morris, et al. "Global Self-Esteem and Specific Self-Esteem: Different Concepts, Different Outcomes." *American Sociological Review* 60, no. 1 (1995) 141–56.

Scanlon, Margaret, and David Buckingham. "Debating the Digital Curriculum: Intersections of the Public and the Private in Educational and Cultural Policy." *London Review of Education* 1, no. 3 (2003) 191–205.

Schwab, Joseph J. "The Practical: A Language for Curriculum." In *School Review* 78 (1969) 1–23. Reprinted in *The Curriculum Studies Reader*, edited by David J. Flinders and Stephen J. Thornton, 103–17. New York: RoutledgeFalmer, 2004.

Schwartz, Morey. "For Whom Do We Write the Curriculum?" *Journal of Curriculum Studies* 38, no. 4 (2006) 449–57.

Scott, Kieran. "The Local Church as an Ecology of Human Development." *Religious Education* 76, no. 2 (1981) 142–61.

———. "Religious Education and Professional Religious Education: A Conflict of Interest?" *Religious Education* 77, no. 6 (1982) 587–603.

———. "Three Traditions of Religious Education." *Religious Education* 79, no. 3 (1984) 323–39.

———. "Youth Education as Problematizing Political Forms." *Religious Education* 77, no. 2 (1982) 197–210.

Sears, James T., and J. Dan Marshall. "Generational Influences on Contemporary Curriculum Thought." *Journal of Curriculum Studies* 32, no. 2 (2000) 199–214.

Seol, Byung-Soo. "The Sydney Korean Community and 'The I.M.F. Drifting People.'" *People and Place* 7, no. 2 (1997) 23–33.

Sever, Rita. "Patterns of Coping with the Task at Schools." In *Children of Perestroika in Israel*, edited by Tamar Horowitz, 178–89. Lanham, MD: University Press of America, 1999.

Seymour, Jack L. "Approaches to Christian Education." In *Contemporary Approaches to Christian Education*, edited by Jack L. Seymour and Donald E. Miller, 11–34. Nashville: Abingdon, 1982.

———. "The Clue to Christian Religious Education: Uniting Theology and Education, 1950 to the Present." *Religious Education* 99, no. 3 (2004) 272–86.

———. "The Future of the Past: History and Policy-Making in Religious Education." *Religious Education* 81, no. 1 (1986) 113–33.

———. "Religious Education and the Future of Religious Education." *Religious Education* 100, no. 4 (2005) 337–39.

Seymour, Jack L., and Carol A. Wehrheim. "Faith Seeking Understanding: Interpretation as a Task of Christian Education." In *Contemporary Approaches to Christian*

Education, edited by Jack L. Seymour and Donald E. Miller, 123–44. Nashville: Abingdon, 1982.

Sharan, Shlomo. *Cooperative Learning: Theory and Research*. New York: Praeger, 1990.

Shin, Eui Hang. "Religion and Adaptation of Immigrants: The Case of Revival Meetings in Korean-American Churches." *Development and Society* 31, no. 1 (2002) 125–62.

Shin, Sun-Young. "The Functions of Code-Switching in a Korean Sunday School." *Heritage Language Journal* 7, no. 1 (2010) 91–116.

Shkedi, Asher. "Curriculum and Teachers: An Encounter of Languages and Literatures." *Journal of Curriculum Studies* 38, no. 6 (2006) 719–35.

Silva, Tomaz Tadeu Da. "The Poetics and Politics of Curriculum as Representation." *Pedagogy, Culture & Society* 7, no. 1 (1999) 7–33.

Slattery, Patrick. "Postmodern Curriculum Research and Alternative Forms of Data Representation." Occasional Paper of the Curriculum and Pedagogy Institute of the University of Alberta. Edmonton: University of Alberta, 1997.

Slattery, Patrick, and Dana Rapp. *Ethics and the Foundations of Education: Teaching Convictions in a Postmodern World*. Boston: Allyn & Bacon, 2002.

Slavin, Robert. *Cooperative Learning: Theory, Research, and Practice*. Engliwood Cliffs, NJ: Prentice Hall, 1990.

Smith, David L., and Terence J. Lovat. *Curriculum: Action on Reflection*. 4th ed. Tuggerah, Australia: Social Science, 2003.

Smith, Glenn Gordon, and Hermann Kurthen. "Front-Stage and Back-Stage in Hybrid E-Learning Face-to-Face Courses." *International Journal on E-Learning* 6, no. 3 (2007) 455–74.

Song, Miri. *Choosing Ethnic Identity*. Cambridge, UK: Polity, 2003.

Speedy, Graeme. "The Concept of Organizing Principle in Christian Education Curriculum." M.Ed. diss., University of Melbourne, 1965.

Stryker, Sheldon. "Identity Theory and Personality Theory: Mutual Relevance." *Journal of Personality* 75, no. 6 (2007) 1083–102.

Svahn, Fredrik. "The Sociomateriality of Competing Technological Regimes in Digital Innovation." In *The 32nd Information Systems Research Seminar in Scandinavia: Inclusive Design*, edited by Judith Molka-Danielsen, 23–40. Molde University College, Molde, Norway, August 9–12, 2009.

Swidler, Leonard. "Confucianism for Modern Persons in Dialogue with Christianity and Modernity." *Journal of Ecumenical Studies* 40 (2003) 1225–38.

Tajfel, Henri. *Human Groups and Social Categories*. Cambridge: Cambridge University Press, 1981.

Tanner, Daniel, and Laurel Tanner. *Curriculum Development: Theory into Practice*. 2nd ed. New York: Macmillan, 1980.

Terwel, J. "Curriculum Differentiation: Multiple Perspectives and Developments in Education." *Journal of Curriculum Studies* 37, no. 6 (2005) 653–70.

Texas Catholic Conference Education Department. "Minimum Requirements for Teachers of Religion/Theology." Pharr Oratory of St. Philip Neri School System. www.oratoryschools.org/oshome/jobs/tcced2-3.pdf.

Tomlinson, John. "Globalization and Cultural Identity." In *The Global Transformations Reader: An Introduction to the Globalization Debate*, edited by David Held and Anthony McGrew, 269–77. Malden, MA: Blackwell, 2003.

Torrance, Thomas F. *Karl Barth, Biblical and Evangelical Theologian*. Edinburgh: T. & T. Clark, 1990.

Torres, Claudio Vaz, and Amalia Raquel Pérez-Nebra. "The Influence of Human Values on Holiday Destination Choice in Australia and Brazil." *Brazilian Administration Review* 4, no. 3 (2007) 63–76.

Tuli, Kapil, et al. "Rethinking Customer Solutions: From Product Bundles to Relational Processes." *Journal of Marketing* 71 (2007) 1–17.

Tyler, Ralph W. *Basic Principles of Curriculum and Instruction*. Chicago: University of Chicago Press, 1949.

Vandiver, Beverly J., et al. "Cross's Negrescence Model: From Theory to Scale to Theory." *Journal of Multicultural Counseling and Development* 29, no. 3 (2001) 174–200.

Verkuyten, Maykel. "Ethnic Group Identification and Group Evaluation among Minority and Majority Groups: Testing the Multiculturalism Hypothesis." *Social Development* 88, no. 1 (2005) 121–38.

Vries, Wouter de, et al. "Bauman's (Post) Modernism and Globalization: Geographical Approaches." Radboud University Nijmegen. http://socgeo.ruhosting.nl/html/files/geoapp/Werkstukken/Bauman.pdf.

Vukich, Lee, and Steve Vandegriff. *Timeless Youth Ministry: A Handbook for Successfully Reaching Today's Youth*. Chicago: Moody, 2002.

Walker, Melanie. "Pedagogies of Beginning." In *Reclaiming Universities from a Runaway World*, edited by Melanie Walker and Jon Nixon, 131–46. Maidenhead, UK: SRHE / Open University Press, 2004.

Webster, John. "Eberhad Jüngel: The Humanity of God and the Humanity of Man." *Evangel* 2, no. 2 (1984) 4–6.

Westerhoff, John H., III. "Calling Forth the Future." *Religious Education* 75, no. 1 (1980) 51–57.

———. "The Church and Education Debate." *Religious Education* 67, no. 1 (1972) 49–59.

———. "The Church and the Family." *Religious Education* 78, no. 2 (1983) 249–74.

———. "A Discipline in Crisis." *Religious Education* 74, no. 1 (1979) 7–15.

———. "Religious Education for the Maypole Dancers." *Religious Education* 68, no. 5 (1973) 569–85.

———. "Scripture and Education: Challenges Facing Religious Educators." *Religious Education* 77, no. 5 (1982) 472–76.

———. *Tomorrow's Church: A Community of Change*. Waco, TX: Word, 1976.

———. "Values for Today's Children." *Religious Education* 75, no. 3 (1980) 249–59.

———. *Will Our Children Have Faith?* Melbourne: Dove, 1976.

Willis, Robert E. *The Ethics of Karl Barth*. Leiden: Brill, 1971.

Wood, Donald. *Barth's Theology of Interpretation*. Brookfield, VT: Ashgate, 2007.

Wraga, William, and Peter Hlebowitsh. "Toward a Renaissance in Curriculum Theory and Development in the USA." *Journal of Curriculum Studies* 35, no. 4 (2003) 425–37.

Wright, Andrew. *Religion, Education and Post-modernity*. London: RoutledgeFalmer, 2004.

Wuebben, Jon. *Content Is Currency: Developing Powerful Content for Web and Mobile*. Boston: Brealey, 2011.

Wyckoff, D. Campbell. "Curriculum Theory and Practice." In *Foundations for Christian Education in an Era of Change*, edited by Marvin J. Taylor, 127–37. Nashville: Abingdon, 1976.

———. *The Task of Christian Education*. Philadelphia: Westminster, 1955.

———. *Theory and Design of Christian Education Curriculum*. Philadelphia: Westminster, 1961.

———. *Theory and Design of Christian Education Curriculum*. Translated by Kook-Whan Kim. Seoul: Sung Kwang, 1990.

Xu, Zhichang. "When Hybrid Learning Meets Blended Teaching: Online Computer-Mediated Communication (CMC) Discourse and Classroom Face-to-Face (FTF) Discourse Analysis." In *Hybrid Learning and Education*, edited by Fong Joseph et al., 157–67. Proceedings of the First International Conference on Hybrid Learning, Hong Kong, August 13–15, 2008. Berlin: Springer, 2008.

Yang, Kum Hee. "Gyoyukui gwanjeomeseo ikneun kalbinui gyohoeron" [Reading Calvin's understanding of church with educational perspective]. *Jangsin Nondan* 17 (2001) 464–84.

Yang, Myung Duk. "Hanho gan chogi injeok gyoryuwa hanin sahoeui hyeongseong 1880–1967" [The early exchanges of human resources between Korea and Australia and the formation of Korean community in Australia 1880–1967]." In *Hoju hanin osipnyeonsa* [50-year history of Koreans in Australia], edited by Hoju hanin osipnyeonsa Pyeonchan wiwonhoe, 18–37. Seoul: Doseo-chulpan jinheung, 2008.

———. "Hanindeului jonggyo hwaldong" [The religious activity of Koreans in Australia]. In *Hoju hanin osipnyeonsa* [50-year history of Koreans in Australia], edited by Hoju hanin osipnyeonsa Pyeonchan wiwonhoe, 142–63. Seoul: Doseo-chulpan jinheung, 2008.

Yardi, Sarita. "Whispers in the Classroom." In *Digital Youth, Innovation, and the Unexpected*, edited by Tara McPherson, 143–64. Cambridge: MIT Press, 2008.

Yeh, Christine J. "Age, Acculturation, Cultural Adjustment, and Mental Health Symptoms of Chinese, Korean, and Japanese Immigrant Youths." *Cultural Diversity and Ethnic Minority Psychology* 9, no. 1 (2003) 34–48.

Yeh, Christine J., and Karen Huang. "The Collectivistic Nature of Ethnic Identity Development among Asian-American College Students." *Adolescence* 31, no. 123 (1996) 645–61.

Yinger, John M. "Ethnicity in Complex Societies." In *The Uses of Controversy in Sociology*, edited by L. A. Coser and O. N. Larsen, 197–216. New York: Free Press, 1976.

Young, Michael. "Durkheim, Vygotsky and the Curriculum of the Future." *London Review of Education* 1, no. 2 (2003) 100–117.

www.ingramcontent.com/pod-product-compliance
Lightning Source LLC
Chambersburg PA
CBHW050436240426
43661CB00055B/2399